UNIX™ TIME-SHARING SYSTEM:

UNIX PROGRAMMER'S MANUAL

UNIX™ TIME-SHARING SYSTEM:

UNIX PROGRAMMER'S MANUAL

Revised and Expanded Version

Bell Telephone Laboratories, Incorporated
Murray Hill, New Jersey

HOLT, RINEHART AND WINSTON

New York   Chicago   San Francisco   Philadelphia
Montreal   Toronto   London   Sydney   Tokyo
Mexico City   Rio de Janeiro   Madrid

Library of Congress Cataloging in Publication Data

Bell Telephone Laboratories, inc.
  UNIX time-sharing system.

  Includes index.
  1. UNIX (Computer system)   I. Title.
QA76.8.U65B44   1982   001.64'404   82-15498

ISBN 0-03-061742-1

Printed in the United States of America
Published simultaneously in Canada
3 4 5 6   014   9 8 7 6 5 4 3

CBS COLLEGE PUBLISHING
Holt, Rinehart and Winston
The Dryden Press
Saunders College Publishing

CONTENTS

PREFACE

This new form of the Seventh Edition manual attests to the gratifying popularity of the UNIX Operating System. Delivered with no support and with an amateurishly published manual, this elegant and productive system has nevertheless earned worldwide respect, sometimes bordering on adulation.

Thousands of users today work from faint reproductions of reproductions of the original manual, whose ragged pages dangle and slide out of beat-up ring binders. The new form remedies the physical difficulties, while preserving the familiar style and content. Dozens of errors have been corrected, an index keyed to page numbers has been constructed, and a quick reference section has been incorporated.

Volume 1 is intended as reference material. In the interest of brevity it contains few examples, and in the interest of quick retrieval in continual use is ordered by UNIX terminology, not by functional progression as a primer might be. General tutorial information and more detailed descriptions of major programming languages and utility programs, such as C, FORTRAN, or the *troff* typesetting package, will be found in Volume 2, forthcoming from Holt in this new form.

INTRODUCTION TO VOLUME 1

This volume gives descriptions of the publicly available features of the UNIX† system. It does not attempt to provide perspective or tutorial information upon the UNIX operating system, its facilities, or its implementation. Various documents on those topics are contained in Volume 2. In particular, for an overview see 'The UNIX Time-Sharing System' by Ritchie and Thompson; for a tutorial see 'UNIX for Beginners' by Kernighan.

Within the area it surveys, this volume attempts to be timely, complete and concise. Where the latter two objectives conflict, the obvious is often left unsaid in favor of brevity. It is intended that each program be described as it is, not as it should be. Inevitably, this means that various sections will soon be out of date.

The volume is divided into nine sections:

1. Commands
2. System calls
3. Subroutines
4. Special files
5. File formats and conventions
6. Games
7. Macro packages and language conventions
8. Maintenance
9. Quick UNIX Reference

Commands are programs intended to be invoked directly by the user, in contradistinction to subroutines, which are intended to be called by the user's programs. Commands generally reside in directory /bin (for binary programs). Some programs also reside in /usr/bin, to save space in /bin. These directories are searched automatically by the command interpreter.

System calls are entries into the UNIX supervisor. Every system call has one or more C language interfaces described in section 2. The underlying assembly language interface, coded with opcode *sys*, a synonym for *trap*, is given as well.

An assortment of subroutines is available; they are described in section 3. The primary libraries in which they are kept are described in *intro*(3). The functions are described in terms of C, but most will work with Fortran as well.

The special files section 4 discusses the characteristics of each system 'file' that actually refers to an I/O device. The names in this section refer to the DEC device names for the hardware, instead of the names of the special files themselves.

The file formats and conventions section 5 documents the structure of particular kinds of files; for example, the form of the output of the loader and assembler is given. Excluded are files used by only one command, for example the assembler's intermediate files.

Games have been relegated to section 6 to keep them from contaminating the more staid information of section 1.

Section 7 is a miscellaneous collection of information necessary to writing in various specialized languages: character codes, macro packages for typesetting, etc.

The maintenance section 8 discusses procedures not intended for use by the ordinary user. These procedures often involve use of commands of section 1, where an attempt has been made to single

---

† UNIX is a Trademark of Bell Laboratories.

out peculiarly maintenance-flavored commands by marking them 1M.

Each section consists of a number of independent entries of a page or so each. The name of the entry is in the upper corners of its pages, together with the section number, and sometimes a letter characteristic of a subcategory, e.g. graphics is 1G, and the math library is 3M. Entries within each section are alphabetized. The page numbers of each entry start at 1; it is infeasible to number consecutively the pages of a document like this that is republished in many variant forms.

All entries are based on a common format, not all of whose subsections will always appear.

The *name* subsection lists the exact names of the commands and subroutines covered under the entry and gives a very short description of their purpose.

The *synopsis* summarizes the use of the program being described. A few conventions are used, particularly in the Commands subsection:

Boldface words are considered literals, and are typed just as they appear.

Square brackets [ ] around an argument indicate that the argument is optional. When an argument is given as 'name', it always refers to a file name.

Ellipses '...' are used to show that the previous argument-prototype may be repeated.

A final convention is used by the commands themselves. An argument beginning with a minus sign '−' is often taken to mean some sort of option-specifying argument even if it appears in a position where a file name could appear. Therefore, it is unwise to have files whose names begin with '−'.

The *description* subsection discusses in detail the subject at hand.

The *files* subsection gives the names of files which are built into the program.

A *see also* subsection gives pointers to related information.

A *diagnostics* subsection discusses the diagnostic indications which may be produced. Messages which are intended to be self-explanatory are not listed.

The *bugs* subsection gives known bugs and sometimes deficiencies. Occasionally also the suggested fix is described.

In section 2 an *assembler* subsection carries the assembly language system interface.

At the beginning of the volume is a table of contents, organized by section and alphabetically within each section.

HOW TO GET STARTED

This section sketches the basic information you need to get started on UNIX: how to log in and log out, how to communicate through your terminal, and how to run a program. See 'UNIX for Beginners' in Volume 2 for a more complete introduction to the system.

Logging in. You must call UNIX from an appropriate terminal. UNIX terminals are typified by the TTY 43, the GE Terminet 300, the DASI 300S and 450, and most video terminals such as the Datamedia 5120 or HP 2640. You must also have a valid user name, which may be obtained, together with the telephone number, from the system administrators. The same telephone number serves terminals operating at all the standard speeds. After a data connection is established, the login procedure depends on what kind of terminal you are using.

300-baud terminals: Such terminals include the GE Terminet 300 and most display terminals run with popular modems. These terminals generally have a speed switch which should be set at '300' (or '30' for 30 characters per second) and a half/full duplex switch which should be set at full-duplex. (This switch will often have to be changed since many other systems require half-duplex). When a connection is established, the system types 'login:'; you type your user name, followed by the 'return' key. If you have a password, the system asks for it and turns off the printer on the terminal so the password will not appear. After you have logged in, the 'return', 'new line', or 'linefeed' keys will give exactly the same results.

1200- and 150-baud terminals: If there is a half/full duplex switch, set it at full-duplex. When you have established a data connection, the system types out a few garbage characters (the 'login:' message at the wrong speed). Depress the 'break' (or 'interrupt') key; this is a speed-independent signal to UNIX that a different speed terminal is in use. The system then will type 'login:,' this time at another speed. Continue depressing the break key until 'login:' appears in clear, then respond with your user name. From the TTY 37 terminal, and any other which has the 'newline' function (combined carriage return and linefeed), terminate each line you type with the 'new line' key, otherwise use the 'return' key.

Hard-wired terminals. Hard-wired terminals usually begin at the right speed, up to 9600 baud; otherwise the preceding instructions apply.

For all these terminals, it is important that you type your name in lower-case if possible; if you type upper-case letters, UNIX will assume that your terminal cannot generate lower-case letters and will translate all subsequent upper-case letters to lower case.

The evidence that you have successfully logged in is that the Shell program will type a '$' to you. (The Shell is described below under 'How to run a program.')

For more information, consult *stty*(1), which tells how to adjust terminal behavior, *getty*(8), which discusses the login sequence in more detail, and *tty*(4), which discusses terminal I/O.

Logging out. There are three ways to log out:

> You can simply hang up the phone.

> You can log out by typing an end-of-file indication (EOT character, control-d) to the Shell. The Shell will terminate and the 'login: ' message will appear again.

> You can also log in directly as another user by giving a *login*(1) command.

How to communicate through your terminal. When you type characters, a gnome deep in the system gathers your characters and saves them in a secret place. The characters will not be given to a program until you type a return (or newline), as described above in *Logging in.*

UNIX terminal I/O is full-duplex. It has full read-ahead, which means that you can type at any time, even while a program is typing at you. Of course, if you type during output, the printed output will have the input characters interspersed. However, whatever you type will be saved up and interpreted in correct sequence. There is a limit to the amount of read-ahead, but it is generous and not likely to be exceeded unless the system is in trouble. When the read-ahead limit is exceeded, the system throws away all the saved characters.

The character '@' in typed input kills all the preceding characters in the line, so typing mistakes can be repaired on a single line. Also, the character '#' erases the last character typed. Successive uses of '#' erase characters back to, but not beyond, the beginning of the line. '@' and '#' can be transmitted to a program by preceding them with '\'. (So, to erase '\', you need two '#'s). These conventions can be changed by the *stty*(1) command.

The 'break' or 'interrupt' key causes an *interrupt signal,* as does the The ASCII 'delete' (or 'rubout') character, which is not passed to programs. This signal generally causes whatever program you are running to terminate. It is typically used to stop a long printout that you don't want. However, programs can arrange either to ignore this signal altogether, or to be notified when it happens (instead of being terminated). The editor, for example, catches interrupts and stops what it is doing, instead of terminating, so that an interrupt can be used to halt an editor printout without losing the file being edited.

The *quit* signal is generated by typing the ASCII FS character. (FS appears many places on different terminals, most commonly as control-\ or control-|.) It not only causes a running program to terminate but also generates a file with the core image of the terminated process. Quit is useful for debugging.

Besides adapting to the speed of the terminal, UNIX tries to be intelligent about whether you have a terminal with the newline function or whether it must be simulated with carriage-return and line-feed. In the latter case, all input carriage returns are turned to newline characters (the standard line delimiter) and both a carriage return and a line feed are echoed to the terminal. If you get into the wrong mode, the *stty*(1) command will rescue you.

Tab characters are used freely in UNIX source programs. If your terminal does not have the tab function, you can arrange to have them turned into spaces during output, and echoed as spaces during input. The system assumes that tabs are set every eight columns. Again, the *stty* (1) command will set or reset this mode. Also, the command *tabs* (1) will set the tab stops automatically on many terminals.

How to run a program; the Shell. When you have successfully logged in, a program called the Shell is listening to your terminal. The Shell reads typed-in lines, splits them up into a command name and arguments, and executes the command. A command is simply an executable program. The Shell looks first in your current directory (see below) for a program with the given name, and if none is there, then in a system directory. There is nothing special about system-provided commands except that they are kept in a directory where the Shell can find them.

The command name is always the first word on an input line; it and its arguments are separated from one another by spaces.

When a program terminates, the Shell will ordinarily regain control and type a '$' at you to indicate that it is ready for another command.

The Shell has many other capabilities, which are described in detail in section *sh* (1).

The current directory. UNIX has a file system arranged in a hierarchy of directories. When the system administrator gave you a user name, he also created a directory for you (ordinarily with the same name as your user name). When you log in, any file name you type is by default in this directory. Since you are the owner of this directory, you have full permission to read, write, alter, or destroy its contents. Permissions to have your will with other directories and files will have been granted or denied to you by their owners. As a matter of observed fact, few UNIX users protect their files from destruction, let alone perusal, by other users.

To change the current directory (but not the set of permissions you were endowed with at login) use *cd* (1).

Path names. To refer to files not in the current directory, you must use a path name. Full path names begin with '/', the name of the root directory of the whole file system. After the slash comes the name of each directory containing the next sub-directory (followed by a '/') until finally the file name is reached. For example, */usr/lem/filex* refers to the file *filex* in the directory *lem; lem* is itself a subdirectory of *usr; usr* springs directly from the root directory.

If your current directory has subdirectories, the path names of files therein begin with the name of the subdirectory with no prefixed '/'.

A path name may be used anywhere a file name is required.

Important commands which modify the contents of files are *cp* (1), *mv* (1), and *rm* (1), which respectively copy, move (i.e. rename) and remove files. To find out the status of files or directories, use *ls* (1). See *mkdir* (1) for making directories and *rmdir* (in *rm* (1)) for destroying them.

For a fuller discussion of the file system, see 'The UNIX Time-Sharing System,' by Ken Thompson and Dennis Ritchie. It may also be useful to glance through section 2 of this manual, which discusses system calls, even if you don't intend to deal with the system at that level.

Writing a program. To enter the text of a source program into a UNIX file, use the editor *ed* (1). The three principal languages in UNIX are provided by the C compiler *cc* (1), the Fortran compiler *f77* (1), and the assembler *as* (1). After the program text has been entered through the editor and written on a file, you can give the file to the appropriate language processor as an argument. The output of the language processor will be left on a file in the current directory named 'a.out'. (If the output is precious, use *mv* to move it to a less exposed name soon.) If you wrote in assembly language, you will probably need to load the program with library subroutines; see *ld* (1). The other two language processors call the loader automatically.

When you have finally gone through this entire process without provoking any diagnostics, the resulting program can be run by giving its name to the Shell in response to the '$' prompt.

Your programs can receive arguments from the command line just as system programs do, see *exec* (2).

Text processing. Almost all text is entered through the editor *ed* (1). The commands most often used to write text on a terminal are: *cat, pr, roff* and *nroff,* all in section 1.

The *cat* command simply dumps ASCII text on the terminal, with no processing at all. The *pr* command paginates the text, supplies headings, and has a facility for multi-column output. *Nroff* is an elaborate text formatting program. Used naked, it requires careful forethought, but for ordinary documents it has been tamed; see *ms* (7). *Roff* is a simpler text formatting program, and requires somewhat less forethought.

Troff prepares documents for a Graphics Systems phototypesetter; it is very similar to *nroff,* and often works from exactly the same source text. It was used to produce this manual.

Status inquiries. Various commands exist to provide you with useful information. *Who* (1) prints a list of users presently logged in. *Date* (1) prints the current time and date. *Ls* (1) will list the files in your directory or give summary information about particular files.

Surprises. Certain commands provide inter-user communication. Even if you do not plan to use them, it would be well to learn something about them, because someone else may aim them at you.

To communicate with another user currently logged in, *write* (1) is used; *mail* (1) will leave a message whose presence will be announced to another user when he next logs in. The write-ups in the manual also suggest how to respond to the two commands if you are a target.

When you log in, a message-of-the-day may greet you before the first '$'.

CONVERTING FROM THE 6TH EDITION

There follows a catalogue of significant, mostly incompatible, changes that will affect old users converting to the 7th edition. No attempt is made to list all new facilities, or even all minor, but easily spotted changes, just the bare essentials without which it will be almost impossible to do anything.

Addressing files. Byte addresses in files are now long (32-bit) integers. Accordingly *seek* has been replaced by *lseek* (2). Every program that contains a *seek* must be modified. *Stat* and *fstat* (2) have been affected similarly, since file lengths are now 32- rather than 24-bit quantities.

Assembly language. System entry points are no longer built in symbols. Their values must be obtained from *lusrlincludelsys.s,* see *intro* (2). All system calls modify r0. This means that sequences like

```
    mov     file,r0
    sys     lseek,0,0,2
    sys     write,buf,n
```

will no longer work. (In fact, *lseek* now modifies r1 as well, so be doubly cautious.)

The *sleep* (2) entry point is gone; see the more general facility, *alarm,* plus *pause.*

Few library functions have assembly language entry points any more. You will have to simulate the C calling sequence.

Stty and gtty. These system calls have been extensively altered, see *ioctl* (2) and *tty* (4).

Archive files. The format of files produced by *ar* (1) has been altered. To convert to the new style, use *arcv* (1).

C language, lint. The official syntax for initialization requires an equal sign = before an initializer, and brackets { } around compound initial values; arrays and structures are now initialized honestly. Two-address operators, such as = + and = -, are now written + = and -= to avoid ambiguities, although the old style is still accepted. You will also certainly want to learn about

```
    long integers
    type definitions
    casts (for type conversion)
    unions (for more honest storage sharing)
    #include <filename> (which searches in standard places)
```

The program *lint*(1) checks for obsolete syntax and does strong type checking of C programs, singly or in groups that are expected to be loaded together. It is indispensable for conversion work.

Fortran. The old *fc* is replaced by *f77*, a true compiler for Fortran 77, compatible with C. There are substantial changes in the language; see 'A Portable Fortran 77 Compiler' in Volume 2.

Stream editor. The program *sed*(1) is adapted to massive, repetitive editing jobs of the sort encountered in converting to the new system. It is well worth learning.

Standard I/O. The old *fopen, getc, putc* complex and the old −*lp* package are both dead, and even *getchar* has changed. All have been replaced by the clean, highly efficient, *stdio*(3) package. The first things to know are that *getchar*(3) returns the integer EOF (−1), which is not a possible byte value, on end of file, that 518-byte buffers are out, and that there is a defined FILE data type.

Make. The program *make*(1) handles the recompilation and loading of software in an orderly way from a 'makefile' recipe given for each piece of software. It remakes only as much as the modification dates of the input files show is necessary. The makefiles will guide you in building your new system.

Shell, chdir. F. L. Bauer once said Algol 68 is the Everest that must be climbed by every computer scientist because it is there. So it is with the shell for UNIX users. Everything beyond simple command invocation from a terminal is different. Even *chdir* is now spelled *cd*. You will want to study *sh*(1) long and hard.

Debugging. *Adb*(1) is a far more capable replacement for the debugger *db*. The first-time user should be especially careful about distinguishing / and ? in *adb* commands, and watching to make sure that the *x* whose value he asked for is the real *x*, and not just some absolute location equal to the stack offset of some automatic *x*. You can always use the 'true' name, _*x*, to pin down a C external variable.

Dsw. This little-known, but indispensable facility has been taken over by *rm* −*ri*.

Boot procedures. Needless to say, these are all different. See section 8 of this volume, and 'Setting up UNIX' in Volume 2.

UNIX™ TIME-SHARING SYSTEM:

UNIX PROGRAMMER'S MANUAL

Section 1
COMMANDS

NAME

    intro — introduction to commands

DESCRIPTION

    This section describes publicly accessible commands in alphabetic order. Certain distinctions of purpose are made in the headings:

    (1)   Commands of general utility.

    (1C)   Commands for communication with other systems.

    (1G)   Commands used primarily for graphics and computer-aided design.

    (1M)   Commands used primarily for system maintenance.

    The word 'local' at the foot of a page means that the command is not intended for general distribution.

SEE ALSO

DIAGNOSTICS

    Section (6) for computer games.

    How to get started, in the Introduction.

DIAGNOSTICS

    Upon termination each command returns two bytes of status, one supplied by the system giving the cause for termination, and (in the case of 'normal' termination) one supplied by the program, see *wait* and *exit*(2). The former byte is 0 for normal termination, the latter is customarily 0 for successful execution, nonzero to indicate troubles such as erroneous parameters, bad or inaccessible data, or other inability to cope with the task at hand. It is called variously 'exit code', 'exit status' or 'return code', and is described only where special conventions are involved.

NAME
    ac — login accounting

SYNOPSIS
    ac [−**w** wtmp] [−**p**] [−**d**] [people] ...

DESCRIPTION
Ac produces a printout giving connect time for each user who has logged in during the life of the current *wtmp* file. A total is also produced. −**w** is used to specify an alternate *wtmp* file. −**p** prints individual totals; without this option, only totals are printed. −**d** causes a printout for each midnight to midnight period. Any *people* will limit the printout to only the specified login names. If no *wtmp* file is given, */usr/adm/wtmp* is used.

The accounting file */usr/adm/wtmp* is maintained by *init* and *login*. Neither of these programs creates the file, so if it does not exist no connect-time accounting is done. To start accounting, it should be created with length 0. On the other hand if the file is left undisturbed it will grow without bound, so periodically any information desired should be collected and the file truncated.

FILES
    /usr/adm/wtmp

SEE ALSO
    init(8), login(1), utmp(5).

NAME

adb — debugger

SYNOPSIS

adb [−**w**] [objfil [corfil]]

DESCRIPTION

Adb is a general purpose debugging program. It may be used to examine files and to provide a controlled environment for the execution of UNIX programs.

Objfil is normally an executable program file, preferably containing a symbol table; if not then the symbolic features of *adb* cannot be used although the file can still be examined. The default for *objfil* is **a.out.** *Corfil* is assumed to be a core image file produced after executing *objfil*; the default for *corfil* is **core.**

Requests to *adb* are read from the standard input and responses are to the standard output. If the −**w** flag is present then both *objfil* and *corfil* are created if necessary and opened for reading and writing so that files can be modified using *adb*. *Adb* ignores QUIT; INTERRUPT causes return to the next *adb* command.

In general requests to *adb* are of the form

[*address*] [, *count*] [*command*] [;]

If *address* is present then *dot* is set to *address*. Initially *dot* is set to 0. For most commands *count* specifies how many times the command will be executed. The default *count* is 1. *Address* and *count* are expressions.

The interpretation of an address depends on the context it is used in. If a subprocess is being debugged then addresses are interpreted in the usual way in the address space of the subprocess. For further details of address mapping see ADDRESSES.

EXPRESSIONS

. The value of *dot*.

+ The value of *dot* incremented by the current increment.

^ The value of *dot* decremented by the current increment.

" The last *address* typed.

integer An octal number if *integer* begins with a 0; a hexadecimal number if preceded by **#**; otherwise a decimal number.

integer.fraction
A 32 bit floating point number.

`cccc` The ASCII value of up to 4 characters. \ may be used to escape a `.

< *name*
The value of *name*, which is either a variable name or a register name. *Adb* maintains a number of variables (see VARIABLES) named by single letters or digits. If *name* is a register name then the value of the register is obtained from the system header in *corfil*. The register names are **r0 ... r5 sp pc ps**.

symbol A *symbol* is a sequence of upper or lower case letters, underscores or digits, not starting with a digit. The value of the *symbol* is taken from the symbol table in *objfil*. An initial _ or ~ will be prepended to *symbol* if needed.

_ *symbol*
In C, the 'true name' of an external symbol begins with _. It may be necessary to utter this name to disinguish it from internal or hidden variables of a program.

routine . name
>   The address of the variable *name* in the specified C routine. Both *routine* and *name* are *symbols*. If *name* is omitted the value is the address of the most recently activated C stack frame corresponding to *routine*.

(exp)   The value of the expression *exp*.

Monadic operators

∗exp   The contents of the location addressed by *exp* in *corfil*.

@exp   The contents of the location addressed by *exp* in *objfil*.

−exp   Integer negation.

~exp   Bitwise complement.

Dyadic operators are left associative and are less binding than monadic operators.

e1 +e2   Integer addition.

e1 −e2   Integer subtraction.

e1 ∗e2   Integer multiplication.

e1 %e2   Integer division.

e1 &e2   Bitwise conjunction.

e1 |e2   Bitwise disjunction.

e1 #e2   *E1* rounded up to the next multiple of *e2*.

COMMANDS

Most commands consist of a verb followed by a modifier or list of modifiers. The following verbs are available. (The commands '?' and '/' may be followed by '∗'; see ADDRESSES for further details.)

?f   Locations starting at *address* in *objfil* are printed according to the format *f*.

/f   Locations starting at *address* in *corfil* are printed according to the format *f*.

=f   The value of *address* itself is printed in the styles indicated by the format *f*. (For **i** format '?' is printed for the parts of the instruction that reference subsequent words.)

A *format* consists of one or more characters that specify a style of printing. Each format character may be preceded by a decimal integer that is a repeat count for the format character. While stepping through a format *dot* is incremented temporarily by the amount given for each format letter. If no format is given then the last format is used. The format letters available are as follows.

o	2	Print 2 bytes in octal. All octal numbers output by *adb* are preceded by 0.
O	4	Print 4 bytes in octal.
q	2	Print in signed octal.
Q	4	Print long signed octal.
d	2	Print in decimal.
D	4	Print long decimal.
x	2	Print 2 bytes in hexadecimal.
X	4	Print 4 bytes in hexadecimal.
u	2	Print as an unsigned decimal number.
U	4	Print long unsigned decimal.
f	4	Print the 32 bit value as a floating point number.
F	8	Print double floating point.
b	1	Print the addressed byte in octal.

c 1   Print the addressed character.

C 1   Print the addressed character using the following escape convention. Character values 000 to 040 are printed as @ followed by the corresponding character in the range 0100 to 0140. The character @ is printed as @@.

s *n*   Print the addressed characters until a zero character is reached.

S *n*   Print a string using the @ escape convention. *n* is the length of the string including its zero terminator.

Y 4   Print 4 bytes in date format (see *ctime*(3)).

i n   Print as PDP11 instructions. *n* is the number of bytes occupied by the instruction. This style of printing causes variables 1 and 2 to be set to the offset parts of the source and destination respectively.

a 0   Print the value of *dot* in symbolic form. Symbols are checked to ensure that they have an appropriate type as indicated below.

    /   local or global data symbol
    ?   local or global text symbol
    =   local or global absolute symbol

p 2   Print the addressed value in symbolic form using the same rules for symbol lookup as **a**.

t 0   When preceded by an integer tabs to the next appropriate tab stop. For example, **8t** moves to the next 8-space tab stop.

r 0   Print a space.

n 0   Print a newline.

"..." 0 Print the enclosed string.

    ^   *Dot* is decremented by the current increment. Nothing is printed.

    +   *Dot* is incremented by 1. Nothing is printed.

    −   *Dot* is decremented by 1. Nothing is printed.

newline

If the previous command temporarily incremented *dot*, make the increment permanent. Repeat the previous command with a *count* of 1.

[?/]l *value mask*

Words starting at *dot* are masked with *mask* and compared with *value* until a match is found. If **L** is used then the match is for 4 bytes at a time instead of 2. If no match is found then *dot* is unchanged; otherwise *dot* is set to the matched location. If *mask* is omitted then −1 is used.

[?/]w *value* ...

Write the 2-byte *value* into the addressed location. If the command is **W**, write 4 bytes. Odd addresses are not allowed when writing to the subprocess address space.

[?/]m *b1 e1 f1*[?/]

New values for (*b1*, *e1*, *f1*) are recorded. If less than three expressions are given then the remaining map parameters are left unchanged. If the '?' or '/' is followed by '∗' then the second segment (*b2*, *e2*, *f2*) of the mapping is changed. If the list is terminated by '?' or '/' then the file (*objfil* or *corfil* respectively) is used for subsequent requests. (So that, for example, '/m?' will cause '/' to refer to *objfil*.)

>*name* *Dot* is assigned to the variable or register named.

!   A shell is called to read the rest of the line following '!'.

$*modifier*

Miscellaneous commands. The available *modifiers* are:

    <*f*   Read commands from the file *f* and return.

>*f*   Send output to the file *f*, which is created if it does not exist.

r   Print the general registers and the instruction addressed by **pc**. *Dot* is set to **pc**.

f   Print the floating registers in single or double length. If the floating point status of **ps** is set to double (0200 bit) then double length is used anyway.

b   Print all breakpoints and their associated counts and commands.

a   ALGOL 68 stack backtrace. If *address* is given then it is taken to be the address of the current frame (instead of **r4**). If *count* is given then only the first *count* frames are printed.

c   C stack backtrace. If *address* is given then it is taken as the address of the current frame (instead of **r5**). If **C** is used then the names and (16 bit) values of all automatic and static variables are printed for each active function. If *count* is given then only the first *count* frames are printed.

e   The names and values of external variables are printed.

w   Set the page width for output to *address* (default 80).

s   Set the limit for symbol matches to *address* (default 255).

o   All integers input are regarded as octal.

d   Reset integer input as described in EXPRESSIONS.

q   Exit from *adb*.

v   Print all non zero variables in octal.

m   Print the address map.

:*modifier*

  Manage a subprocess. Available modifiers are:

b*c*   Set breakpoint at *address*. The breakpoint is executed *count*−1 times before causing a stop. Each time the breakpoint is encountered the command *c* is executed. If this command sets *dot* to zero then the breakpoint causes a stop.

d   Delete breakpoint at *address*.

r   Run *objfil* as a subprocess. If *address* is given explicitly then the program is entered at this point; otherwise the program is entered at its standard entry point. *count* specifies how many breakpoints are to be ignored before stopping. Arguments to the subprocess may be supplied on the same line as the command. An argument starting with < or > causes the standard input or output to be established for the command. All signals are turned on on entry to the subprocess.

c*s*   The subprocess is continued with signal *s c s*, see *signal*(2). If *address* is given then the subprocess is continued at this address. If no signal is specified then the signal that caused the subprocess to stop is sent. Breakpoint skipping is the same as for **r**.

s*s*   As for **c** except that the subprocess is single stepped *count* times. If there is no current subprocess then *objfil* is run as a subprocess as for **r**. In this case no signal can be sent; the remainder of the line is treated as arguments to the subprocess.

k   The current subprocess, if any, is terminated.

VARIABLES

  Adb provides a number of variables. Named variables are set initially by *adb* but are not used subsequently. Numbered variables are reserved for communication as follows.

0   The last value printed.

1   The last offset part of an instruction source.

2   The previous value of variable 1.

On entry the following are set from the system header in the *corfil*. If *corfil* does not appear to be a **core** file then these values are set from *objfil*.

b   The base address of the data segment.

d   The data segment size.

e   The entry point.

m   The 'magic' number (0405, 0407, 0410 or 0411).

s   The stack segment size.

t   The text segment size.

ADDRESSES

The address in a file associated with a written address is determined by a mapping associated with that file. Each mapping is represented by two triples (*b1*, *e1*, *f1*) and (*b2*, *e2*, *f2*) and the *file address* corresponding to a written *address* is calculated as follows.

$$b1 \leq address < e1 \implies file\ address = address + f1 - b1,\ \text{otherwise,}$$

$$b2 \leq address < e2 \implies file\ address = address + f2 - b2,$$

otherwise, the requested *address* is not legal. In some cases (e.g. for programs with separated I and D space) the two segments for a file may overlap. If a **?** or **/** is followed by an **∗** then only the second triple is used.

The initial setting of both mappings is suitable for normal **a.out** and **core** files. If either file is not of the kind expected then, for that file, *b1* is set to 0, *e1* is set to the maximum file size and *f1* is set to 0; in this way the whole file can be examined with no address translation.

So that *adb* may be used on large files all appropriate values are kept as signed 32 bit integers.

FILES

     /dev/mem

     /dev/swap

     a.out

     core

SEE ALSO

     ptrace(2), a.out(5), core(5)

DIAGNOSTICS

'Adb' when there is no current command or format. Comments about inaccessible files, syntax errors, abnormal termination of commands, etc. Exit status is 0, unless last command failed or returned nonzero status.

BUGS

A breakpoint set at the entry point is not effective on initial entry to the program.

When single stepping, system calls do not count as an executed instruction.

Local variables whose names are the same as an external variable may foul up the accessing of the external.

NAME

ar − archive and library maintainer

SYNOPSIS

ar key [posname] afile name ...

DESCRIPTION

Ar maintains groups of files combined into a single archive file. Its main use is to create and update library files as used by the loader. It can be used, though, for any similar purpose.

Key is one character from the set **drqtpmx**, optionally concatenated with one or more of **vuaibcl**. *Afile* is the archive file. The *names* are constituent files in the archive file. The meanings of the *key* characters are:

d Delete the named files from the archive file.

r Replace the named files in the archive file. If the optional character **u** is used with **r**, then only those files with modified dates later than the archive files are replaced. If an optional positioning character from the set **abi** is used, then the *posname* argument must be present and specifies that new files are to be placed after (**a**) or before (**b** or **i**) *posname*. Otherwise new files are placed at the end.

q Quickly append the named files to the end of the archive file. Optional positioning characters are invalid. The command does not check whether the added members are already in the archive. Useful only to avoid quadratic behavior when creating a large archive piece-by-piece.

t Print a table of contents of the archive file. If no names are given, all files in the archive are tabled. If names are given, only those files are tabled.

p Print the named files in the archive.

m Move the named files to the end of the archive. If a positioning character is present, then the *posname* argument must be present and, as in **r**, specifies where the files are to be moved.

x Extract the named files. If no names are given, all files in the archive are extracted. In neither case does **x** alter the archive file.

v Verbose. Under the verbose option, *ar* gives a file-by-file description of the making of a new archive file from the old archive and the constituent files. When used with **t**, it gives a long listing of all information about the files. When used with **p**, it precedes each file with a name.

c Create. Normally *ar* will create *afile* when it needs to. The create option suppresses the normal message that is produced when *afile* is created.

l Local. Normally *ar* places its temporary files in the directory /tmp. This option causes them to be placed in the local directory.

FILES

/tmp/v*   temporaries

SEE ALSO

ld(1), ar(5), lorder(1)

BUGS

If the same file is mentioned twice in an argument list, it may be put in the archive twice.

NAME

      arcv − convert archives to new format

SYNOPSIS

      arcv file ...

DESCRIPTION

      Arcv converts archive files (see *ar*(1), *ar*(5)) from 6th edition to 7th edition format. The conversion is done in place, and the command refuses to alter a file not in old archive format.

      Old archives are marked with a magic number of 0177555 at the start; new archives have 0177545.

FILES

      /tmp/v*, temporary copy

SEE ALSO

      ar(1), ar(5)

NAME

  as − assembler

SYNOPSIS

  as [−] [−**o** objfile] file ...

DESCRIPTION

  As assembles the concatenation of the named files. If the optional first argument − is used, all undefined symbols in the assembly are treated as global.

  The output of the assembly is left on the file *objfile;* if that is omitted, **a.out** is used. It is executable if no errors occurred during the assembly, and if there were no unresolved external references.

FILES

  /lib/as2   pass 2 of the assembler
  /tmp/atm[1-3]?temporary
  a.out   object

SEE ALSO

  ld(1), nm(1), adb(1), a.out(5)
  UNIX Assembler Manual by D. M. Ritchie

DIAGNOSTICS

  When an input file cannot be read, its name followed by a question mark is typed and assembly ceases. When syntactic or semantic errors occur, a single-character diagnostic is typed out together with the line number and the file name in which it occurred. Errors in pass 1 cause cancellation of pass 2. The possible errors are:

)   Parentheses error
  ]   Parentheses error
  <   String not terminated properly
  *   Indirection used illegally
  a   **Error in address**
  b   **Branch instruction is odd or too remote**
  e   **Error in expression**
  f   **Error in local ('f' or 'b') type symbol**
  g   **Garbage (unknown) character**
  i   **End of file inside an if**
  m   **Multiply defined symbol as label**
  o   **Word quantity assembled at odd address**
  p   '.' different in pass 1 and 2
  r   Relocation error
  u   Undefined symbol
  x   Syntax error

BUGS

  Syntax errors can cause incorrect line numbers in following diagnostics.

NAME

at — execute commands at a later time

SYNOPSIS

at time [day] [file]

DESCRIPTION

At squirrels away a copy of the named *file* (standard input default) to be used as input to *sh*(1) at a specified later time. A *cd*(1) command to the current directory is inserted at the beginning, followed by assignments to all environment variables. When the script is run, it uses the user and group ID of the creator of the copy file.

The *time* is 1 to 4 digits, with an optional following 'A', 'P', 'N' or 'M' for AM, PM, noon or midnight. One and two digit numbers are taken to be hours, three and four digits to be hours and minutes. If no letters follow the digits, a 24 hour clock time is understood.

The optional *day* is either (1) a month name followed by a day number, or (2) a day of the week; if the word 'week' follows invocation is moved seven days further off. Names of months and days may be recognizably truncated. Examples of legitimate commands are

        at 8am jan 24
        at 1530 fr week

At programs are executed by periodic execution of the command */usr/lib/atrun* from *cron*(8). The granularity of *at* depends upon how often *atrun* is executed.

Standard output or error output is lost unless redirected.

FILES

/usr/spool/at/yy.ddd.hhhh.uu

activity to be performed at hour *hhhh* of year day *ddd* of year *yy*. *uu* is a unique number.
/usr/spool/at/lasttimedone contains *hhhh* for last hour of activity.
/usr/spool/at/past directory of activities now in progress
/usr/lib/atrun program that executes activities that are due
pwd(1)

SEE ALSO

calendar(1), cron(8)

DIAGNOSTICS

Complains about various syntax errors and times out of range.

BUGS

Due to the granularity of the execution of */usr/lib/atrun*, there may be bugs in scheduling things almost exactly 24 hours into the future.

NAME

awk − pattern scanning and processing language

SYNOPSIS

awk [−F*c*] [prog] [file] ...

DESCRIPTION

Awk scans each input *file* for lines that match any of a set of patterns specified in *prog*. With each pattern in *prog* there can be an associated action that will be performed when a line of a *file* matches the pattern. The set of patterns may appear literally as *prog*, or in a file specified as −**f** *file*.

Files are read in order; if there are no files, the standard input is read. The file name '−' means the standard input. Each line is matched against the pattern portion of every pattern-action statement; the associated action is performed for each matched pattern.

An input line is made up of fields separated by white space. (This default can be changed by using FS, *vide infra*.) The fields are denoted $1, $2, ... ; $0 refers to the entire line.

A pattern-action statement has the form

        pattern { action }

A missing { action } means print the line; a missing pattern always matches.

An action is a sequence of statements. A statement can be one of the following:

        if (conditional) statement [else statement]
        while (conditional) statement
        for (expression ; conditional ; expression) statement
        break
        continue
        { [statement] ... }
        variable = expression
        print [expression-list] [>expression]
        printf format [, expression-list] [>expression]
        next   # skip remaining patterns on this input line
        exit   # skip the rest of the input

Statements are terminated by semicolons, newlines or right braces. An empty expression-list stands for the whole line. Expressions take on string or numeric values as appropriate, and are built using the operators +, −, *, /, %, and concatenation (indicated by a blank). The C operators ++, −−, +=, −=, *=, /=, and %= are also available in expressions. Variables may be scalars, array elements (denoted x[i]) or fields. Variables are initialized to the null string. Array subscripts may be any string, not necessarily numeric; this allows for a form of associative memory. String constants are quoted "...".

The *print* statement prints its arguments on the standard output (or on a file if >*file* is present), separated by the current output field separator, and terminated by the output record separator. The *printf* statement formats its expression list according to the format (see *printf*(3)).

The built-in function *length* returns the length of its argument taken as a string, or of the whole line if no argument. There are also built-in functions *exp*, *log*, *sqrt*, and *int*. The last truncates its argument to an integer. *substr(s, m, n)* returns the *n*-character substring of *s* that begins at position *m*. The function *sprintf(fmt, expr, expr, ...)* formats the expressions according to the *printf*(3) format given by *fmt* and returns the resulting string.

Patterns are arbitrary Boolean combinations (!, ||, &&, and parentheses) of regular expressions and relational expressions. Regular expressions must be surrounded by slashes and are as in *egrep*. Isolated regular expressions in a pattern apply to the entire line. Regular expressions may also occur in relational expressions.

A pattern may consist of two patterns separated by a comma; in this case, the action is performed for all lines between an occurrence of the first pattern and the next occurrence of the second.

A relational expression is one of the following:

> expression matchop regular-expression
> expression relop expression

where a relop is any of the six relational operators in C, and a matchop is either ˜ (for contains) or !˜ (for does not contain). A conditional is an arithmetic expression, a relational expression, or a Boolean combination of these.

The special patterns BEGIN and END may be used to capture control before the first input line is read and after the last. BEGIN must be the first pattern, END the last.

A single character *c* may be used to separate the fields by starting the program with

> BEGIN { FS = "c" }

or by using the −F*c* option.

Other variable names with special meanings include NF, the number of fields in the current record; NR, the ordinal number of the current record; FILENAME, the name of the current input file; OFS, the output field separator (default blank); ORS, the output record separator (default newline); and OFMT, the output format for numbers (default "%.6g").

EXAMPLES

Print lines longer than 72 characters:

Print first two fields in opposite order:

> { print $2, $1 }

Add up first column, print sum and average:

> { s += $1 }
> END   { print "sum is", s, " average is", s/NR }

Print fields in reverse order:

> { for (i = NF; i > 0; −−i) print $i }

Print all lines between start/stop pairs:

> /start/, /stop/

Print all lines whose first field is different from previous one:

> $1 != prev { print; prev = $1 }

SEE ALSO

lex(1), sed(1)

A. V. Aho, B. W. Kernighan, P. J. Weinberger, *Awk − a pattern scanning and processing language*

BUGS

There are no explicit conversions between numbers and strings. To force an expression to be treated as a number add 0 to it; to force it to be treated as a string concatenate "" to it.

NAME

bas — basic

SYNOPSIS

bas [file]

DESCRIPTION

Bas is a dialect of Basic. If a file argument is provided, the file is used for input before the terminal is read. *Bas* accepts lines of the form:

statement

integer statement

Integer numbered statements (known as internal statements) are stored for later execution. They are stored in sorted ascending order. Non-numbered statements are immediately executed. The result of an immediate expression statement (that does not have '=' as its highest operator) is printed. Interrupts suspend computation.

Statements have the following syntax:

expression

The expression is executed for its side effects (assignment or function call) or for printing as described above.

comment

This statement is ignored. It is used to interject commentary in a program.

done

Return to system level.

dump

The name and current value of every variable is printed.

edit

The UNIX editor, *ed,* is invoked with the *file* argument. After the editor exits, this file is recompiled.

for name = expression expression statement

for name = expression expression

next

The *for* statement repetitively executes a statement (first form) or a group of statements (second form) under control of a named variable. The variable takes on the value of the first expression, then is incremented by one on each loop, not to exceed the value of the second expression.

goto expression

The expression is evaluated, truncated to an integer and execution goes to the corresponding integer numbered statment. If executed from immediate mode, the internal statements are compiled first.

if expression statement

if expression

[else

fi

The statement (first form) or group of statements (second form) is executed if the expression evaluates to non-zero. In the second form, an optional **else** allows for a group of statements to be executed when the first group is not.

list [expression [expression]]

is used to print out the stored internal statements. If no arguments are given, all internal statements are printed. If one argument is given, only that internal statement is listed. If two arguments are given, all internal statements inclusively between the arguments are printed.

print list

The list of expressions and strings are concatenated and printed. (A string is delimited by " characters.)

prompt list

Prompt is the same as *print* except that no newline character is printed.

return [expression]

The expression is evaluated and the result is passed back as the value of a function call. If no expression is given, zero is returned.

run

The internal statements are compiled. The symbol table is re-initialized. The random number generator is reset. Control is passed to the lowest numbered internal statement.

save [expression [expression]]

Save is like *list* except that the output is written on the *file* argument. If no argument is given on the command, **b.out** is used.

Expressions have the following syntax:

name

A name is used to specify a variable. Names are composed of a letter followed by letters and digits. The first four characters of a name are significant.

number

A number is used to represent a constant value. A number is written in Fortran style, and contains digits, an optional decimal point, and possibly a scale factor consisting of an **e** followed by a possibly signed exponent.

(expression)

Parentheses are used to alter normal order of evaluation.

_ expression

The result is the negation of the expression.

expression operator expression

Common functions of two arguments are abbreviated by the two arguments separated by an operator denoting the function. A complete list of operators is given below.

expression ([expression [, expression] ...])

Functions of an arbitrary number of arguments can be called by an expression followed by the arguments in parentheses separated by commas. The expression evaluates to the line number of the entry of the function in the internally stored statements. This causes the internal statements to be compiled. If the expression evaluates negative, a builtin function is called. The list of builtin functions appears below.

name [expression [, expression] ...]

Each expression is truncated to an integer and used as a specifier for the name. The result is syntactically identical to a name. **a[1,2]** is the same as **a[1][2]**. The truncated expressions are restricted to values between 0 and 32767.

The following is the list of operators:

=   = is the assignment operator. The left operand must be a name or an array element. The result is the right operand. Assignment binds right to left,

& | & (logical and) has result zero if either of its arguments are zero. It has result one if both its arguments are non-zero. | (logical or) has result zero if both of its arguments are zero. It has result one if either of its arguments are non-zero.

$< \quad <= \quad > \quad >= \quad == \quad <>$

The relational operators ($<$ less than, $<=$ less than or equal, $>$ greater than, $>=$ greater than or equal, $==$ equal to, $<>$ not equal to) return one if their arguments are in the specified relation. They return zero otherwise. Relational operators at the same level extend as follows: a>b>c is the same as a>b&b>c.

$+ \quad -$ Add and subtract.

$* \; /$ Multiply and divide.

$\hat{\ }$ Exponentiation.

The following is a list of builtin functions:

arg(i) is the value of the *i* -th actual parameter on the current level of function call.

exp(x) is the exponential function of *x*.

log(x) is the natural logarithm of *x*.

sqr(x) is the square root of *x*.

sin(x) is the sine of *x* (radians).

cos(x) is the cosine of *x* (radians).

atn(x) is the arctangent of *x*. Its value is between $-\pi/2$ and $\pi/2$.

rnd( ) is a uniformly distributed random number between zero and one.

expr( )

is the only form of program input. A line is read from the input and evaluated as an expression. The resultant value is returned.

abs(x) is the absolute value of *x*.

int(x) returns *x* truncated (towards 0) to an integer.

FILES
/tmp/btm?   temporary
b.out   save file
/bin/ed for **edit**

DIAGNOSTICS
Syntax errors cause the incorrect line to be typed with an underscore where the parse failed. All other diagnostics are self explanatory.

BUGS
Has been known to give core images.
Catches interrupts even when they are turned off.

NAME

basename — strip filename affixes

SYNOPSIS

basename string [suffix]

DESCRIPTION

Basename deletes any prefix ending in '/' and the *suffix*, if present in *string*, from *string*, and prints the result on the standard output. It is normally used inside substitution marks ` ` in shell procedures.

This shell procedure invoked with the argument */usr/src/cmd/cat.c* compiles the named file and moves the output to *cat* in the current directory:

```
cc $1
mv a.out `basename $1 .c`
```

SEE ALSO

sh(1)

NAME

bc − arbitrary-precision arithmetic language

SYNOPSIS

bc [−c] [−l] [file ...]

DESCRIPTION

Bc is an interactive processor for a language which resembles C but provides unlimited precision arithmetic. It takes input from any files given, then reads the standard input. The −l argument stands for the name of an arbitrary precision math library. The syntax for *bc* programs is as follows; L means letter a-z, E means expression, S means statement.

Comments
>   are enclosed in /* and */.

Names
>   simple variables: L
>   array elements: L [E]
>   The words 'ibase', 'obase', and 'scale'

Other operands
>   arbitrarily long numbers with optional sign and decimal point.
>   (E)
>   sqrt (E)
>   length (E)   number of significant decimal digits
>   scale (E)   number of digits right of decimal point
>   L (E , ... , E)

Operators
>   + − * / % ^ (% is remainder; ^ is power)
>   ++ −−   (prefix and postfix; apply to names)
>   == <= >= != < >
>   = =+ =− =* =/ =% =^

Statements
>   E
>   { S ; ... ; S }
>   if (E) S
>   while (E) S
>   for (E ; E ; E) S
>   null statement
>   break
>   quit

Function definitions
>   define L (L ,..., L) {
>   auto L, ... , L
>   S; ... S
>   return (E)
>   }

Functions in −l math library
>   s(x)   sine
>   c(x)   cosine
>   e(x)   exponential
>   l(x)   log
>   a(x)   arctangent
>   j(n,x)   Bessel function

All function arguments are passed by value.

The value of a statement that is an expression is printed unless the main operator is an assignment. Either semicolons or newlines may separate statements. Assignment to *scale* influences the number of digits to be retained on arithmetic operations in the manner of *dc*(1). Assignments to *ibase* or *obase* set the input and output number radix respectively.

The same letter may be used as an array, a function, and a simple variable simultaneously. All variables are global to the program. 'Auto' variables are pushed down during function calls. When using arrays as function arguments or defining them as automatic variables empty square brackets must follow the array name.

For example

```
scale = 20
define e(x){
        auto a, b, c, i, s
        a = 1
        b = 1
        s = 1
        for(i=1; 1==1; i++){
                a = a*x
                b = b*i
                c = a/b
                if(c == 0) return(s)
                s = s+c
        }
}
```

defines a function to compute an approximate value of the exponential function and

```
        for(i=1; i<=10; i++) e(i)
```

prints approximate values of the exponential function of the first ten integers.

Bc is actually a preprocessor for *dc*(1), which it invokes automatically, unless the −c (compile only) option is present. In this case the *dc* input is sent to the standard output instead.

FILES

    /usr/lib/lib.b mathematical library
    dc(1)   desk calculator proper

SEE ALSO

    dc(1)
    L. L. Cherry and R. Morris, *BC − An arbitrary precision desk-calculator language*

BUGS

    No &&, ǀǀ, or ! operators.
    For statement must have all three E's.
    Quit is interpreted when read, not when executed.

NAME

    cal − print calendar

SYNOPSIS

    cal [month] year

DESCRIPTION

    Cal prints a calendar for the specified year. If a month is also specified, a calendar just for that
month is printed. *Year* can be between 1 and 9999. The *month* is a number between 1 and 12.
The calendar produced is that for England and her colonies.

    Try September 1752.

BUGS

    The year is always considered to start in January even though this is historically naive.
Beware that 'cal 78' refers to the early Christian era, not the 20th century.

NAME

    calendar — reminder service

SYNOPSIS

    calendar [−]

DESCRIPTION

    Calendar consults the file 'calendar' in the current directory and prints out lines that contain today's or tomorrow's date anywhere in the line. Most reasonable month-day dates such as 'Dec. 7,' 'december 7,' '12/7,' etc., are recognized, but not '7 December' or '7/12'. On weekends 'tomorrow' extends through Monday.

    When an argument is present, *calendar* does its job for every user who has a file 'calendar' in his login directory and sends him any positive results by *mail*(1). Normally this is done daily in the wee hours under control of *cron*(8).

FILES

    calendar
    /usr/lib/calendar to figure out today's and tomorrow's dates
    /etc/passwd
    /tmp/cal*
    egrep, sed, mail subprocesses

SEE ALSO

    at(1), cron(8), mail(1)

BUGS

    Your calendar must be public information for you to get reminder service.
    Calendar's extended idea of 'tomorrow' doesn't account for holidays.

NAME

cat — catenate and print

SYNOPSIS

cat [**−u**] file ...

DESCRIPTION

Cat reads each *file* in sequence and writes it on the standard output. Thus

      cat file

prints the file and

      cat file1 file2 >file3

concatenates the first two files and places the result on the third.

If no *file* is given, or if the argument '−' is encountered, *cat* reads from the standard input. Output is buffered in 512-byte blocks unless the standard output is a terminal or the −**u** option is present.

SEE ALSO

pr(1), cp(1)

BUGS

Beware of 'cat a b >a' and 'cat a b >b', which destroy input files before reading them.

NAME
cb — C program beautifier

SYNOPSIS
cb

DESCRIPTION
Cb places a copy of the C program from the standard input on the standard output with spacing and indentation that displays the structure of the program.

BUGS

NAME

cc, pcc — C compiler

SYNOPSIS

cc [option] ... file ...

pcc [option] ... file ...

DESCRIPTION

Cc is the UNIX C compiler. It accepts several types of arguments:

Arguments whose names end with '.c' are taken to be C source programs; they are compiled, and each object program is left on the file whose name is that of the source with '.o' substituted for '.c'. The '.o' file is normally deleted, however, if a single C program is compiled and loaded all at one go.

In the same way, arguments whose names end with '.s' are taken to be assembly source programs and are assembled, producing a '.o' file.

The following options are interpreted by *cc*. See *ld*(1) for load-time options.

−c   Suppress the loading phase of the compilation, and force an object file to be produced even if only one program is compiled.

−p   Arrange for the compiler to produce code which counts the number of times each routine is called; also, if loading takes place, replace the standard startup routine by one which automatically calls *monitor*(3) at the start and arranges to write out a *mon.out* file at normal termination of execution of the object program. An execution profile can then be generated by use of *prof*(1).

−f   In systems without hardware floating-point, use a version of the C compiler which handles floating-point constants and loads the object program with the floating-point interpreter. Do not use if the hardware is present.

−O   Invoke an object-code optimizer.

−S   Compile the named C programs, and leave the assembler-language output on corresponding files suffixed '.s'.

−P   Run only the macro preprocessor and place the result for each '.c' file in a corresponding '.i' file and has no '#' lines in it.

−E   Run only the macro preprocessor and send the result to the standard output. The output is intended for compiler debugging; it is unacceptable as input to *cc*.

−o *output*

     Name the final output file *output*. If this option is used the file 'a.out' will be left undisturbed.

−D*name*=*def*

−D*name*

     Define the *name* to the preprocessor, as if by '#define'. If no definition is given, the name is defined as 1.

−U*name*

     Remove any initial definition of *name*.

−I*dir*   '#include' files whose names do not begin with '/' are always sought first in the directory of the *file* argument, then in directories named in −I options, then in directories on a standard list.

−B*string*

     Find substitute compiler passes in the files named *string* with the suffixes cpp, c0, c1 and c2. If *string* is empty, use a standard backup version.

−t[p012]
> Find only the designated compiler passes in the files whose names are constructed by a −**B** option. In the absence of a −**B** option, the *string* is taken to be '/usr/c/'.

Other arguments are taken to be either loader option arguments, or C-compatible object programs, typically produced by an earlier *cc* run, or perhaps libraries of C-compatible routines. These programs, together with the results of any compilations specified, are loaded (in the order given) to produce an executable program with name **a.out.**

The major purpose of the 'portable C compiler', *pcc*, is to serve as a model on which to base other compilers. *Pcc* does not support options −**f**, −**E**, −**B**, and −**t**. It provides, in addition to the language of *cc*, unsigned char type data and initialized bit fields.

FILES

file.c	input file
file.o	object file
a.out	loaded output
/tmp/ctm?	temporaries for *cc*
/lib/cpp	preprocessor
/lib/c[01]	compiler for *cc*
/usr/c/oc[012]	backup compiler for *cc*
/usr/c/ocpp	backup preprocessor
/lib/fc[01]	floating-point compiler
/lib/c2	optional optimizer
/lib/crt0.o	runtime startoff
/lib/mcrt0.o	startoff for profiling
/lib/fcrt0.o	startoff for floating-point interpretation
/lib/libc.a	standard library, see *intro*(3)
/usr/include	standard directory for '#include' files
/tmp/pc*	temporaries for *pcc*
/usr/lib/ccom	compiler for *pcc*

SEE ALSO

> B. W. Kernighan and D. M. Ritchie, *The C Programming Language,* Prentice-Hall, 1978
> D. M. Ritchie, *C Reference Manual*
> monitor(3), prof(1), adb(1), ld(1)

DIAGNOSTICS

> The diagnostics produced by C itself are intended to be self-explanatory. Occasional messages may be produced by the assembler or loader. Of these, the most mystifying are from the assembler, *as*(1), in particular 'm', which means a multiply-defined external symbol (function or data).

BUGS

> *Pcc* is little tried on the PDP11; specialized code generated for that machine has not been well shaken down. The −**O** optimizer was designed to work with *cc*; its use with *pcc* is suspect.

NAME

    cd — change working directory

SYNOPSIS

    cd directory

DESCRIPTION

    Directory becomes the new working directory. The process must have execute (search) permission in *directory*.

    Because a new process is created to execute each command, *cd* would be ineffective if it were written as a normal command. It is therefore recognized and executed by the Shell.

SEE ALSO

    sh(1), pwd(1), chdir(2)

NAME

chmod − change mode

SYNOPSIS

chmod mode file ...

DESCRIPTION

The mode of each named file is changed according to *mode,* which may be absolute or symbolic. An absolute *mode* is an octal number constructed from the OR of the following modes:

4000	set user ID on execution
2000	set group ID on execution
1000	sticky bit, see *chmod*(2)
0400	read by owner
0200	write by owner
0100	execute (search in directory) by owner
0070	read, write, execute (search) by group
0007	read, write, execute (search) by others

A symbolic *mode* has the form:

[*who*] *op permission* [*op permission*] ...

The *who* part is a combination of the letters **u** (for user's permissions), **g** (group) and **o** (other). The letter **a** stands for **ugo.** If *who* is omitted, the default is *a* but the setting of the file creation mask (see umask(2)) is taken into account.

Op can be + to add *permission* to the file's mode, − to take away *permission* and = to assign *permission* absolutely (all other bits will be reset).

Permission is any combination of the letters **r** (read), **w** (write), **x** (execute), **s** (set owner or group id) and **t** (save text − sticky). Letters **u, g** or **o** indicate that *permission* is to be taken from the current mode. Omitting *permission* is only useful with = to take away all permissions.

The first example denies write permission to others, the second makes a file executable:

chmod o−w file
chmod +x file

Multiple symbolic modes separated by commas may be given. Operations are performed in the order specified. The letter **s** is only useful with **u** or **g.**

Only the owner of a file (or the super-user) may change its mode.

SEE ALSO

ls(1), chmod(2), chown (1), stat(2), umask(2)

NAME

chown, chgrp — change owner or group

SYNOPSIS

chown owner file ...

chgrp group file ...

DESCRIPTION

Chown changes the owner of the *files* to *owner*. The owner may be either a decimal UID or a login name found in the password file.

Chgrp changes the group-ID of the *files* to *group*. The group may be either a decimal GID or a group name found in the group-ID file.

Only the super-user can change owner or group, in order to simplify as yet unimplemented accounting procedures.

FILES

/etc/passwd

/etc/group

SEE ALSO

chown(2), passwd(5), group(5)

NAME

clri — clear i-node

SYNOPSIS

clri filesystem i-number ...

DESCRIPTION

Clri writes zeros on the i-nodes with the decimal *i-numbers* on the *filesystem*. After *clri*, any blocks in the affected file will show up as 'missing' in an *icheck*(1) of the *filesystem*.

Read and write permission is required on the specified file system device. The i-node becomes allocatable.

The primary purpose of this routine is to remove a file which for some reason appears in no directory. If it is used to zap an i-node which does appear in a directory, care should be taken to track down the entry and remove it. Otherwise, when the i-node is reallocated to some new file, the old entry will still point to that file. At that point removing the old entry will destroy the new file. The new entry will again point to an unallocated i-node, so the whole cycle is likely to be repeated again and again.

SEE ALSO

icheck(1)

BUGS

If the file is open, *clri* is likely to be ineffective.

NAME

cmp − compare two files

SYNOPSIS

cmp [−l] [−s] file1 file2

DESCRIPTION

The two files are compared. (If *file1* is '−', the standard input is used.) Under default options, *cmp* makes no comment if the files are the same; if they differ, it announces the byte and line number at which the difference occurred. If one file is an initial subsequence of the other, that fact is noted.

Options:

−l   Print the byte number (decimal) and the differing bytes (octal) for each difference.

−s   Print nothing for differing files; return codes only.

SEE ALSO

diff(1), comm(1)

DIAGNOSTICS

Exit code 0 is returned for identical files, 1 for different files, and 2 for an inaccessible or missing argument.

NAME

col — filter reverse line feeds

SYNOPSIS

col [−bfx]

DESCRIPTION

Col reads the standard input and writes the standard output. It performs the line overlays implied by reverse line feeds (ESC-7 in ASCII) and by forward and reverse half line feeds (ESC-9 and ESC-8). *Col* is particularly useful for filtering multicolumn output made with the '.rt' command of *nroff* and output resulting from use of the *tbl*(1) preprocessor.

Although *col* accepts half line motions in its input, it normally does not emit them on output. Instead, text that would appear between lines is moved to the next lower full line boundary. This treatment can be suppressed by the −**f** (fine) option; in this case the output from *col* may contain forward half line feeds (ESC-9), but will still never contain either kind of reverse line motion.

If the −**b** option is given, *col* assumes that the output device in use is not capable of backspacing. In this case, if several characters are to appear in the same place, only the last one read will be taken.

The control characters SO (ASCII code 017), and SI (016) are assumed to start and end text in an alternate character set. The character set (primary or alternate) associated with each printing character read is remembered; on output, SO and SI characters are generated where necessary to maintain the correct treatment of each character.

Col normally converts white space to tabs to shorten printing time. If the −**x** option is given, this conversion is suppressed.

All control characters are removed from the input except space, backspace, tab, return, newline, ESC (033) followed by one of 789, SI, SO, and VT (013). This last character is an alternate form of full reverse line feed, for compatibility with some other hardware conventions. All other non-printing characters are ignored.

SEE ALSO

troff(1), tbl(1), greek(1)

BUGS

Can't back up more than 128 lines.
No more than 800 characters, including backspaces, on a line.

NAME

comm — select or reject lines common to two sorted files

SYNOPSIS

comm [— [**123**]] file1 file2

DESCRIPTION

Comm reads *file1* and *file2,* which should be ordered in ASCII collating sequence, and produces a three column output: lines only in *file1;* lines only in *file2;* and lines in both files. The filename '—' means the standard input.

Flags 1, 2, or 3 suppress printing of the corresponding column. Thus **comm** —**12** prints only the lines common to the two files; **comm** —**23** prints only lines in the first file but not in the second; **comm** —**123** is a no-op.

SEE ALSO

cmp(1), diff(1), uniq(1)

NAME

cp — copy

SYNOPSIS

cp file1 file2

cp file ... directory

DESCRIPTION

File1 is copied onto *file2*. The mode and owner of *file2* are preserved if it already existed; the mode of the source file is used otherwise.

In the second form, one or more *files* are copied into the *directory* with their original file-names.

Cp refuses to copy a file onto itself.

SEE ALSO

cat(1), pr(1), mv(1)

NAME

crypt — encode/decode

SYNOPSIS

crypt [password]

DESCRIPTION

Crypt reads from the standard input and writes on the standard output. The *password* is a key that selects a particular transformation. If no *password* is given, *crypt* demands a key from the terminal and turns off printing while the key is being typed in. *Crypt* encrypts and decrypts with the same key:

        crypt key <clear >cypher
        crypt key <cypher | pr

will print the clear.

Files encrypted by *crypt* are compatible with those treated by the editor *ed* in encryption mode.

The security of encrypted files depends on three factors: the fundamental method must be hard to solve; direct search of the key space must be infeasible; 'sneak paths' by which keys or clear-text can become visible must be minimized.

Crypt implements a one-rotor machine designed along the lines of the German Enigma, but with a 256-element rotor. Methods of attack on such machines are known, but not widely; moreover the amount of work required is likely to be large.

The transformation of a key into the internal settings of the machine is deliberately designed to be expensive, i.e. to take a substantial fraction of a second to compute. However, if keys are restricted to (say) three lower-case letters, then encrypted files can be read by expending only a substantial fraction of five minutes of machine time.

Since the key is an argument to the *crypt* command, it is potentially visible to users executing *ps*(1) or a derivative. To minimize this possibility, *crypt* takes care to destroy any record of the key immediately upon entry. No doubt the choice of keys and key security are the most vulnerable aspect of *crypt*.

FILES

/dev/tty for typed key

SEE ALSO

ed(1), makekey(8)

BUGS

There is no warranty of merchantability nor any warranty of fitness for a particular purpose nor any other warranty, either express or implied, as to the accuracy of the enclosed materials or as to their suitability for any particular purpose. Accordingly, Bell Telephone Laboratories assumes no responsibility for their use by the recipient. Further, Bell Laboratories assumes no obligation to furnish any assistance of any kind whatsoever, or to furnish any additional information or documentation.

NAME
cu − call UNIX

SYNOPSIS
cu telno [−t] [−s speed] [−a acu] [−l line]

DESCRIPTION
Cu calls up another UNIX system, a terminal, or possibly a non-UNIX system. It manages an interactive conversation with possible transfers of text files. *Telno* is the telephone number, with minus signs at appropriate places for delays. The −t flag is used to dial out to a terminal. *Speed* gives the transmission speed (110, 134, 150, 300, 1200); 300 is the default value.

The −a and −l values may be used to specify pathnames for the ACU and communications line devices. They can be used to override the following built-in choices:

−a /dev/cua0 −l /dev/cul0

After making the connection, *cu* runs as two processes: the *send* process reads the standard input and passes most of it to the remote system; the *receive* process reads from the remote system and passes most data to the standard output. Lines beginning with '˜' have special meanings.

The *send* process interprets the following:

˜.	terminate the conversation.
˜EOT	terminate the conversation
˜<file	send the contents of *file* to the remote system, as though typed at the terminal.
˜!	invoke an interactive shell on the local system.
˜!cmd ...	run the command on the local system (via **sh** −c).
˜$cmd ...	run the command locally and send its output to the remote system.
˜%take from [to]	copy file 'from' (on the remote system) to file 'to' on the local system. If 'to' is omitted, the 'from' name is used both places.
˜%put from [to]	copy file 'from' (on local system) to file 'to' on remote system. If 'to' is omitted, the 'from' name is used both places.
˜˜...	send the line '˜...'.

The *receive* process handles output diversions of the following form:

˜>[>][:]file
zero or more lines to be written to file
˜>

In any case, output is diverted (or appended, if '>>' used) to the file. If ':' is used, the diversion is *silent*, i.e., it is written only to the file. If ':' is omitted, output is written both to the file and to the standard output. The trailing '˜>' terminates the diversion.

The use of ˜**put** requires *stty* and *cat* on the remote side. It also requires that the current erase and kill characters on the remote system be identical to the current ones on the local system. Backslashes are inserted at appropriate places.

The use of ˜**take** requires the existence of *echo* and *tee* on the remote system. Also, **stty tabs** mode is required on the remote system if tabs are to be copied without expansion.

FILES
/dev/cua0
/dev/cul0
/dev/null

SEE ALSO

dn(4), tty(4)

DIAGNOSTICS

Exit code is zero for normal exit, nonzero (various values) otherwise.

BUGS

The syntax is unique.

NAME
date — print and set the date

SYNOPSIS
date [yymmddhhmm [.ss]]

DESCRIPTION
If no argument is given, the current date and time are printed. If an argument is given, the current date is set. *yy* is the last two digits of the year; the first *mm* is the month number; *dd* is the day number in the month; *hh* is the hour number (24 hour system); the second *mm* is the minute number; *.ss* is optional and is the seconds. For example:

    date 10080045

sets the date to Oct 8, 12:45 AM. The year, month and day may be omitted, the current values being the defaults. The system operates in GMT. *Date* takes care of the conversion to and from local standard and daylight time.

FILES
/usr/adm/wtmp to record time-setting

SEE ALSO
utmp(5)

DIAGNOSTICS
'No permission' if you aren't the super-user and you try to change the date; 'bad conversion' if the date set is syntactically incorrect.

NAME

dc — desk calculator

SYNOPSIS

dc [file]

DESCRIPTION

Dc is an arbitrary precision arithmetic package. Ordinarily it operates on decimal integers, but one may specify an input base, output base, and a number of fractional digits to be maintained. The overall structure of *dc* is a stacking (reverse Polish) calculator. If an argument is given, input is taken from that file until its end, then from the standard input. The following constructions are recognized:

number
>   The value of the number is pushed on the stack. A number is an unbroken string of the digits 0-9. It may be preceded by an underscore _ to input a negative number. Numbers may contain decimal points.

+ − / * % ^
>   The top two values on the stack are added (+), subtracted (−), multiplied (*), divided (/), remaindered (%), or exponentiated (^). The two entries are popped off the stack; the result is pushed on the stack in their place. Any fractional part of an exponent is ignored.

s*x*
>   The top of the stack is popped and stored into a register named *x*, where *x* may be any character. If the **s** is capitalized, *x* is treated as a stack and the value is pushed on it.

l*x*
>   The value in register *x* is pushed on the stack. The register *x* is not altered. All registers start with zero value. If the **l** is capitalized, register *x* is treated as a stack and its top value is popped onto the main stack.

d
>   The top value on the stack is duplicated.

p
>   The top value on the stack is printed. The top value remains unchanged. **P** interprets the top of the stack as an ascii string, removes it, and prints it.

f
>   All values on the stack and in registers are printed.

q
>   exits the program. If executing a string, the recursion level is popped by two. If **q** is capitalized, the top value on the stack is popped and the string execution level is popped by that value.

x
>   treats the top element of the stack as a character string and executes it as a string of dc commands.

X
>   replaces the number on the top of the stack with its scale factor.

[...] puts the bracketed ascii string onto the top of the stack.

<*x* >*x* =*x*
>   The top two elements of the stack are popped and compared. Register *x* is executed if they obey the stated relation.

v
>   replaces the top element on the stack by its square root. Any existing fractional part of the argument is taken into account, but otherwise the scale factor is ignored.

!
>   interprets the rest of the line as a UNIX command.

c
>   All values on the stack are popped.

i
>   The top value on the stack is popped and used as the number radix for further input. **I** pushes the input base on the top of the stack.

o   The top value on the stack is popped and used as the number radix for further output.

O   pushes the output base on the top of the stack.

k   the top of the stack is popped, and that value is used as a non-negative scale factor: the appropriate number of places are printed on output, and maintained during multiplication, division, and exponentiation. The interaction of scale factor, input base, and output base will be reasonable if all are changed together.

z   The stack level is pushed onto the stack.

Z   replaces the number on the top of the stack with its length.

?   A line of input is taken from the input source (usually the terminal) and executed.

; :   are used by *bc* for array operations.

An example which prints the first ten values of n! is

```
[la1+dsa*pla10>y]sy
0sa1
lyx
```

SEE ALSO

bc(1), which is a preprocessor for *dc* providing infix notation and a C-like syntax which implements functions and reasonable control structures for programs.

DIAGNOSTICS

'x is unimplemented' where x is an octal number.
'stack empty' for not enough elements on the stack to do what was asked.
'Out of space' when the free list is exhausted (too many digits).
'Out of headers' for too many numbers being kept around.
'Out of pushdown' for too many items on the stack.
'Nesting Depth' for too many levels of nested execution.

NAME

dcheck — file system directory consistency check

SYNOPSIS

dcheck [−i numbers] [filesystem]

DESCRIPTION

Dcheck reads the directories in a file system and compares the link-count in each i-node with the number of directory entries by which it is referenced. If the file system is not specified, a set of default file systems is checked.

The −i flag is followed by a list of i-numbers; when one of those i-numbers turns up in a directory, the number, the i-number of the directory, and the name of the entry are reported.

The program is fastest if the raw version of the special file is used, since the i-list is read in large chunks.

FILES

Default file systems vary with installation.

SEE ALSO

icheck(1), filsys(5), clri(1), ncheck(1)

DIAGNOSTICS

When a file turns up for which the link-count and the number of directory entries disagree, the relevant facts are reported. Allocated files which have 0 link-count and no entries are also listed. The only dangerous situation occurs when there are more entries than links; if entries are removed, so the link-count drops to 0, the remaining entries point to thin air. They should be removed. When there are more links than entries, or there is an allocated file with neither links nor entries, some disk space may be lost but the situation will not degenerate.

BUGS

Since *dcheck* is inherently two-pass in nature, extraneous diagnostics may be produced if applied to active file systems.

NAME

dd — convert and copy a file

SYNOPSIS

dd [option=value] ...

DESCRIPTION

Dd copies the specified input file to the specified output with possible conversions. The standard input and output are used by default. The input and output block size may be specified to take advantage of raw physical I/O.

option	values
if=	input file name; standard input is default
of=	output file name; standard output is default
ibs=*n*	input block size *n* bytes (default 512)
obs=*n*	output block size (default 512)
bs=*n*	set both input and output block size, superseding *ibs* and *obs;* also, if no conversion is specified, it is particularly efficient since no copy need be done
cbs=*n*	conversion buffer size
skip=*n*	skip *n* input records before starting copy
files=*n*	copy *n* files from (tape) input
seek=*n*	seek *n* records from beginning of output file before copying
count=*n*	copy only *n* input records
conv=ascii	convert EBCDIC to ASCII
ebcdic	convert ASCII to EBCDIC
ibm	slightly different map of ASCII to EBCDIC
lcase	map alphabetics to lower case
ucase	map alphabetics to upper case
swab	swap every pair of bytes
noerror	do not stop processing on an error
sync	pad every input record to *ibs*
... , ...	several comma-separated conversions

Where sizes are specified, a number of bytes is expected. A number may end with **k, b** or **w** to specify multiplication by 1024, 512, or 2 respectively; a pair of numbers may be separated by **x** to indicate a product.

Cbs is used only if *ascii* or *ebcdic* conversion is specified. In the former case *cbs* characters are placed into the conversion buffer, converted to ASCII, and trailing blanks trimmed and newline added before sending the line to the output. In the latter case ASCII characters are read into the conversion buffer, converted to EBCDIC, and blanks added to make up an output record of size *cbs*.

After completion, *dd* reports the number of whole and partial input and output blocks.

For example, to read an EBCDIC tape blocked ten 80-byte EBCDIC card images per record into the ASCII file *x*:

dd if=/dev/rmt0 of=x ibs=800 cbs=80 conv=ascii,lcase

Note the use of raw magtape. *Dd* is especially suited to I/O on the raw physical devices because it allows reading and writing in arbitrary record sizes.

To skip over a file before copying from magnetic tape do

(dd of=/dev/null; dd of=x) </dev/rmt0

SEE ALSO

cp(1), tr(1)

DIAGNOSTICS

    f+p records in(out): numbers of full and partial records read(written)

BUGS

    The ASCII/EBCDIC conversion tables are taken from the 256 character standard in the CACM Nov, 1968. The 'ibm' conversion, while less blessed as a standard, corresponds better to certain IBM print train conventions. There is no universal solution.

    Newlines are inserted only on conversion to ASCII; padding is done only on conversion to EBCDIC. These should be separate options.

NAME

> deroff − remove nroff, troff, tbl and eqn constructs

SYNOPSIS

> **deroff** [−w] file ...

DESCRIPTION

> *Deroff* reads each file in sequence and removes all *nroff* and *troff* command lines, backslash constructions, macro definitions, *eqn* constructs (between '.EQ' and '.EN' lines or between delimiters), and table descriptions and writes the remainder on the standard output. *Deroff* follows chains of included files ('.so' and '.nx' commands); if a file has already been included, a '.so' is ignored and a '.nx' terminates execution. If no input file is given, *deroff* reads from the standard input file.

> If the −w flag is given, the output is a word list, one 'word' (string of letters, digits, and apostrophes, beginning with a letter; apostrophes are removed) per line, and all other characters ignored. Otherwise, the output follows the original, with the deletions mentioned above.

SEE ALSO

> troff(1), eqn(1), tbl(1)

BUGS

> *Deroff* is not a complete *troff* interpreter, so it can be confused by subtle constructs. Most errors result in too much rather than too little output.

NAME

df − disk free

SYNOPSIS

df [filesystem] ...

DESCRIPTION

Df prints out the number of free blocks available on the *filesystems*. If no file system is specified, the free space on all of the normally mounted file systems is printed.

FILES

Default file systems vary with installation.

SEE ALSO

icheck(1)

NAME

diff — differential file comparator

SYNOPSIS

diff [**−efbh**] file1 file2

DESCRIPTION

Diff tells what lines must be changed in two files to bring them into agreement. If *file1* (*file2*) is '−', the standard input is used. If *file1* (*file2*) is a directory, then a file in that directory whose file-name is the same as the file-name of *file2* (*file1*) is used. The normal output contains lines of these forms:

        n1 a *n3,n4*
        n1,n2 d *n3*
        n1,n2 c *n3,n4*

These lines resemble *ed* commands to convert *file1* into *file2*. The numbers after the letters pertain to *file2*. In fact, by exchanging 'a' for 'd' and reading backward one may ascertain equally how to convert *file2* into *file1*. As in *ed*, identical pairs where $n1 = n2$ or $n3 = n4$ are abbreviated as a single number.

Following each of these lines come all the lines that are affected in the first file flagged by '<', then all the lines that are affected in the second file flagged by '>'.

The −**b** option causes trailing blanks (spaces and tabs) to be ignored and other strings of blanks to compare equal.

The −**e** option produces a script of *a, c* and *d* commands for the editor *ed*, which will recreate *file2* from *file1*. The −**f** option produces a similar script, not useful with *ed*, in the opposite order. In connection with −**e**, the following shell program may help maintain multiple versions of a file. Only an ancestral file ($1) and a chain of version-to-version *ed* scripts ($2,$3,...) made by *diff* need be on hand. A 'latest version' appears on the standard output.

        (shift; cat $*; echo ´1,$p´) | ed − $1

Except in rare circumstances, *diff* finds a smallest sufficient set of file differences.

Option −**h** does a fast, half-hearted job. It works only when changed stretches are short and well separated, but does work on files of unlimited length. Options −**e** and −**f** are unavailable with −**h**.

FILES

/tmp/d?????
/usr/lib/diffh for −**h**

SEE ALSO

cmp(1), comm(1), ed(1)

DIAGNOSTICS

Exit status is 0 for no differences, 1 for some, 2 for trouble.

BUGS

Editing scripts produced under the −**e** or −**f** option are naive about creating lines consisting of a single '.'.

NAME

diff3 — 3-way differential file comparison

SYNOPSIS

diff3 [**−ex3**] file1 file2 file3

DESCRIPTION

Diff3 compares three versions of a file, and publishes disagreeing ranges of text flagged with these codes:

====	all three files differ
====1	*file1* is different
====2	*file2* is different
====3	*file3* is different

The type of change suffered in converting a given range of a given file to some other is indicated in one of these ways:

f : *n1* **a**   Text is to be appended after line number *n1* in file *f*, where *f* = 1, 2, or 3.

f : *n1* , *n2* **c**   Text is to be changed in the range line *n1* to line *n2*. If *n1* = *n2*, the range may be abbreviated to *n1*.

The original contents of the range follows immediately after a **c** indication. When the contents of two files are identical, the contents of the lower-numbered file is suppressed.

Under the −e option, *diff3* publishes a script for the editor *ed* that will incorporate into *file1* all changes between *file2* and *file3*, *i.e.* the changes that normally would be flagged ==== and ====3. Option −x (−3) produces a script to incorporate only changes flagged ==== (====3). The following command will apply the resulting script to 'file1'.

(cat script; echo ´1,$p´) | ed − file1

FILES

/tmp/d3?????
/usr/lib/diff3

SEE ALSO

diff(1)

BUGS

Text lines that consist of a single '.' will defeat −e.
Files longer than 64K bytes won't work.

NAME
    du − summarize disk usage

SYNOPSIS
    du [−s] [−a] [name ...]

DESCRIPTION
Du gives the number of blocks contained in all files and (recursively) directories within each specified directory or file *name*. If *name* is missing, '.' is used.

The optional argument −s causes only the grand total to be given. The optional argument −a causes an entry to be generated for each file. Absence of either causes an entry to be generated for each directory only.

A file which has two links to it is only counted once.

BUGS
Non-directories given as arguments (not under −a option) are not listed.
If there are too many distinct linked files, *du* counts the excess files multiply.

NAME

dump — incremental file system dump

SYNOPSIS

dump [key [argument ...] filesystem]

DESCRIPTION

Dump copies to magnetic tape all files changed after a certain date in the *filesystem*. The *key* specifies the date and other options about the dump. *Key* consists of characters from the set **0123456789fusd.**

f   Place the dump on the next *argument* file instead of the tape.

u   If the dump completes successfully, write the date of the beginning of the dump on file '/etc/ddate'. This file records a separate date for each filesystem and each dump level.

0—9 This number is the 'dump level'. All files modified since the last date stored in the file '/etc/ddate' for the same filesystem at lesser levels will be dumped. If no date is determined by the level, the beginning of time is assumed; thus the option **0** causes the entire filesystem to be dumped.

s   The size of the dump tape is specified in feet. The number of feet is taken from the next *argument*. When the specified size is reached, the dump will wait for reels to be changed. The default size is 2300 feet.

d   The density of the tape, expressed in BPI, is taken from the next *argument*. This is used in calculating the amount of tape used per write. The default is 1600.

If no arguments are given, the *key* is assumed to be **9u** and a default file system is dumped to the default tape.

Now a short suggestion on how perform dumps. Start with a full level 0 dump

      dump 0u

Next, periodic level 9 dumps should be made on an exponential progression of tapes. (Sometimes called Tower of Hanoi — 1 2 1 3 1 2 1 4 ... tape 1 used every other time, tape 2 used every fourth, tape 3 used every eighth, etc.)

      dump 9u

When the level 9 incremental approaches a full tape (about 78000 blocks at 1600 BPI blocked 20), a level 1 dump should be made.

      dump 1u

After this, the exponential series should progress as uninterrupted. These level 9 dumps are based on the level 1 dump which is based on the level 0 full dump. This progression of levels of dump can be carried as far as desired.

FILES

default filesystem and tape vary with installation.
/etc/ddate: record dump dates of filesystem/level.

SEE ALSO

restor(1), dump(5), dumpdir(1)

DIAGNOSTICS

If the dump requires more than one tape, it will ask you to change tapes. Reply with a newline when this has been done.

BUGS

Sizes are based on 1600 BPI blocked tape. The raw magtape device has to be used to approach these densities. Read errors on the filesystem are ignored. Write errors on the magtape are usually fatal.

NAME

　　dumpdir − print the names of files on a dump tape

SYNOPSIS

　　dumpdir [**f** filename]

DESCRIPTION

　　Dumpdir is used to read magtapes dumped with the *dump* command and list the names and inode numbers of all the files and directories on the tape.

　　The **f** option causes *filename* as the name of the tape instead of the default.

FILES

　　default tape unit varies with installation
　　rst*

SEE ALSO

　　dump(1), restor(1)

DIAGNOSTICS

　　If the dump extends over more than one tape, it may ask you to change tapes. Reply with a new-line when the next tape has been mounted.

BUGS

　　There is redundant information on the tape that could be used in case of tape reading problems. Unfortunately, *dumpdir* doesn't use it.

NAME

  echo − echo arguments

SYNOPSIS

  echo [−**n**] [arg] ...

DESCRIPTION

  Echo writes its arguments separated by blanks and terminated by a newline on the standard output. If the flag −**n** is used, no newline is added to the output.

  Echo is useful for producing diagnostics in shell programs and for writing constant data on pipes. To send diagnostics to the standard error file, do 'echo ... 1>&2'. delim $$

NAME
ed — text editor

SYNOPSIS
ed [−] [−**x**] [name]

DESCRIPTION
Ed is the standard text editor.

If a *name* argument is given, *ed* simulates an *e* command (see below) on the named file; that is to say, the file is read into *ed's* buffer so that it can be edited. If −**x** is present, an *x* command is simulated first to handle an encrypted file. The optional − suppresses the printing of character counts by *e, r,* and *w* commands.

Ed operates on a copy of any file it is editing; changes made in the copy have no effect on the file until a *w* (write) command is given. The copy of the text being edited resides in a temporary file called the *buffer*.

Commands to *ed* have a simple and regular structure: zero or more *addresses* followed by a single character *command,* possibly followed by parameters to the command. These addresses specify one or more lines in the buffer. Missing addresses are supplied by default.

In general, only one command may appear on a line. Certain commands allow the addition of text to the buffer. While *ed* is accepting text, it is said to be in *input mode*. In this mode, no commands are recognized; all input is merely collected. Input mode is left by typing a period '.' alone at the beginning of a line.

Ed supports a limited form of *regular expression* notation. A regular expression specifies a set of strings of characters. A member of this set of strings is said to be *matched* by the regular expression. In the following specification for regular expressions the word 'character' means any character but newline.

1.   Any character except a special character matches itself. Special characters are the regular expression delimiter plus \ [. and sometimes ˆ * $.

2.   A . matches any character.

3.   A \ followed by any character except a digit or ( ) matches that character.

4.   A nonempty string *s* bracketed [*s*] (or [ˆ*s*]) matches any character in (or not in) *s*. In *s*, \ has no special meaning, and] may only appear as the first letter. A substring *a−b*, with *a* and *b* in ascending ASCII order, stands for the inclusive range of ASCII characters.

5.   A regular expression of form 1-4 followed by * matches a sequence of 0 or more matches of the regular expression.

6.   A regular expression, *x*, of form 1-8, bracketed \(*x*\) matches what *x* matches.

7.   A \ followed by a digit *n* matches a copy of the string that the bracketed regular expression beginning with the *n*th \(matched.

8.   A regular expression of form 1-8, *x*, followed by a regular expression of form 1-7, *y* matches a match for *x* followed by a match for *y*, with the *x* match being as long as possible while still permitting a *y* match.

9.   A regular expression of form 1-8 preceded by   (or followed by $), is constrained to matches that begin at the left (or end at the right) end of a line.

10.   A regular expression of form 1-9 picks out the longest among the leftmost matches in a line.

11.   An empty regular expression stands for a copy of the last regular expression encountered.

Regular expressions are used in addresses to specify lines and in one command (see *s* below) to specify a portion of a line which is to be replaced. If it is desired to use one of the regular expression metacharacters as an ordinary character, that character may be preceded by '\'. This also applies to the character bounding the regular expression (often '/') and to '\' itself.

To understand addressing in *ed* it is necessary to know that at any time there is a *current line*. Generally speaking, the current line is the last line affected by a command; however, the exact effect on the current line is discussed under the description of the command. Addresses are constructed as follows.

1.　　The character '.' addresses the current line.

2.　　The character '$' addresses the last line of the buffer.

3.　　A decimal number *n* addresses the *n*-th line of the buffer.

4.　　'*x*' addresses the line marked with the name *x*, which must be a lower-case letter. Lines are marked with the *k* command described below.

5.　　A regular expression enclosed in slashes '/' addresses the line found by searching forward from the current line and stopping at the first line containing a string that matches the regular expression. If necessary the search wraps around to the beginning of the buffer.

6.　　A regular expression enclosed in queries '?' addresses the line found by searching backward from the current line and stopping at the first line containing a string that matches the regular expression. If necessary the search wraps around to the end of the buffer.

7.　　An address followed by a plus sign '+' (or a minus sign '−') owed by a decimal number specifies that address plus (or minus) the indicated number of lines. The plus sign may be omitted.

8.　　If an address begins with '+' or '−' the addition or subtraction is taken with respect to the current line; e.g. '−5' is understood to mean '.−5'.

9.　　If an address ends with '+' (or '−'), then 1 is added (or subtracted). As a consequence of this rule and rule 8, the address '−' refers to the line before the current line. Moreover, trailing '+' and '−' characters have cumulative effect, so '−−' refers to the current line less 2.

10.　To maintain compatibility with earlier versions of the editor, the character '^' in addresses is equivalent to '−'.

Commands may require zero, one, or two addresses. Commands which require no addresses regard the presence of an address as an error. Commands which accept one or two addresses assume default addresses when insufficient are given. If more addresses are given than such a command requires, the last one or two (depending on what is accepted) are used.

Addresses are separated from each other typically by a comma ','. They may also be separated by a semicolon ';'. In this case the current line '.' is set to the previous address before the next address is interpreted. This feature can be used to determine the starting line for forward and backward searches ('/', '?'). The second address of any two-address sequence must correspond to a line following the line corresponding to the first address.

In the following list of *ed* commands, the default addresses are shown in parentheses. The parentheses are not part of the address, but are used to show that the given addresses are the default.

As mentioned, it is generally illegal for more than one command to appear on a line. However, most commands may be suffixed by 'p' or by 'l', in which case the current line is either printed or listed respectively in the way discussed below.

(.)a
<text>
.

   The append command reads the given text and appends it after the addressed line. '.' is
   left on the last line input, if there were any, otherwise at the addressed line. Address '0'
   is legal for this command; text is placed at the beginning of the buffer.

(.,.)c
<text>
.

   The change command deletes the addressed lines, then accepts input text which replaces
   these lines. '.' is left at the last line input; if there were none, it is left at the line preceding the deleted lines.

(.,.)d

   The delete command deletes the addressed lines from the buffer. The line originally after
   the last line deleted becomes the current line; if the lines deleted were originally at the
   end, the new last line becomes the current line.

e filename

   The edit command causes the entire contents of the buffer to be deleted, and then the
   named file to be read in. '.' is set to the last line of the buffer. The number of characters
   read is typed. 'filename' is remembered for possible use as a default file name in a subsequent r or w command. If 'filename' is missing, the remembered name is used.

E filename

   This command is the same as e, except that no diagnostic results even when no w has
   been given since the last buffer alteration.

f filename

   The filename command prints the currently remembered file name. If 'filename' is given,
   the currently remembered file name is changed to 'filename'.

(1,$) g/regular expression/command list

   In the global command, the first step is to mark every line which matches the given regular expression. Then for every such line, the given command list is executed with '.' initially set to that line. A single command or the first of multiple commands appears on the
   same line with the global command. All lines of a multi-line list except the last line must
   be ended with '\'. A, i, and c commands and associated input are permitted; the '.' terminating input mode may be omitted if it would be on the last line of the command list.
   The commands g and v are not permitted in the command list.

(.)i
<text>
.

   This command inserts the given text before the addressed line. '.' is left at the last line
   input, or, if there were none, at the line before the addressed line. This command differs
   from the a command only in the placement of the text.

(.,.+1)j

   This command joins the addressed lines into a single line; intermediate newlines simply
   disappear. '.' is left at the resulting line.

(.)kx

   The mark command marks the addressed line with name x, which must be a lower-case letter. The address form ''x' then addresses this line.

(.,.)l
  The list command prints the addressed lines in an unambiguous way: non-graphic characters are printed in two-digit octal, and long lines are folded. The *l* command may be
  placed on the same line after any non-i/o command.

(.,.) m*a*
  The move command repositions the addressed lines after the line addressed by *a*. The
  last of the moved lines becomes the current line.

(.,.) p
  The print command prints the addressed lines. '.' is left at the last line printed. The *p*
  command may be placed on the same line after any non-i/o command.

(.,.) P
  This command is a synonym for *p*.

q   The quit command causes *ed* to exit. No automatic write of a file is done.

Q   This command is the same as *q*, except that no diagnostic results even when no *w* has
      been given since the last buffer alteration.

($) r filename
  The read command reads in the given file after the addressed line. If no file name is
  given, the remembered file name, if any, is used (see *e* and *f* commands). The file name
  is remembered if there was no remembered file name already. Address '0' is legal for *r*
  and causes the file to be read at the beginning of the buffer. If the read is successful, the
  number of characters read is typed. '.' is left at the last line read in from the file.

(.,.) s/regular expression/replacement/   or,
(.,.) s/regular expression/replacement/g
  The substitute command searches each addressed line for an occurrence of the specified
  regular expression. On each line in which a match is found, all matched strings are
  replaced by the replacement specified, if the global replacement indicator 'g' appears after
  the command. If the global indicator does not appear, only the first occurrence of the
  matched string is replaced. It is an error for the substitution to fail on all addressed lines.
  Any character other than space or new-line may be used instead of '/' to delimit the regular expression and the replacement. '.' is left at the last line substituted.

  An ampersand '&' appearing in the replacement is replaced by the string matching the
  regular expression. The special meaning of '&' in this context may be suppressed by
  preceding it by '\'. The characters '\n' where *n* is a digit, are replaced by the text
  matched by the *n*-th regular subexpression enclosed between '\(' and '\)'. When nested,
  parenthesized subexpressions are present, *n* is determined by counting occurrences of '\('
  starting from the left.

  Lines may be split by substituting new-line characters into them. The new-line in the
  replacement string must be escaped by preceding it by '\'.

(.,.) t*a*
  This command acts just like the *m* command, except that a copy of the addressed lines is
  placed after address *a* (which may be 0). '.' is left on the last line of the copy.

(.,.) u
  The undo command restores the preceding contents of the current line, which must be
  the last line in which a substitution was made.

(1, $) v/regular expression/command list
  This command is the same as the global command *g* except that the command list is executed with '.' initially set to every line *except* those matching the regular expression.

(1, $) w filename

The write command writes the addressed lines onto the given file. If the file does not exist, it is created mode 666 (readable and writable by everyone). The file name is remembered if there was no remembered file name already. If no file name is given, the remembered file name, if any, is used (see *e* and *f* commands). '.' is unchanged. If the command is successful, the number of characters written is printed.

(1,$)W filename

This command is the same as *w*, except that the addressed lines are appended to the file.

x   A key string is demanded from the standard input. Later *r, e* and *w* commands will encrypt and decrypt the text with this key by the algorithm of *crypt*(1). An explicitly empty key turns off encryption.

($) =

The line number of the addressed line is typed. '.' is unchanged by this command.

!<shell command>

The remainder of the line after the '!' is sent to *sh*(1) to be interpreted as a command. '.' is unchanged.

(.+1) <newline>

An address alone on a line causes the addressed line to be printed. A blank line alone is equivalent to '.+1p'; it is useful for stepping through text.

If an interrupt signal (ASCII DEL) is sent, *ed* prints a '?' and returns to its command level.

Some size limitations: 512 characters per line, 256 characters per global command list, 127 characters per file name, and 128K characters in the temporary file. The limit on the number of lines depends on the amount of core: each line takes 1 word.

When reading a file, *ed* discards ASCII NUL characters *and all characters after the last newline*. It refuses to read files containing non-ASCII characters.

FILES

/tmp/e*

ed.hup: work is saved here if terminal hangs up

SEE ALSO

B. W. Kernighan, *A Tutorial Introduction to the ED Text Editor*
B. W. Kernighan, *Advanced editing on UNIX*
sed(1), crypt(1)

DIAGNOSTICS

'?name' for inaccessible file; '?' for errors in commands; '?TMP' for temporary file overflow.

To protect against throwing away valuable work, a *q* or *e* command is considered to be in error, unless a *w* has occurred since the last buffer change. A second *q* or *e* will be obeyed regardless.

BUGS

A *!* command cannot be subject to a *g* command.

NAME

xsend, xget, enroll — secret mail

SYNOPSIS

xsend person
xget
enroll

DESCRIPTION

These commands implement a secure communication channel; it is like *mail*(1), but no one can read the messages except the intended recipient. The method embodies a public-key cryptosystem using knapsacks.

To receive messages, use *enroll*; it asks you for a password that you must subsequently quote in order to receive secret mail.

To receive secret mail, use *xget*. It asks for your password, then gives you the messages.

To send secret mail, use *xsend* in the same manner as the ordinary mail command. (However, it will accept only one target). A message announcing the receipt of secret mail is also sent by ordinary mail.

FILES

/usr/spool/secretmail/*.key: keys /usr/spool/secretmail/*.[0-9]: messages

SEE ALSO

mail (1)

BUGS

It should be integrated with ordinary mail. The announcement of secret mail makes traffic analysis possible.

NAME

eqn, neqn, checkeq − typeset mathematics

SYNOPSIS

eqn [−**dxy**] [−**pn**] [−**sn**] [−**fn**] [−**Tdest**] [file] ...

checkeq [file] ...

DESCRIPTION

Eqn is a *troff(1)* preprocessor for typesetting mathematics on a phototypesetter, *neqn* on terminals. Usage is almost always

eqn file ... | troff
neqn file ... | nroff

If no files are specified, these programs read from the standard input. *Eqn* prepares output for the typesetter named in the −T option (Mergenthaler Linotron 202 default, see *troff*(1)).

A line beginning with '.EQ' marks the start of an equation; the end of an equation is marked by a line beginning with '.EN'. Neither of these lines is altered, so they may be defined in macro packages to get centering, numbering, etc. It is also possible to set two characters as 'delimiters'; subsequent text between delimiters is also treated as *eqn* input. Delimiters may be set to characters *x* and *y* with the command-line argument −**d**xy or (more commonly) with 'delim *xy*' between .EQ and .EN. The left and right delimiters may be identical. Delimiters are turned off by 'delim off'. All text that is neither between delimiters nor between .EQ and .EN is passed through untouched.

The program *checkeq* reports missing or unbalanced delimiters and .EQ/.EN pairs.

Tokens within *eqn* are separated by spaces, tabs, newlines, braces, double quotes, tildes or circumflexes. Braces {} are used for grouping; generally speaking, anywhere a single character like *x* could appear, a complicated construction enclosed in braces may be used instead. Tilde ˜ represents a full space in the output, circumflex ˆ half as much, and tab represents an ordinary *troff* tab character.

Subscripts and superscripts are produced with the keywords **sub** and **sup.** Thus *x sub i* makes x_i, *a sub i sup 2* produces a_i^2, and *e sup {x sup 2 + y sup 2}* gives $e^{x^2+y^2}$.

Fractions are made with **over**: *a over b* yields $\frac{a}{b}$.

sqrt makes square roots: *1 over sqrt {ax sup 2 +bx+c}* results in $\frac{1}{\sqrt{ax^2+bx+c}}$.

The keywords **from** and **to** introduce lower and upper limits on arbitrary things: $\lim_{n\to\infty}\sum_0^n x_i$ is made with *lim from {n−> inf } sum from 0 to n x sub i.*

Left and right brackets, braces, etc., of the right height are made with **left** and **right**: *left [x sup 2 + y sup 2 over alpha right] ˜=˜1* produces $\left[x^2+\frac{y^2}{\alpha}\right] = 1$. The **right** clause is optional. Legal characters after **left** and **right** are braces, brackets, bars, **c** and **f** for ceiling and floor, and "" for nothing at all (useful for a right-side-only bracket).

Vertical piles of things are made with **pile, lpile, cpile,** and **rpile**: *pile {a above b above c}* produces $\begin{array}{c}a\\b\\c\end{array}$. There can be an arbitrary number of elements in a pile. **lpile** left-justifies, **pile** and **cpile** center, with different vertical spacing, and **rpile** right justifies.

Matrices are made with **matrix**: *matrix { lcol { x sub i above y sub 2 } ccol { 1 above 2 } }* produces $\begin{array}{cc}x_i & 1\\y_2 & 2\end{array}$. In addition, there is **rcol** for a right-justified column.

Diacritical marks are made with **dot, dotdot, hat, tilde, bar, vec, dyad**, and **under**: *x dot = f(t) bar* is $\dot{x}=\overline{f(t)}$, *y dotdot bar `=` n under* is $\overline{\ddot{y}} = \underline{n}$, and *x vec `=` y dyad* is $\vec{x} = \vec{y}$.

Sizes and font can be changed with **size** *n* or **size** $\pm n$, **roman**, **italic**, **bold**, and **font** *n*. Size and fonts can be changed globally in a document by **gsize** *n* and **gfont** *n*, or by the command-line arguments $-\text{s}n$ and $-\text{f}n$.

Normally subscripts and superscripts are reduced by 3 point sizes from the previous size; this may be changed by the command-line argument $-\text{p}n$.

Successive display arguments can be lined up. Place **mark** before the desired lineup point in the first equation; place **lineup** at the place that is to line up vertically in subsequent equations.

Shorthands may be defined or existing keywords redefined with **define**: *define thing % replacement %* defines a new token called *thing* which will be replaced by *replacement* whenever it appears thereafter. The % may be any character that does not occur in *replacement*.

Keywords like *sum* ($\sum$) *int* ($\int$) *inf* (∞) and shorthands like $>= (\geq)$ $-> (\rightarrow)$, and $!= (\neq)$ are recognized. Greek letters are spelled out in the desired case, as in *alpha* or *GAMMA*. Mathematical words like sin, cos, log are made Roman automatically. *Troff*(1) four-character escapes like \(bs (⊛) can be used anywhere. Strings enclosed in double quotes "..." are passed through untouched; this permits keywords to be entered as text, and can be used to communicate with *troff* when all else fails.

SEE ALSO

troff(1), tbl(1), ms(7), eqnchar(7)
B. W. Kernighan and L. L. Cherry, *Typesetting Mathematics—User's Guide*
J. F. Ossanna, *NROFF/TROFF User's Manual*

BUGS

To embolden digits, parens, etc., it is necessary to quote them, as in 'bold "12.3"'.

NAME

expr — evaluate arguments as an expression

SYNOPSIS

expr arg ...

DESCRIPTION

The arguments are taken as an expression. After evaluation, the result is written on the standard output. Each token of the expression is a separate argument.

The operators and keywords are listed below. The list is in order of increasing precedence, with equal precedence operators grouped.

expr | expr

yields the first *expr* if it is neither null nor '0', otherwise yields the second *expr*.

expr & expr

yields the first *expr* if neither *expr* is null or '0', otherwise yields '0'.

expr relop expr

where *relop is one of* $< \ \ <= \ \ = \ \ != \ \ >= \ \ >$, yields '1' if the indicated comparison is true, '0' if false. The comparison is numeric if both *expr* are integers, otherwise lexicographic.

expr + expr
expr - expr

addition or subtraction of the arguments.

expr * expr
expr / expr
expr % expr

multiplication, division, or remainder of the arguments.

expr : expr

The matching operator compares the string first argument with the regular expression second argument; regular expression syntax is the same as that of *ed*(1). The \(... \) pattern symbols can be used to select a portion of the first argument. Otherwise, the matching operator yields the number of characters matched ('0' on failure).

(expr)

parentheses for grouping.

Examples:

To add 1 to the Shell variable *a*:

a=`expr $a + 1`

To find the filename part (least significant part) of the pathname stored in variable *a*, which may or may not contain '/':

expr $a : ´.*/\(.*\)´ ⌐ $a

Note the quoted Shell metacharacters.

SEE ALSO

ed(1), sh(1), test(1)

DIAGNOSTICS

Expr returns the following exit codes:

    0   if the expression is neither null nor '0',
    1   if the expression is null or '0',
    2   for invalid expressions.

NAME
> f77 — Fortran 77 compiler

SYNOPSIS
> **f77** [option] ... file ...

DESCRIPTION
> *F77* is the UNIX Fortran 77 compiler. It accepts several types of arguments:
>
> Arguments whose names end with '.f' are taken to be Fortran 77 source programs; they are compiled, and each object program is left on the file in the current directory whose name is that of the source with '.o' substituted for '.f'.
>
> Arguments whose names end with '.r' or '.e' are taken to be Ratfor or EFL source programs, respectively; these are first transformed by the appropriate preprocessor, then compiled by f77.
>
> In the same way, arguments whose names end with '.c' or '.s' are taken to be C or assembly source programs and are compiled or assembled, producing a '.o' file.
>
> The following options have the same meaning as in *cc*(1). See *ld*(1) for load-time options.
>
> −c   Suppress loading and produce '.o' files for each source file.
>
> −p   Prepare object files for profiling, see *prof*(1).
>
> −O   Invoke an object-code optimizer.
>
> −S   Compile the named programs, and leave the assembler-language output on corresponding files suffixed '.s'. (No '.o' is created.).
>
> −f   Use a floating point interpreter (for PDP11's that lack 11/70-style floating point).
>
> −o output
> >   Name the final output file *output* instead of 'a.out'.
>
> The following options are peculiar to *f77*.
>
> −onetrip
> >   Compile DO loops that are performed at least once if reached. (Fortran 77 DO loops are not performed at all if the upper limit is smaller than the lower limit.)
>
> −u   Make the default type of a variable 'undefined' rather than using the default Fortran rules.
>
> −C   Compile code to check that subscripts are within declared array bounds.
>
> −w   Suppress all warning messages. If the option is '−w66', only Fortran 66 compatibility warnings are suppressed.
>
> −F   Apply EFL and Ratfor preprocessor to relevant files, put the result in the file with the suffix changed to '.f', but do not compile.
>
> −m   Apply the M4 preprocessor to each '.r' or '.e' file before transforming it with the Ratfor or EFL preprocessor.
>
> −E*x*   Use the string *x* as an EFL option in processing '.e' files.
>
> −R*x*   Use the string *x* as a Ratfor option in processing '.r' files.
>
> Other arguments are taken to be either loader option arguments, or F77-compatible object programs, typically produced by an earlier run, or perhaps libraries of F77-compatible routines. These programs, together with the results of any compilations specified, are loaded (in the order given) to produce an executable program with name 'a.out'.

FILES
> file.[fresc]   input file
> file.o   object file

          a.out   loaded output
          /usr/lib/f77pass1compiler
          /lib/c1   pass 2
          /lib/c2   optional optimizer
          /usr/lib/libF77.a intrinsic function library
          /usr/lib/libI77.a Fortran I/O library
          /lib/libc.a   C library, see section 3

SEE ALSO

S. I. Feldman, P. J. Weinberger, *A Portable Fortran 77 Compiler*
prof(1), cc(1), ld(1)

DIAGNOSTICS

The diagnostics produced by *f77* itself are intended to be self-explanatory. Occasional messages
may be produced by the loader.

BUGS

The Fortran 66 subset of the language has been exercised extensively; the newer features have
not.

NAME

factor, primes — factor a number, generate large primes

SYNOPSIS

factor [number]

primes

DESCRIPTION

When *factor* is invoked without an argument, it waits for a number to be typed in. If you type in a positive number less than 2^{56} (about 7.2×10^{16}) it will factor the number and print its prime factors; each one is printed the proper number of times. Then it waits for another number. It exits if it encounters a zero or any non-numeric character.

If *factor* is invoked with an argument, it factors the number as above and then exits.

Maximum time to factor is proportional to $\sqrt{n}$ and occurs when *n* is prime or the square of a prime. It takes 1 minute to factor a prime near 10^{14} on a PDP11.

When *primes* is invoked, it waits for a number to be typed in. If you type in a positive number less than 2^{56} it will print all primes greater than or equal to this number.

DIAGNOSTICS

'Ouch.' for input out of range or for garbage input.

NAME

  file — determine file type

SYNOPSIS

  file file ...

DESCRIPTION

  File performs a series of tests on each argument in an attempt to classify it. If an argument appears to be ascii, *file* examines the first 512 bytes and tries to guess its language.

BUGS

  It often makes mistakes. In particular it often suggests that command files are C programs.

NAME

find — find files

SYNOPSIS

find pathname-list   expression

DESCRIPTION

Find recursively descends the directory hierarchy for each pathname in the *pathname-list* (i.e., one or more pathnames) seeking files that match a boolean *expression* written in the primaries given below. In the descriptions, the argument n is used as a decimal integer where $+n$ means more than n, $-n$ means less than n and n means exactly n.

−name filename

True if the *filename* argument matches the current file name. Normal Shell argument syntax may be used if escaped (watch out for '[', '?' and '*').

−perm onum

True if the file permission flags exactly match the octal number *onum* (see *chmod*(1)). If *onum* is prefixed by a minus sign, more flag bits (017777, see *stat*(2)) become significant and the flags are compared: *(flags&onum)==onum*.

−type c   True if the type of the file is *c*, where *c* is **b, c, d** or **f** for block special file, character special file, directory or plain file.

−links n   True if the file has *n* links.

−user uname

True if the file belongs to the user *uname* (login name or numeric user ID).

−group gname

True if the file belongs to group *gname* (group name or numeric group ID).

−size n   True if the file is *n* blocks long (512 bytes per block).

−inum n   True if the file has inode number *n*.

−atime n   True if the file has been accessed in *n* days.

−mtime n

True if the file has been modified in *n* days.

−exec command

True if the executed command returns a zero value as exit status. The end of the command must be punctuated by an escaped semicolon. A command argument '{}' is replaced by the current pathname.

−ok command

Like **−exec** except that the generated command is written on the standard output, then the standard input is read and the command executed only upon response **y**.

−print   Always true; causes the current pathname to be printed.

−newer file

True if the current file has been modified more recently than the argument *file*.

The primaries may be combined using the following operators (in order of decreasing precedence):

1) A parenthesized group of primaries and operators (parentheses are special to the Shell and must be escaped).

2) The negation of a primary ('!' is the unary *not* operator).

3) Concatenation of primaries (the *and* operation is implied by the juxtaposition of two primaries).

4)   Alternation of primaries ('−**o**' is the *or* operator).

EXAMPLE

To remove all files named 'a.out' or '*.o' that have not been accessed for a week:

find / \(−name a.out −o −name '*.o' \) −atime +7 −exec rm {} \;

FILES

/etc/passwd
/etc/group

SEE ALSO

sh(1), test(1), filsys(5)

BUGS

The syntax is painful.

NAME

graph — draw a graph

SYNOPSIS

graph [option] ...

DESCRIPTION

Graph with no options takes pairs of numbers from the standard input as abscissas and ordinates of a graph. Successive points are connected by straight lines. The graph is encoded on the standard output for display by the *plot*(1) filters.

If the coordinates of a point are followed by a nonnumeric string, that string is printed as a label beginning on the point. Labels may be surrounded with quotes "...", in which case they may be empty or contain blanks and numbers; labels never contain newlines.

The following options are recognized, each as a separate argument.

- −a　　Supply abscissas automatically (they are missing from the input); spacing is given by the next argument (default 1). A second optional argument is the starting point for automatic abscissas (default 0 or lower limit given by −x).

- −b　　Break (disconnect) the graph after each label in the input.

- −c　　Character string given by next argument is default label for each point.

- −g　　Next argument is grid style, 0 no grid, 1 frame with ticks, 2 full grid (default).

- −l　　Next argument is label for graph.

- −m　　Next argument is mode (style) of connecting lines: 0 disconnected, 1 connected (default). Some devices give distinguishable line styles for other small integers.

- −s　　Save screen, don't erase before plotting.

- −x [l]

　　　　If l is present, x axis is logarithmic. Next 1 (or 2) arguments are lower (and upper) *x* limits. Third argument, if present, is grid spacing on *x* axis. Normally these quantities are determined automatically.

- −y [l]

　　　　Similarly for *y*.

- −h　　Next argument is fraction of space for height.

- −w　　Similarly for width.

- −r　　Next argument is fraction of space to move right before plotting.

- −u　　Similarly to move up before plotting.

- −t　　Transpose horizontal and vertical axes. (Option −x now applies to the vertical axis.)

A legend indicating grid range is produced with a grid unless the −s option is present.

If a specified lower limit exceeds the upper limit, the axis is reversed.

SEE ALSO

spline(1), plot(1)

BUGS

Graph stores all points internally and drops those for which there isn't room.

Segments that run out of bounds are dropped, not windowed.

Logarithmic axes may not be reversed.

NAME

grep, egrep, fgrep — search a file for a pattern

SYNOPSIS

grep [option] ... expression [file] ...

egrep [option] ... [expression] [file] ...

fgrep [option] ... [strings] [file]

DESCRIPTION

Commands of the *grep* family search the input *files* (standard input default) for lines matching a pattern. Normally, each line found is copied to the standard output; unless the —**h** flag is used, the file name is shown if there is more than one input file.

Grep patterns are limited regular expressions in the style of *ed*(1); it uses a compact nondeterministic algorithm. *Egrep* patterns are full regular expressions; it uses a fast deterministic algorithm that sometimes needs exponential space. *Fgrep* patterns are fixed strings; it is fast and compact.

The following options are recognized.

—**v**   All lines but those matching are printed.

—**c**   Only a count of matching lines is printed.

—**l**   The names of files with matching lines are listed (once) separated by newlines.

—**n**   Each line is preceded by its line number in the file.

—**b**   Each line is preceded by the block number on which it was found. This is sometimes useful in locating disk block numbers by context.

—**s**   No output is produced, only status.

—**h**   Do not print filename headers with output lines.

—**y**   Lower case letters in the pattern will also match upper case letters in the input (*grep* only).

—**e** *expression*

Same as a simple *expression* argument, but useful when the *expression* begins with a —.

—**f** *file* The regular expression (*egrep*) or string list (*fgrep*) is taken from the *file*.

—**x**   (Exact) only lines matched in their entirety are printed (*fgrep* only).

Care should be taken when using the characters $ * [^ | ? ´ " ( ) and \ in the *expression* as they are also meaningful to the Shell. It is safest to enclose the entire *expression* argument in single quotes ´´.

Fgrep searches for lines that contain one of the (newline-separated) *strings*.

Egrep accepts extended regular expressions. In the following description 'character' excludes newline:

A \ followed by a single character matches that character.

The character ^ ($) matches the beginning (end) of a line.

A . matches any character.

A single character not otherwise endowed with special meaning matches that character.

A string enclosed in brackets [] matches any single character from the string. Ranges of ASCII character codes may be abbreviated as in 'a—z0—9'. A] may occur only as the first character of the string. A literal — must be placed where it can't be mistaken as a range indicator.

A regular expression followed by * (+, ?) matches a sequence of 0 or more (1 or more, 0 or 1) matches of the regular expression.

Two regular expressions concatenated match a match of the first followed by a match of the second.

Two regular expressions separated by | or newline match either a match for the first or a match for the second.

A regular expression enclosed in parentheses matches a match for the regular expression.

The order of precedence of operators at the same parenthesis level is [ ] then *+? then concatenation then | and newline.

SEE ALSO

ed(1), sed(1), sh(1)

DIAGNOSTICS

Exit status is 0 if any matches are found, 1 if none, 2 for syntax errors or inaccessible files.

BUGS

Ideally there should be only one *grep*, but we don't know a single algorithm that spans a wide enough range of space-time tradeoffs.

Lines are limited to 256 characters; longer lines are truncated.

NAME
    icheck — file system storage consistency check

SYNOPSIS
    icheck [**−s**]   [**−b** numbers] [filesystem]

DESCRIPTION
    Icheck examines a file system, builds a bit map of used blocks, and compares this bit map against the free list maintained on the file system. If the file system is not specified, a set of default file systems is checked. The normal output of *icheck* includes a report of

    The total number of files and the numbers of regular, directory, block special and character special files.

    The total number of blocks in use and the numbers of single-, double-, and triple-indirect blocks and directory blocks.

    The number of free blocks.

    The number of blocks missing; i.e. not in any file nor in the free list.

    The −s option causes *icheck* to ignore the actual free list and reconstruct a new one by rewriting the super-block of the file system. The file system should be dismounted while this is done; if this is not possible (for example if the root file system has to be salvaged) care should be taken that the system is quiescent and that it is rebooted immediately afterwards so that the old, bad in-core copy of the super-block will not continue to be used. Notice also that the words in the super-block which indicate the size of the free list and of the i-list are believed. If the super-block has been curdled these words will have to be patched. The −s option causes the normal output reports to be suppressed.

    Following the −b option is a list of block numbers; whenever any of the named blocks turns up in a file, a diagnostic is produced.

    Icheck is faster if the raw version of the special file is used, since it reads the i-list many blocks at a time.

FILES
    Default file systems vary with installation.

SEE ALSO
    dcheck(1), ncheck(1), filsys(5), clri(1)

DIAGNOSTICS
    For duplicate blocks and bad blocks (which lie outside the file system) *icheck* announces the difficulty, the i-number, and the kind of block involved. If a read error is encountered, the block number of the bad block is printed and *icheck* considers it to contain 0. 'Bad freeblock' means that a block number outside the available space was encountered in the free list. '*n* dups in free' means that *n* blocks were found in the free list which duplicate blocks either in some file or in the earlier part of the free list.

BUGS
    Since *icheck* is inherently two-pass in nature, extraneous diagnostics may be produced if applied to active file systems.
    It believes even preposterous super-blocks and consequently can get core images.

NAME

iostat — report I/O statistics

SYNOPSIS

iostat [option] ... [interval [count]]

DESCRIPTION

Iostat delves into the system and reports certain statistics kept about input-output activity. Information is kept about up to three different disks (RF, RK, RP) and about typewriters. For each disk, IO completions and number of words transferred are counted; for typewriters collectively, the number of input and output characters are counted. Also, each sixtieth of a second, the state of each disk is examined and a tally is made if the disk is active. The tally goes into one of four categories, depending on whether the system is executing in user mode, in 'nice' (background) user mode, in system mode, or idle. From all these numbers and from the known transfer rates of the devices it is possible to determine information such as the degree of IO overlap and average seek times for each device.

The optional *interval* argument causes *iostat* to report once each *interval* seconds. The first report is for all time since a reboot and each subsequent report is for the last interval only.

The optional *count* argument restricts the number of reports.

With no option argument *iostat* reports for each disk the number of transfers per minute, the milliseconds per average seek, and the milliseconds per data transfer exclusive of seek time. It also gives the percentage of time the system has spend in each of the four categories mentioned above.

The following options are available:

—**t**   Report the number of characters of terminal IO per second as well.

—**i**   Report the percentage of time spend in each of the four categories mentioned above, the percentage of time each disk was active (seeking or transferring), the percentage of time any disk was active, and the percentage of time spent in 'IO wait:' idle, but with a disk active.

—**s**   Report the raw timing information: 32 numbers indicating the percentage of time spent in each of the possible configurations of 4 system states and 8 IO states (3 disks each active or not).

—**b**   Report on the usage of IO buffers.

FILES

/dev/mem, /unix

NAME

join — relational database operator

SYNOPSIS

join [options] file1 file2

DESCRIPTION

Join forms, on the standard output, a join of the two relations specified by the lines of *file1* and *file2*. If *file1* is '−', the standard input is used.

File1 and *file2* must be sorted in increasing ASCII collating sequence on the fields on which they are to be joined, normally the first in each line.

There is one line in the output for each pair of lines in *file1* and *file2* that have identical join fields. The output line normally consists of the common field, then the rest of the line from *file1*, then the rest of the line from *file2*.

Fields are normally separated by blank, tab or newline. In this case, multiple separators count as one, and leading separators are discarded.

These options are recognized:

−**a***n*   In addition to the normal output, produce a line for each unpairable line in file *n*, where *n* is 1 or 2.

−e *s*   Replace empty output fields by string *s*.

−**j***n m*   Join on the *m*th field of file *n*. If *n* is missing, use the *m*th field in each file.

−o *list*   Each output line comprises the fields specifed in *list*, each element of which has the form *n.m*, where *n* is a file number and *m* is a field number.

−t*c*   Use character *c* as a separator (tab character). Every appearance of *c* in a line is significant.

SEE ALSO

sort(1), comm(1), awk(1)

BUGS

With default field separation, the collating sequence is that of *sort* −*b*; with −*t*, the sequence is that of a plain sort.

The conventions of *join, sort, comm, uniq, look* and *awk*(1) are wildly incongruous.

NAME
kill — terminate a process with extreme prejudice

SYNOPSIS
kill [−signo] processid ...

DESCRIPTION
Kill sends signal 15 (terminate) to the specified processes. If a signal number preceded by '−' is given as first argument, that signal is sent instead of terminate (see *signal*(2)). This will kill processes that do not catch the signal; in particular 'kill −9 ...' is a sure kill.

By convention, if process number 0 is specified, all members in the process group (i.e. processes resulting from the current login) are signaled.

The killed processes must belong to the current user unless he is the super-user. To shut the system down and bring it up single user the super-user may use 'kill −1 1'; see *init*(8).

The process number of an asynchronous process started with '&' is reported by the shell. Process numbers can also be found by using *ps*(1).

SEE ALSO
ps(1), kill(2), signal(2)

NAME

lex — generator of lexical analysis programs

SYNOPSIS

lex [−tvfn] [file] ...

DESCRIPTION

Lex generates programs to be used in simple lexical analyis of text. The input *files* (standard input default) contain regular expressions to be searched for, and actions written in C to be executed when expressions are found.

A C source program, 'lex.yy.c' is generated, to be compiled thus:

        cc lex.yy.c −ll

This program, when run, copies unrecognized portions of the input to the output, and executes the associated C action for each regular expression that is recognized.

The following *lex* program converts upper case to lower, removes blanks at the end of lines, and replaces multiple blanks by single blanks.

        %%
        [A−Z] putchar(yytext[0]+´a´−´A´);
        [ ]+$
        [ ]+   putchar(´ ´);

The options have the following meanings.

−t   Place the result on the standard output instead of in file 'lex.yy.c'.

−v   Print a one-line summary of statistics of the generated analyzer.

−n   Opposite of −v; −n is default.

−f   'Faster' compilation: don't bother to pack the resulting tables; limited to small programs.

SEE ALSO

yacc(1)

M. E. Lesk and E. Schmidt, *LEX — Lexical Analyzer Generator*

NAME

lint — a C program verifier

SYNOPSIS

lint [**−abchnpuvx**] file ...

DESCRIPTION

Lint attempts to detect features of the C program *files* which are likely to be bugs, or non-portable, or wasteful. It also checks the type usage of the program more strictly than the compilers. Among the things which are currently found are unreachable statements, loops not entered at the top, automatic variables declared and not used, and logical expressions whose value is constant. Moreover, the usage of functions is checked to find functions which return values in some places and not in others, functions called with varying numbers of arguments, and functions whose values are not used.

By default, it is assumed that all the *files* are to be loaded together; they are checked for mutual compatibility. Function definitions for certain libraries are available to *lint*; these libraries are referred to by a conventional name, such as '-lm', in the style of *ld*(1).

Any number of the options in the following list may be used. The −D, −U, and −I options of *cc*(1) are also recognized as separate arguments.

p   Attempt to check portability to the *IBM* and *GCOS* dialects of C.

h   Apply a number of heuristic tests to attempt to intuit bugs, improve style, and reduce waste.

b   Report *break* statements that cannot be reached. (This is not the default because, unfortunately, most *lex* and many *yacc* outputs produce dozens of such comments.)

v   Suppress complaints about unused arguments in functions.

x   Report variables referred to by extern declarations, but never used.

a   Report assignments of long values to int variables.

c   Complain about casts which have questionable portability.

u   Do not complain about functions and variables used and not defined, or defined and not used (this is suitable for running *lint* on a subset of files out of a larger program).

n   Do not check compatibility against the standard library.

Exit(2) and other functions which do not return are not understood; this causes various lies.

Certain conventional comments in the C source will change the behavior of *lint*:

/*NOTREACHED*/

at appropriate points stops comments about unreachable code.

/*VARARGS*n**/

suppresses the usual checking for variable numbers of arguments in the following function declaration. The data types of the first *n* arguments are checked; a missing *n* is taken to be 0.

/*NOSTRICT*/

shuts off strict type checking in the next expression.

/*ARGSUSED*/

turns on the −v option for the next function.

/*LINTLIBRARY*/

at the beginning of a file shuts off complaints about unused functions in this file.

FILES

/usr/lib/lint[12] programs

/usr/lib/llib-lc declarations for standard functions
/usr/lib/llib-port declarations for portable functions

SEE ALSO

cc(1)

S. C. Johnson, *Lint, a C Program Checker*

NAME

ln − make a link

SYNOPSIS

ln name1 [name2]

DESCRIPTION

A link is a directory entry referring to a file; the same file (together with its size, all its protection information, etc.) may have several links to it. There is no way to distinguish a link to a file from its original directory entry; any changes in the file are effective independently of the name by which the file is known.

Ln creates a link to an existing file *name1*. If *name2* is given, the link has that name; otherwise it is placed in the current directory and its name is the last component of *name1*.

It is forbidden to link to a directory or to link across file systems.

SEE ALSO

rm(1)

NAME

login — sign on

SYNOPSIS

login [username]

DESCRIPTION

The *login* command is used when a user initially signs on, or it may be used at any time to change from one user to another. The latter case is the one summarized above and described here. See 'How to Get Started' for how to dial up initially.

If *login* is invoked without an argument, it asks for a user name, and, if appropriate, a password. Echoing is turned off (if possible) during the typing of the password, so it will not appear on the written record of the session.

After a successful login, accounting files are updated and the user is informed of the existence of *.mail* and message-of-the-day files. *Login* initializes the user and group IDs and the working directory, then executes a command interpreter (usually *sh*(1)) according to specifications found in a password file. Argument 0 of the command interpreter is '−sh.

Login is recognized by *sh*(1) and executed directly (without forking).

FILES

/etc/utmp	accounting
/usr/adm/wtmp	accounting
/usr/mail/*	mail
/etc/motd	message-of-the-day
/etc/passwd	password file

SEE ALSO

init(8), newgrp(1), getty(8), mail(1), passwd(1), passwd(5)

DIAGNOSTICS

'Login incorrect,' if the name or the password is bad.
'No Shell', 'cannot open password file', 'no directory': consult a programming counselor.

NAME

look − find lines in a sorted list

SYNOPSIS

look [−**df**] string [file]

DESCRIPTION

Look consults a sorted *file* and prints all lines that begin with *string*. It uses binary search.

The options **d** and **f** affect comparisons as in *sort*(1):

d   'Dictionary' order: only letters, digits, tabs and blanks participate in comparisons.

f   Fold. Upper case letters compare equal to lower case.

If no *file* is specified, */usr/dict/words* is assumed with collating sequence −**df.**

FILES

/usr/dict/words

SEE ALSO

sort(1), grep(1)

NAME

lookall — look through all text files on UNIX

SYNOPSIS

lookall [−Cn]

DESCRIPTION

Lookall accepts keywords from the standard input, performs a search similar to that of *refer*(1), and writes the result on the standard output. *Lookall* consults, however, an index to all the text files on the system rather than just bibliographies. Only the first 50 words of each file (roughly) were used to make the indexes. Blank lines are taken as delimiters between queries.

The -Cn option specifies a coordination level search: up to n keywords may be missing from the answers, and the answers are listed with those containing the most keywords first.

The command sequence in */usr/dict/lookall/makindex* regenerates the index.

FILES

The directory */usr/dict/lookall* contains the index files.

DIAGNOSTICS

'Warning: index precedes file ...' means that a file has been changed since the index was made and it may be retrieved (or not retrieved) erroneously.

BUGS

Coordination level searching doesn't work as described: only those acceptable items with the smallest number of missing keywords are retrieved.

NAME
    lorder — find ordering relation for an object library

SYNOPSIS
    lorder file ...

DESCRIPTION
    The input is one or more object or library archive (see *ar*(1)) *files.* The standard output is a list of pairs of object file names, meaning that the first file of the pair refers to external identifiers defined in the second. The output may be processed by *tsort*(1) to find an ordering of a library suitable for one-pass access by *ld*(1).

    This brash one-liner intends to build a new library from existing '.o' files.

        ar cr library `lorder *.o | tsort`

FILES
    *symref, *symdef
    nm(1), sed(1), sort(1), join(1)

SEE ALSO
    tsort(1), ld(1), ar(1)

BUGS
    The names of object files, in and out of libraries, must end with '.o'; nonsense results otherwise.

NAME

ls — list contents of directory

SYNOPSIS

ls [**—ltasdrucifg**] name ...

DESCRIPTION

For each directory argument, *ls* lists the contents of the directory; for each file argument, *ls* repeats its name and any other information requested. The output is sorted alphabetically by default. When no argument is given, the current directory is listed. When several arguments are given, the arguments are first sorted appropriately, but file arguments appear before directories and their contents. There are several options:

—l   List in long format, giving mode, number of links, owner, size in bytes, and time of last modification for each file. (See below.) If the file is a special file the size field will instead contain the major and minor device numbers.

—t   Sort by time modified (latest first) instead of by name, as is normal.

—a   List all entries; usually '.' and '..' are suppressed.

—s   Give size in blocks, including indirect blocks, for each entry.

—d   If argument is a directory, list only its name, not its contents (mostly used with —l to get status on directory).

—r   Reverse the order of sort to get reverse alphabetic or oldest first as appropriate.

—u   Use time of last access instead of last modification for sorting (—t) or printing (—l).

—c   Use time of last modification to inode (mode, etc.) instead of last modification to file for sorting (—t) or printing (—l).

—i   Print i-number in first column of the report for each file listed.

—f   Force each argument to be interpreted as a directory and list the name found in each slot. This option turns off —l, —t, —s, and —r, and turns on —a; the order is the order in which entries appear in the directory.

—g   Give group ID instead of owner ID in long listing.

The mode printed under the —l option contains 11 characters which are interpreted as follows: the first character is

d   if the entry is a directory;
b   if the entry is a block-type special file;
c   if the entry is a character-type special file;
—   if the entry is a plain file.

The next 9 characters are interpreted as three sets of three bits each. The first set refers to owner permissions; the next to permissions to others in the same user-group; and the last to all others. Within each set the three characters indicate permission respectively to read, to write, or to execute the file as a program. For a directory, 'execute' permission is interpreted to mean permission to search the directory for a specified file. The permissions are indicated as follows:

r   if the file is readable;
w   if the file is writable;
x   if the file is executable;
—   if the indicated permission is not granted.

The group-execute permission character is given as **s** if the file has set-group-ID mode; likewise the user-execute permission character is given as **s** if the file has set-user-ID mode.

The last character of the mode (normally 'x' or '−') is **t** if the 1000 bit of the mode is on. See *chmod*(1) for the meaning of this mode.

When the sizes of the files in a directory are listed, a total count of blocks, including indirect blocks is printed.

FILES

/etc/passwd to get user ID's for 'ls −l'.
/etc/group to get group ID's for 'ls −g'.

NAME
    m4 — macro processor

SYNOPSIS
    m4 [files]

DESCRIPTION
M4 is a macro processor intended as a front end for Ratfor, C, and other languages. Each of the argument files is processed in order; if there are no arguments, or if an argument is '−', the standard input is read. The processed text is written on the standard output.

Macro calls have the form

        name(arg1,arg2, . . . , argn)

The '(' must immediately follow the name of the macro. If a defined macro name is not followed by a '(', it is deemed to have no arguments. Leading unquoted blanks, tabs, and newlines are ignored while collecting arguments. Potential macro names consist of alphabetic letters, digits, and underscore '_', where the first character is not a digit.

Left and right single quotes (` ') are used to quote strings. The value of a quoted string is the string stripped of the quotes.

When a macro name is recognized, its arguments are collected by searching for a matching right parenthesis. Macro evaluation proceeds normally during the collection of the arguments, and any commas or right parentheses which happen to turn up within the value of a nested call are as effective as those in the original input text. After argument collection, the value of the macro is pushed back onto the input stream and rescanned.

M4 makes available the following built-in macros. They may be redefined, but once this is done the original meaning is lost. Their values are null unless otherwise stated.

define   The second argument is installed as the value of the macro whose name is the first argument. Each occurrence of $n in the replacement text, where n is a digit, is replaced by the n-th argument. Argument 0 is the name of the macro; missing arguments are replaced by the null string.

undefine   removes the definition of the macro named in its argument.

ifdef   If the first argument is defined, the value is the second argument, otherwise the third. If there is no third argument, the value is null. The word *unix* is predefined on UNIX versions of *m4*.

changequote
            Change quote characters to the first and second arguments. *Changequote* without arguments restores the original values (i.e., ` ').

divert   *M4* maintains 10 output streams, numbered 0-9. The final output is the concatenation of the streams in numerical order; initially stream 0 is the current stream. The *divert* macro changes the current output stream to its (digit-string) argument. Output diverted to a stream other than 0 through 9 is discarded.

undivert   causes immediate output of text from diversions named as arguments, or all diversions if no argument. Text may be undiverted into another diversion. Undiverting discards the diverted text.

divnum   returns the value of the current output stream.

dnl   reads and discards characters up to and including the next newline.

ifelse   has three or more arguments. If the first argument is the same string as the second, then the value is the third argument. If not, and if there are more than four arguments, the process is repeated with arguments 4, 5, 6 and 7. Otherwise, the value is either the fourth string, or, if it is not present, null.

incr   returns the value of its argument incremented by 1. The value of the argument is calculated by interpreting an initial digit-string as a decimal number.

eval   evaluates its argument as an arithmetic expression, using 32-bit arithmetic. Operators include +, −, *, /, %, ^ (exponentiation); relationals; parentheses.

len   returns the number of characters in its argument.

index   returns the position in its first argument where the second argument begins (zero origin), or −1 if the second argument does not occur.

substr   returns a substring of its first argument. The second argument is a zero origin number selecting the first character; the third argument indicates the length of the substring. A missing third argument is taken to be large enough to extend to the end of the first string.

translit   transliterates the characters in its first argument from the set given by the second argument to the set given by the third. No abbreviations are permitted.

include   returns the contents of the file named in the argument.

sinclude   is identical to *include*, except that it says nothing if the file is inaccessible.

syscmd   executes the UNIX command given in the first argument. No value is returned.

maketemp   fills in a string of XXXXX in its argument with the current process id.

errprint   prints its argument on the diagnostic output file.

dumpdef   prints current names and definitions, for the named items, or for all if no arguments are given.

SEE ALSO

B. W. Kernighan and D. M. Ritchie, *The M4 Macro Processor*

NAME

mail — send or receive mail among users

SYNOPSIS

mail person ...

mail [−r] [−q] [−p] [−f file]

DESCRIPTION

Mail with no argument prints a user's mail, message-by-message, in last-in, first-out order; the optional argument −r causes first-in, first-out order. If the −p flag is given, the mail is printed with no questions asked; otherwise, for each message, *mail* reads a line from the standard input to direct disposition of the message.

newline
    Go on to next message.

d   Delete message and go on to the next.

p   Print message again.

−   Go back to previous message.

s [*file*] ...
    Save the message in the named *files* ('mbox' default).

w [*file*] ...
    Save the message, without a header, in the named *files* ('mbox' default).

m [*person*] ...
    Mail the message to the named *persons* (yourself is default).

EOT (control-D)
    Put unexamined mail back in the mailbox and stop.

q   Same as EOT.

x   Exit, without changing the mailbox file.

!command
    Escape to the Shell to do command.

?   Print a command summary.

An interrupt stops the printing of the current letter. The optional argument −q causes *mail* to exit after interrupts without changing the mailbox.

When *persons* are named, *mail* takes the standard input up to an end-of-file (or a line with just '.') and adds it to each *person's* 'mail' file. The message is preceded by the sender's name and a postmark. Lines that look like postmarks are prepended with '>'. A *person* is usually a user name recognized by *login*(1). To denote a recipient on a remote system, prefix *person* by the system name and exclamation mark (see *uucp*(1)).

The −f option causes the named file, e.g. 'mbox', to be printed as if it were the mail file.

Each user owns his own mailbox, which is by default generally readable but not writable. The command does not delete an empty mailbox nor change its mode, so a user may make it unreadable if desired.

When a user logs in he is informed of the presence of mail.

FILES

/usr/spool/mail/*   mailboxes
/etc/passwd   to identify sender and locate persons
mbox   saved mail
/tmp/ma*   temp file

       dead.letter   unmailable text
       uux(1)

SEE ALSO

       xsend(1), write(1), uucp(1)

BUGS

       There is a locking mechanism intended to prevent two senders from accessing the same mailbox, but it is not perfect and races are possible.

NAME

make − maintain program groups

SYNOPSIS

make [−f makefile] [option] ... file ...

DESCRIPTION

Make executes commands in *makefile* to update one or more target *names*. *Name* is typically a program. If no −f option is present, 'makefile' and 'Makefile' are tried in order. If *makefile* is '−', the standard input is taken. More than one −f option may appear

Make updates a target if it depends on prerequisite files that have been modified since the target was last modified, or if the target does not exist.

Makefile contains a sequence of entries that specify dependencies. The first line of an entry is a blank-separated list of targets, then a colon, then a list of prerequisite files. Text following a semicolon, and all following lines that begin with a tab, are shell commands to be executed to update the target.

Sharp and newline surround comments.

The following makefile says that 'pgm' depends on two files 'a.o' and 'b.o', and that they in turn depend on '.c' files and a common file 'incl'.

```
pgm: a.o b.o
        cc a.o b.o −lm −o pgm
a.o: incl a.c
        cc −c a.c
b.o: incl b.c
        cc −c b.c
```

Makefile entries of the form

```
string1 = string2
```

are macro definitions. Subsequent appearances of *$(string1)* are replaced by *string2*. If *string1* is a single character, the parentheses are optional.

Make infers prerequisites for files for which *makefile* gives no construction commands. For example, a '.c' file may be inferred as prerequisite for a '.o' file and be compiled to produce the '.o' file. Thus the preceding example can be done more briefly:

```
pgm: a.o b.o
        cc a.o b.o −lm −o pgm
a.o b.o: incl
```

Prerequisites are inferred according to selected suffixes listed as the 'prerequisites' for the special name '.SUFFIXES'; multiple lists accumulate; an empty list clears what came before. Order is significant; the first possible name for which both a file and a rule as described in the next paragraph exist is inferred. The default list is

```
.SUFFIXES: .out .o .c .e .r .f .y .l .s
```

The rule to create a file with suffix $s2$ that depends on a similarly named file with suffix $s1$ is specified as an entry for the 'target' $s1s2$. In such an entry, the special macro $* stands for the target name with suffix deleted, $@ for the full target name, $< for the complete list of prerequisites, and $? for the list of prerequisites that are out of date. For example, a rule for making optimized '.o' files from '.c' files is

```
.c.o: ; cc −c −O −o $@ $*.c
```

Certain macros are used by the default inference rules to communicate optional arguments to any resulting compilations. In particular, 'CFLAGS' is used for *cc* and *f77*(1) options,

'LFLAGS' and 'YFLAGS' for *lex* and *yacc*(1) options.

Command lines are executed one at a time, each by its own shell. A line is printed when it is executed unless the special target '.SILENT' is in *makefile,* or the first character of the command is '@'.

Commands returning nonzero status (see *intro*(1)) cause *make* to terminate unless the special target '.IGNORE' is in *makefile* or the command begins with <tab><hyphen>.

Interrupt and quit cause the target to be deleted unless the target depends on the special name '.PRECIOUS'.

Other options:

  −i   Equivalent to the special entry '.IGNORE:'.

  −k   When a command returns nonzero status, abandon work on the current entry, but continue on branches that do not depend on the current entry.

  −n   Trace and print, but do not execute the commands needed to update the targets.

  −t   Touch, i.e. update the modified date of targets, without executing any commands.

  −r   Equivalent to an initial special entry '.SUFFIXES:' with no list.

  −s   Equivalent to the special entry '.SILENT:'.

FILES

      makefile, Makefile

SEE ALSO

      sh(1), touch(1)

      S. I. Feldman *Make − A Program for Maintaining Computer Programs*

BUGS

      Some commands return nonzero status inappropriately. Use −i to overcome the difficulty.

      Commands that are directly executed by the shell, notably *cd*(1), are ineffectual across newlines in *make*.

NAME

man — print sections of this manual

SYNOPSIS

man [option ...] [chapter] title ...

DESCRIPTION

Man locates and prints the section of this manual named *title* in the specified *chapter*. (In this context, the word 'page' is often used as a synonym for 'section'.) The *title* is entered in lower case. The *chapter* number does not need a letter suffix. If no *chapter* is specified, the whole manual is searched for *title* and all occurrences of it are printed.

Options and their meanings are:

−t   Phototypeset the section using *troff*(1).

−n   Print the section on the standard output using *nroff*(1).

−k   Display the output on a Tektronix 4014 terminal using *troff*(1) and *tc*(1).

−e   Appended or prefixed to any of the above causes the manual section to be preprocessed by *neqn* or *eqn*(1); −e alone means **−te**.

−w   Print the path names of the manual sections, but do not print the sections themselves.

(default)

Copy an already formatted manual section to the terminal, or, if none is available, act as **−n**. It may be necessary to use a filter to adapt the output to the particular terminal's characteristics.

Further *options,* e.g. to specify the kind of terminal you have, are passed on to *troff*(1) or *nroff*. *Options* and *chapter* may be changed before each *title*.

For example:

man man

would reproduce this section, as well as any other sections named *man* that may exist in other chapters of the manual, e.g. *man*(7).

FILES

/usr/man/man?/*
/usr/man/cat?/*

SEE ALSO

nroff(1), eqn(1), tc(1), man(7)

BUGS

The manual is supposed to be reproducible either on a phototypesetter or on a terminal. However, on a terminal some information is necessarily lost.

NAME

mesg — permit or deny messages

SYNOPSIS

mesg [**n**] [**y**]

DESCRIPTION

Mesg with argument **n** forbids messages via *write*(1) by revoking non-user write permission on the user's terminal. *Mesg* with argument y reinstates permission. All by itself, *mesg* reports the current state without changing it.

FILES

/dev/tty*

/dev

SEE ALSO

write(1)

DIAGNOSTICS

Exit status is 0 if messages are receivable, 1 if not, 2 on error.

NAME
mkconf − generate configuration tables

SYNOPSIS
mkconf

DESCRIPTION
Mkconf examines a machine configuration table on its standard input. Its output is a pair of files *l.s* and *c.c*. The first is an assembler program that represents the interrupt vectors located in low memory addresses; the second contains initialized block and character device switch tables.

Input to *mkconf* is a sequence of lines. The following describe devices on the machine:

pc	(PC11)
lp	(LP11)
rf	(RS11)
hs	(RS03/RS04)
tc	(TU56)
rk	(RK03/RK05)
tm	(TU10)
rp	(RP03)
hp	(RP04/5/6)
ht	(TU16)
dc*	(DC11)
kl*	(KL11/DL11-ABC)
dl*	(DL11-E)
dp*	(DP11)
dn*	(DN11)
dh*	(DH11)
dhdm*	(DM11-BB)
du*	(DU11)

The devices marked with * may be preceded by a number telling how many are to be included. The console typewrite is automatically included; don't count it as part of the KL or DL specification. Count DN's in units of 4 (1 system unit).

The following lines are also accepted.

root *dev minor*
> The specified block device (e.g. **hp**) is used for the root. *minor* is a decimal number giving the minor device. This line must appear exactly once.

swap *dev minor*
> The specified block device is used for swapping. If not given the root is used.

pipe *dev minor*
> The specified block device is used to store pipes. If not given the root is used.

swplo *number*

nswap *number*
> Sets the origin (block number) and size of the area used for swapping. By default, the not very useful numbers 4000 and 872.

pack Include the packet driver. By default it is left out.

mpx Include the multiplexor driver. By default it is left out.

FILES
l.s, c.c output files

SEE ALSO

'Setting up Unix', in Volume 2.

BUGS

The set of devices it knows about, the set of drivers included, and the set of devices on the machine are mutually incomparable. Some handwork is certain to be necessary. Because of floating vectors that may have been missed, It is mandatory to check the *l.s* file to make sure it corresponds with reality.

NAME
     mkdir − make a directory

SYNOPSIS
     mkdir dirname ...

DESCRIPTION
     Mkdir creates specified directories in mode 777. Standard entries, '.', for the directory itself, and '..' for its parent, are made automatically.

     Mkdir requires write permission in the parent directory.

SEE ALSO
     rm(1)

DIAGNOSTICS
     Mkdir returns exit code 0 if all directories were successfully made. Otherwise it prints a diagnostic and returns nonzero.

NAME

mkfs — construct a file system

SYNOPSIS

/etc/mkfs special proto

DESCRIPTION

Mkfs constructs a file system by writing on the special file *special* according to the directions found in the prototype file *proto*. The prototype file contains tokens separated by spaces or new lines. The first token is the name of a file to be copied onto block zero as the bootstrap program, see *bproc*(8). The second token is a number specifying the size of the created file system. Typically it will be the number of blocks on the device, perhaps diminished by space for swapping. The next token is the number of i-nodes in the i-list. The next set of tokens comprise the specification for the root file. File specifications consist of tokens giving the mode, the user-id, the group id, and the initial contents of the file. The syntax of the contents field depends on the mode.

The mode token for a file is a 6 character string. The first character specifies the type of the file. (The characters **—bcd** specify regular, block special, character special and directory files respectively.) The second character of the type is either **u** or **—** to specify set-user-id mode or not. The third is **g** or **—** for the set-group-id mode. The rest of the mode is a three digit octal number giving the owner, group, and other read, write, execute permissions, see *chmod*(1).

Two decimal number tokens come after the mode; they specify the user and group ID's of the owner of the file.

If the file is a regular file, the next token is a pathname whence the contents and size are copied.

If the file is a block or character special file, two decimal number tokens follow which give the major and minor device numbers.

If the file is a directory, *mkfs* makes the entries . and .. and then reads a list of names and (recursively) file specifications for the entries in the directory. The scan is terminated with the token **$**.

If the prototype file cannot be opened and its name consists of a string of digits, *mkfs* builds a file system with a single empty directory on it. The size of the file system is the value of *proto* interpreted as a decimal number. The number of i-nodes is calculated as a function of the filsystem size. The boot program is left uninitialized.

A sample prototype specification follows:

```
        /usr/mdec/uboot
        4872 55
        d——777 3 1
        usr     d——777 3 1
                sh          ———755 3 1 /bin/sh
                ken         d——755 6 1
                            $
                b0          b——644 3 1 0 0
                c0          c——644 3 1 0 0
                            $
        $
```

SEE ALSO

filsys(5), dir(5), bproc(8)

BUGS

There should be some way to specify links.

NAME

    mknod — build special file

SYNOPSIS

    /etc/mknod name [**c**] [**b**] major minor

DESCRIPTION

    Mknod makes a special file. The first argument is the *name* of the entry. The second is **b** if the special file is block-type (disks, tape) or **c** if it is character-type (other devices). The last two arguments are numbers specifying the *major* device type and the *minor* device (e.g. unit, drive, or line number).

    The assignment of major device numbers is specific to each system. They have to be dug out of the system source file *conf.c*.

SEE ALSO

    mknod(2)

NAME

mount, umount — mount and dismount file system

SYNOPSIS

/etc/mount [special name [**−r**]]

/etc/umount special

DESCRIPTION

Mount announces to the system that a removable file system is present on the device *special*. The file *name* must exist already; it must be a directory (unless the root of the mounted file system is not a directory). It becomes the name of the newly mounted root. The optional last argument indicates that the file system is to be mounted read-only.

Umount announces to the system that the removable file system previously mounted on device *special* is to be removed.

These commands maintain a table of mounted devices. If invoked without an argument, *mount* prints the table.

Physically write-protected and magnetic tape file systems must be mounted read-only or errors will occur when access times are updated, whether or not any explicit write is attempted.

FILES

/etc/mtab: mount table

SEE ALSO

mount(2), mtab(5)

BUGS

Mounting file systems full of garbage will crash the system.
Mounting a root directory on a non-directory makes some apparently good pathnames invalid.

NAME

    mv − move or rename files and directories

SYNOPSIS

    mv file1 file2

    mv file ... directory

DESCRIPTION

    Mv moves (changes the name of) *file1* to *file2*.

    If *file2* already exists, it is removed before *file1* is moved. If *file2* has a mode which forbids writing, *mv* prints the mode (see *chmod*(2)) and reads the standard input to obtain a line; if the line begins with **y**, the move takes place; if not, *mv* exits.

    In the second form, one or more *files* are moved to the *directory* with their original file-names.

    Mv refuses to move a file onto itself.

SEE ALSO

    cp(1), chmod(2)

BUGS

    If *file1* and *file2* lie on different file systems, *mv* must copy the file and delete the original. In this case the owner name becomes that of the copying process and any linking relationship with other files is lost.

    Mv should take −**f** flag, like *rm*, to suppress the question if the target exists and is not writable.

NAME

ncheck — generate names from i-numbers

SYNOPSIS

ncheck [−i numbers] [−a] [−s] [filesystem]

DESCRIPTION

Ncheck with no argument generates a pathname vs. i-number list of all files on a set of default file systems. Names of directory files are followed by '/.'. The −i option reduces the report to only those files whose i-numbers follow. The −a option allows printing of the names '.' and '..', which are ordinarily suppressed. suppressed. The −s option reduces the report to special files and files with set-user-ID mode; it is intended to discover concealed violations of security policy.

A file system may be specified.

The report is in no useful order, and probably should be sorted.

SEE ALSO

dcheck(1), icheck(1), sort(1)

DIAGNOSTICS

When the filesystem structure is improper, '??' denotes the 'parent' of a parentless file and a pathname beginning with '...' denotes a loop.

NAME

      newgrp − log in to a new group

SYNOPSIS

      newgrp group

DESCRIPTION

      Newgrp changes the group identification of its caller, analogously to *login*(1). The same person remains logged in, and the current directory is unchanged, but calculations of access permissions to files are performed with respect to the new group ID.

      A password is demanded if the group has a password and the user himself does not.

      When most users log in, they are members of the group named 'other.' *Newgrp* is known to the shell, which executes it directly without a fork.

FILES

      /etc/group, /etc/passwd

SEE ALSO

      login(1), group(5)

NAME

nice, nohup — run a command at low priority

SYNOPSIS

nice [−*number*] command [arguments]

nohup command [arguments]

DESCRIPTION

Nice executes *command* with low scheduling priority. If the *number* argument is present, the priority is incremented (higher numbers mean lower priorities) by that amount up to a limit of 20. The default *number* is 10.

The super-user may run commands with priority higher than normal by using a negative priority, e.g. '−−10'.

Nohup executes *command* immune to hangup and terminate signals from the controlling terminal. The priority is incremented by 5. *Nohup* should be invoked from the shell with '&' in order to prevent it from responding to interrupts by or stealing the input from the next person who logs in on the same terminal.

FILES

nohup.out standard output and standard error file under *nohup*

SEE ALSO

nice(2)

DIAGNOSTICS

Nice returns the exit status of the subject command.

NAME

    nm − print name list

SYNOPSIS

    nm [**−gnopru**] [file ...]

DESCRIPTION

Nm prints the name list (symbol table) of each object *file* in the argument list. If an argument is an archive, a listing for each object file in the archive will be produced. If no *file* is given, the symbols in 'a.out' are listed.

Each symbol name is preceded by its value (blanks if undefined) and one of the letters U (undefined), A (absolute), T (text segment symbol), D (data segment symbol), B (bss segment symbol), or C (common symbol). If the symbol is local (non-external) the type letter is in lower case. The output is sorted alphabetically.

Options are:

−g   Print only global (external) symbols.

−n   Sort numerically rather than alphabetically.

−o   Prepend file or archive element name to each output line rather than only once.

−p   Don't sort; print in symbol-table order.

−r   Sort in reverse order.

−u   Print only undefined symbols.

SEE ALSO

    ar(1), ar(5), a.out(5)

NAME

od — octal dump

SYNOPSIS

od [−bcdox] [file] [[+]offset[.][b]]

DESCRIPTION

Od dumps *file* in one or more formats as selected by the first argument. If the first argument is missing, −o is default. The meanings of the format argument characters are:

b Interpret bytes in octal.

c Interpret bytes in ASCII. Certain non-graphic characters appear as C escapes: null=\0, backspace=\b, formfeed=\f, newline=\n, return=\r, tab=\t; others appear as 3-digit octal numbers.

d Interpret words in decimal.

o Interpret words in octal.

x Interpret words in hex.

The *file* argument specifies which file is to be dumped. If no file argument is specified, the standard input is used.

The offset argument specifies the offset in the file where dumping is to commence. This argument is normally interpreted as octal bytes. If '.' is appended, the offset is interpreted in decimal. If 'b' is appended, the offset is interpreted in blocks of 512 bytes. If the file argument is omitted, the offset argument must be preceded '+'.

Dumping continues until end-of-file.

SEE ALSO

adb(1)

NAME

    passwd — change login password

SYNOPSIS

    passwd [name]

DESCRIPTION

    This command changes (or installs) a password associated with the user *name* (your own name by default).

    The program prompts for the old password and then for the new one. The caller must supply both. The new password must be typed twice, to forestall mistakes.

    New passwords must be at least four characters long if they use a sufficiently rich alphabet and at least six characters long if monocase. These rules are relaxed if you are insistent enough.

    Only the owner of the name or the super-user may change a password; the owner must prove he knows the old password.

FILES

    /etc/passwd

SEE ALSO

    login(1), passwd(5), crypt(3)

    Robert Morris and Ken Thompson, *Password Security: A Case History*

NAME

plot — graphics filters

SYNOPSIS

plot [−Tterminal [raster]]

DESCRIPTION

These commands read plotting instructions (see *plot*(5)) from the standard input, and in general produce plotting instructions suitable for a particular *terminal* on the standard output.

If no *terminal* type is specified, the environment parameter $TERM (see *environ*(5)) is used. Known *terminals* are:

4014   Tektronix 4014 storage scope.

450   DASI Hyterm 450 terminal (Diablo mechanism).

300   DASI 300 or GSI terminal (Diablo mechanism).

300S   DASI 300S terminal (Diablo mechanism).

ver   Versatec D1200A printer-plotter. This version of *plot* places a scan-converted image in '/usr/tmp/raster' and sends the result directly to the plotter device rather than to the standard output. The optional argument causes a previously scan-converted file *raster* to be sent to the plotter.

FILES

/usr/bin/tek
/usr/bin/t450
/usr/bin/t300
/usr/bin/t300s
/usr/bin/vplot
/usr/tmp/raster

SEE ALSO

plot(3), plot(5)

BUGS

There is no lockout protection for /usr/tmp/raster.

NAME

   pr − print file

SYNOPSIS

   pr [option] ...   [file] ...

DESCRIPTION

Pr produces a printed listing of one or more *files*. The output is separated into pages headed by a date, the name of the file or a specified header, and the page number. If there are no file arguments, *pr* prints its standard input.

Options apply to all following files but may be reset between files:

−*n*   Produce *n*-column output.

+*n*   Begin printing with page *n*.

−**h**   Take the next argument as a page header.

−**w***n*   For purposes of multi-column output, take the width of the page to be *n* characters instead of the default 72.

−**l***n*   Take the length of the page to be *n* lines instead of the default 66.

−**t**   Do not print the 5-line header or the 5-line trailer normally supplied for each page.

−**s***c*   Separate columns by the single character *c* instead of by the appropriate amount of white space. A missing *c* is taken to be a tab.

−**m**   Print all *files* simultaneously, each in one column,

Inter-terminal messages via *write*(1) are forbidden during a *pr*.

FILES

   /dev/tty? to suspend messages.

SEE ALSO

   cat(1)

DIAGNOSTICS

   There are no diagnostics when *pr* is printing on a terminal.

NAME

prep — prepare text for statistical processing

SYNOPSIS

prep [**−dio**] file ...

DESCRIPTION

Prep reads each *file* in sequence and writes it on the standard output, one 'word' to a line. A word is a string of alphabetic characters and imbedded apostrophes, delimited by space or punctuation. Hyphented words are broken apart; hyphens at the end of lines are removed and the hyphenated parts are joined. Strings of digits are discarded.

The following option letters may appear in any order:

−d   Print the word number (in the input stream) with each word.

−i   Take the next *file* as an 'ignore' file. These words will not appear in the output. (They will be counted, for purposes of the −d count.)

−o   Take the next *file* as an 'only' file. Only these words will appear in the output. (All other words will also be counted for the −d count.)

−p   Include punctuation marks (single nonalphanumeric characters) as separate output lines. The punctuation marks are not counted for the −d count.

Ignore and only files contain words, one per line.

SEE ALSO

deroff(1)

NAME

    prof — display profile data

SYNOPSIS

    prof [−v] [−a] [−l] [−low [−high]] [file]

DESCRIPTION

    Prof interprets the file *mon.out* produced by the *monitor* subroutine. Under default modes, the symbol table in the named object file *(a.out* default) is read and correlated with the *mon.out* profile file. For each external symbol, the percentage of time spent executing between that symbol and the next is printed (in decreasing order), together with the number of times that routine was called and the number of milliseconds per call.

    If the −a option is used, all symbols are reported rather than just external symbols. If the −l option is used, the output is listed by symbol value rather than decreasing percentage.

    If the −v option is used, all printing is suppressed and a graphic version of, the profile is produced on the standard output for display by the *plot*(1) filters. The numbers *low* and *high,* by default 0 and 100, cause a selected percentage of the profile to be plotted with accordingly higher resolution.

    In order for the number of calls to a routine to be tallied, the −p option of *cc* must have been given when the file containing the routine was compiled. This option also arranges for the *mon.out* file to be produced automatically.

FILES

    mon.out for profile
    a.out   for namelist

SEE ALSO

    monitor(3), profil(2), cc(1), plot(1)

BUGS

    Beware of quantization errors.

NAME

ps — process status

SYNOPSIS

ps [**aklx**] [namelist]

DESCRIPTION

Ps prints certain indicia about active processes. The **a** option asks for information about all processes with terminals (ordinarily only one's own processes are displayed); **x** asks even about processes with no terminal; **l** asks for a long listing. The short listing contains the process ID, tty letter, the cumulative execution time of the process and an approximation to the command line.

The long listing is columnar and contains

F   Flags associated with the process. 01: in core; 02: system process; 04: locked in core (e.g. for physical I/O); 10: being swapped; 20: being traced by another process.

S   The state of the process. 0: nonexistent; S: sleeping; W: waiting; R: running; I: intermediate; Z: terminated; T: stopped.

UID   The user ID of the process owner.

PID   The process ID of the process; as in certain cults it is possible to kill a process if you know its true name.

PPID   The process ID of the parent process.

CPU   Processor utilization for scheduling.

PRI   The priority of the process; high numbers mean low priority.

NICE   Used in priority computation.

ADDR The core address of the process if resident, otherwise the disk address.

SZ   The size in blocks of the core image of the process.

WCHAN
        The event for which the process is waiting or sleeping; if blank, the process is running.

TTY   The controlling tty for the process.

TIME   The cumulative execution time for the process.

The command and its arguments.

A process that has exited and has a parent, but has not yet been waited for by the parent is marked <defunct>. *Ps* makes an educated guess as to the file name and arguments given when the process was created by examining core memory or the swap area. The method is inherently somewhat unreliable and in any event a process is entitled to destroy this information, so the names cannot be counted on too much.

If the **k** option is specified, the file */usr/sys/core* is used in place of */dev/mem*. This is used for postmortem system debugging. If a second argument is given, it is taken to be the file containing the system's namelist.

FILES

/unix   system namelist
/dev/mem   core memory
/usr/sys/core alternate core file
/dev   searched to find swap device and tty names

SEE ALSO

kill(1)

BUGS

       Things can change while *ps* is running; the picture it gives is only a close approximation to reality.

       Some data printed for defunct processes is irrelevant

NAME

pstat — print system facts

SYNOPSIS

pstat [**−aixptuf**] [suboptions] [file]

DESCRIPTION

Pstat interprets the contents of certain system tables. If *file* is given, the tables are sought there, otherwise in */dev/mem*. The required namelist is taken from */unix*. Options are

−a Under **−p**, describe all process slots rather than just active ones.

−i Print the inode table with the these headings:

LOC The core location of this table entry.

FLAGS Miscellaneous state variables encoded thus:

L	locked
U	update time *filsys*(5)) must be corrected
A	access time must be corrected
M	file system is mounted here
W	wanted by another process (L flag is on)
T	contains a text file
C	changed time must be corrected

CNT Number of open file table entries for this inode.

DEV Major and minor device number of file system in which this inode resides.

INO I-number within the device.

MODE Mode bits, see *chmod*(2).

NLK Number of links to this inode.

UID User ID of owner.

SIZ/DEV

  Number of bytes in an ordinary file, or major and minor device of special file.

−x Print the text table with these headings:

LOC The core location of this table entry.

FLAGS Miscellaneous state variables encoded thus:

T	*ptrace*(2) in effect
W	text not yet written on swap device
L	loading in progress
K	locked
w	wanted (L flag is on)

DADDR Disk address in swap, measured in multiples of 512 bytes.

CADDR Core address, measured in multiples of 64 bytes.

SIZE Size of text segment, measured in multiples of 64 bytes.

IPTR Core location of corresponding inode.

CNT Number of processes using this text segment.

CCNT Number of processes in core using this text segment.

−p Print process table for active processes with these headings:

LOC The core location of this table entry.

S Run state encoded thus:

0	no process
1	waiting for some event
3	runnable

4	being created
5	being terminated
6	stopped under trace

F   Miscellaneous state variables, or-ed together:

01	loaded
02	the scheduler process
04	locked
010	swapped out
020	traced
040	used in tracing
0100	locked in by *lock*(2).

PRI   Scheduling priority, see *nice*(2).

SIGNAL Signals received (signals 1-16 coded in bits 0-15),

UID   Real user ID.

TIM   Time resident in seconds; times over 127 coded as 127.

CPU   Weighted integral of CPU time, for scheduler.

NI   Nice level, see *nice*(2).

PGRP   Process number of root of process group (the opener of the controlling terminal).

PID   The process ID number.

PPID   The process ID of parent process.

ADDR   If in core, the physical address of the 'u-area' of the process measured in multiples of
         64 bytes. If swapped out, the position in the swap area measured in multiples of 512
         bytes.

SIZE   Size of process image in multiples of 64 bytes.

WCHAN Wait channel number of a waiting process.

LINK   Link pointer in list of runnable processes.

TEXTP   If text is pure, pointer to location of text table entry.

CLKT   Countdown for *alarm*(2) measured in seconds.

−t   Print table for terminals (only DH11 and DL11 handled) with these headings:

RAW   Number of characters in raw input queue.

CAN   Number of characters in canonicalized input queue.

OUT   Number of characters in putput queue.

MODE   See *tty*(4).

ADDR   Physical device address.

DEL   Number of delimiters (newlines) in canonicalized input queue.

COL   Calculated column position of terminal.

STATE   Miscellaneous state variables encoded thus:

W	waiting for open to complete
O	open
S	has special (output) start routine
C	carrier is on
B	busy doing output
A	process is awaiting output
X	open for exclusive use
H	hangup on close

PGRP   Process group for which this is controlling terminal.

−u   print information about a user process; the next argument is its address as given by
         ps(1). The process must be in main memory, or the file used can be a core image
         and the address 0.

−f   Print the open file table with these headings:

LOC   The core location of this table entry.

FLG   Miscellaneous state variables encoded thus:

        R   open for reading

        W   open for writing

        P   pipe

CNT   Number of processes that know this open file.

INO   The location of the inode table entry for this file.

OFFS   The file offset, see *lseek*(2).

FILES

/unix   namelist

/dev/mem default source of tables

SEE ALSO

ps(1), stat(2), filsys(5)

K. Thompson, *UNIX Implementation*

NAME
ptx — permuted index

SYNOPSIS
ptx [option] ... [input [output]]

DESCRIPTION
Ptx generates a permuted index to file *input* on file *output* (standard input and output default). It has three phases: the first does the permutation, generating one line for each keyword in an input line. The keyword is rotated to the front. The permuted file is then sorted. Finally, the sorted lines are rotated so the keyword comes at the middle of the page. *Ptx* produces output in the form:

.xx "tail" "before keyword" "keyword and after" "head"

where .xx may be an *nroff* or *troff*(1) macro for user-defined formatting. The *before keyword* and *keyword and after* fields incorporate as much of the line as will fit around the keyword when it is printed at the middle of the page. *Tail* and *head,* at least one of which is an empty string "", are wrapped-around pieces small enough to fit in the unused space at the opposite end of the line. When original text must be discarded, '/' marks the spot.

The following options can be applied:

—f   Fold upper and lower case letters for sorting.

—t   Prepare the output for the phototypesetter; the default line length is 100 characters.

—w *n* Use the next argument, *n,* as the width of the output line. The default line length is 72 characters.

—g *n* Use the next argument, *n,* as the number of characters to allow for each gap among the four parts of the line as finally printed. The default gap is 3 characters.

—o only
    Use as keywords only the words given in the *only* file.

—i ignore
    Do not use as keywords any words given in the *ignore* file. If the *-i* and *-o* options are missing, use /usr/lib/eign as the *ignore* file.

—b break
    Use the characters in the *break* file to separate words. In any case, tab, newline, and space characters are always used as break characters.

—r   Take any leading nonblank characters of each input line to be a reference identifier (as to a page or chapter) separate from the text of the line. Attach that identifier as a 5th field on each output line.

The index for this manual was generated using *ptx.*

FILES
/bin/sort
/usr/lib/eign

BUGS
Line length counts do not account for overstriking or proportional spacing.

NAME

pubindex — make inverted bibliographic index

SYNOPSIS

pubindex [file] ...

DESCRIPTION

Pubindex makes a hashed inverted index to the named *files* for use by *refer*(1). The *files* contain bibliographic references separated by blank lines. A bibliographic reference is a set of lines that contain bibliographic information fields. Each field starts on a line beginning with a '%', followed by a key-letter, followed by a blank, and followed by the contents of the field, which continues until the next line starting with '%'. The most common key-letters and the corresponding fields are:

A	Author name
B	Title of book containing article referenced
C	City
D	Date
d	Alternate date
E	Editor of book containing article referenced
G	Government (CFSTI) order number
I	Issuer (publisher)
J	Journal
K	Other keywords to use in locating reference
M	Technical memorandum number
N	Issue number within volume
O	Other commentary to be printed at end of reference
P	Page numbers
R	Report number
r	Alternate report number
T	Title of article, book, etc.
V	Volume number
X	Commentary unused by *pubindex*

Except for 'A', each field should only be given once. Only relevant fields should be supplied. An example is:

```
%T 5-by-5 Palindromic Word Squares
%A M. D. McIlroy
%J Word Ways
%V 9
%P 199-202
%D 1976
```

FILES

x.ia, x.ib, x.ic where *x* is the first argument.

SEE ALSO

refer(1)

NAME

       pwd — working directory name

SYNOPSIS

       pwd

DESCRIPTION

       Pwd prints the pathname of the working (current) directory.

SEE ALSO

       cd(1)

NAME

quot − summarize file system ownership

SYNOPSIS

quot [option] ... [filesystem]

DESCRIPTION

Quot prints the number of blocks in the named *filesystem* currently owned by each user. If no *filesystem* is named, a default name is assumed. The following options are available:

−**n**   Cause the pipeline **ncheck filesystem** | **sort +0n** | **quot** −**n filesystem** to produce a list of all files and their owners.

−**c**   Print three columns giving file size in blocks, number of files of that size, and cumulative total of blocks in that size or smaller file.

−**f**   Print count of number of files as well as space owned by each user.

FILES

Default file system varies with system.
/etc/passwd to get user names

SEE ALSO

ls(1), du(1)

BUGS

Holes in files are counted as if they actually occupied space.

NAME

  ranlib — convert archives to random libraries

SYNOPSIS

  ranlib archive ...

DESCRIPTION

  Ranlib converts each *archive* to a form which can be loaded more rapidly by the loader, by adding a table of contents named __.**SYMDEF** to the beginning of the archive. It uses *ar*(1) to reconstruct the archive, so that sufficient temporary file space must be available in the file system containing the current directory.

SEE ALSO

  ld(1), ar(1)

BUGS

  Because generation of a library by *ar* and randomization by *ranlib* are separate, phase errors are possible. The loader *ld* warns when the modification date of a library is more recent than the creation of its dictionary; but this means you get the warning even if you only copy the library.

NAME

 ratfor — rational Fortran dialect

SYNOPSIS

 ratfor [option ...] [filename ...]

DESCRIPTION

 Ratfor converts a rational dialect of Fortran into ordinary irrational Fortran. *Ratfor* provides control flow constructs essentially identical to those in C:

 statement grouping:

 { statement; statement; statement }

 decision-making:

 if (condition) statement [else statement]
 switch (integer value) {
 case integer: statement
 ...
 [default:]   statement
 }

 loops: while (condition) statement
 for (expression; condition; expression) statement
 do limits statement
 repeat statement [until (condition)]
 break [n]
 next [n]

 and some syntactic sugar to make programs easier to read and write:

 free form input:

 multiple statements/line; automatic continuation

 comments:

 # this is a comment

 translation of relationals:

 >, >=, etc., become .GT., .GE., etc.

 return (expression)

 returns expression to caller from function

 define: define name replacement

 include:

 include filename

 The option —**h** causes quoted strings to be turned into 27H constructs. —**C** copies comments to the output, and attempts to format it neatly. Normally, continuation lines are marked with a & in column 1; the option —**6x** makes the continuation character **x** and places it in column 6.

 Ratfor is best used with *f77* (1).

SEE ALSO

 f77(1)

 B. W. Kernighan and P. J. Plauger, *Software Tools*, Addison-Wesley, 1976.

NAME

refer, lookbib — find and insert literature references in documents

SYNOPSIS

refer [option] ...

lookbib [file] ...

DESCRIPTION

Lookbib accepts keywords from the standard input and searches a bibliographic data base for references that contain those keywords anywhere in title, author, journal name, etc. Matching references are printed on the standard output. Blank lines are taken as delimiters between queries.

Refer is a preprocessor for *nroff* or *troff*(1) that finds and formats references. The input files (standard input default) are copied to the standard output, except for lines between .[and .] command lines, which are assumed to contain keywords as for *lookbib,* and are replaced by information from the bibliographic data base. The user may avoid the search, override fields from it, or add new fields. The reference data, from whatever source, are assigned to a set of *troff* strings. Macro packages such as *ms*(7) print the finished reference text from these strings. A flag is placed in the text at the point of reference; by default the references are indicated by numbers.

The following options are available:

−**a***r* Reverse the first *r* author names (Jones, J. A. instead of J. A. Jones). If *r* is omitted all author names are reversed.

−**b** Bare mode: do not put any flags in text (neither numbers nor labels).

−**c***string*

Capitalize (with CAPS SMALL CAPS) the fields whose key-letters are in *string*.

−**e** Instead of leaving the references where encountered, accumulate them until a sequence of the form

       .[

       $LIST$

       .]

is encountered, and then write out all references collected so far. Collapse references to the same source.

−**k***x* Instead of numbering references, use labels as specified in a reference data line beginning %*x;* by default *x* is **L**.

−**l***m,n*

Instead of numbering references, use labels made from the senior author's last name and the year of publication. Only the first *m* letters of the last name and the last *n* digits of the date are used. If either *m* or *,n* is omitted the entire name or date respectively is used.

−**p** Take the next argument as a file of references to be searched. The default file is searched last.

−**n** Do not search the default file.

−**s***keys*

Sort references by fields whose key-letters are in the *keys* string; permute reference numbers in text accordingly. Implies −**e**. The key-letters in *keys* may be followed by a number to indicate how many such fields are used, with + taken as a very large number. The default is **AD** which sorts on the senior author and then date; to sort, for example, on all authors and then title use −**sA**+**T**.

To use your own references, put them in the format described in *pubindex*(1) They can be searched more rapidly by running *pubindex*(1) on them before using *refer;* failure to index results in a linear search.

When *refer* is used with *eqn, neqn* or *tbl, refer* should be first, to minimize the volume of data passed through pipes.

FILES

/usr/dict/papers directory of default publication lists and indexes

/usr/lib/refer directory of programs

SEE ALSO

NAME

restor — incremental file system restore

SYNOPSIS

restor key [argument ...]

DESCRIPTION

Restor is used to read magtapes dumped with the *dump* command. The *key* specifies what is to be done. *Key* is one of the characters **rRxt** optionally combined with **f**.

f   Use the first *argument* as the name of the tape instead of the default.

r or R   The tape is read and loaded into the file system specified in *argument*. This should not be done lightly (see below). If the key is **R** *restor* asks which tape of a multi volume set to start on. This allows restor to be interrupted and then restarted (an *icheck* —*s must be done before restart*). ®.TP **x** Each file on the tape named by an *argument* is extracted. The file name has all 'mount' prefixes removed; for example, /usr/bin/lpr is named /bin/lpr on the tape. The file extracted is placed in a file with a numeric name supplied by *restor* (actually the inode number). In order to keep the amount of tape read to a minimum, the following procedure is recommended:

Mount volume 1 of the set of dump tapes.

Type the *restor* command.

Restor will announce whether or not it found the files, give the number it will name the file, and rewind the tape.

It then asks you to 'mount the desired tape volume'. Type the number of the volume you choose. On a multivolume dump the recommended procedure is to mount the last through the first volume in that order. *Restor* checks to see if any of the files requested are on the mounted tape (or a later tape, thus the reverse order) and doesn't read through the tape if no files are. If you are working with a single volume dump or the number of files being restored is large, respond to the query with '1' and *restor* will read the tapes in sequential order.

If you have a hierarchy to restore you can use dumpdir(1) to produce the list of names and a shell script to move the resulting files to their homes.

t   Print the date the tape was written and the date the filesystem was dumped from.

The **r** option should only be used to restore a complete dump tape onto a clear file system or to restore an incremental dump tape onto this. Thus

    /etc/mkfs /dev/rp0 40600
    restor r /dev/rp0

is a typical sequence to restore a complete dump. Another *restor* can be done to get an incremental dump in on top of this.

A *dump* followed by a *mkfs* and a *restor* is used to change the size of a file system.

FILES

default tape unit varies with installation
rst*

SEE ALSO

dump(1), mkfs(1), dumpdir(1)

DIAGNOSTICS

There are various diagnostics involved with reading the tape and writing the disk. There are also diagnostics if the i-list or the free list of the file system is not large enough to hold the dump.

If the dump extends over more than one tape, it may ask you to change tapes. Reply with a new-line when the next tape has been mounted.

BUGS

There is redundant information on the tape that could be used in case of tape reading problems. Unfortunately, *restor* doesn't use it.

NAME
    rev − reverse lines of a file
SYNOPSIS
    rev [file] ...
DESCRIPTION
    Rev copies the named files to the standard output, reversing the order of characters in every
    line. If no file is specified, the standard input is copied.

NAME

rm, rmdir − remove (unlink) files

SYNOPSIS

rm [**−fri**] file ...

rmdir dir ...

DESCRIPTION

Rm removes the entries for one or more files from a directory. If an entry was the last link to the file, the file is destroyed. Removal of a file requires write permission in its directory, but neither read nor write permission on the file itself.

If a file has no write permission and the standard input is a terminal, its permissions are printed and a line is read from the standard input. If that line begins with 'y' the file is deleted, otherwise the file remains. No questions are asked when the **−f** (force) option is given.

If a designated file is a directory, an error comment is printed unless the optional argument **−r** has been used. In that case, *rm* recursively deletes the entire contents of the specified directory, and the directory itself.

If the **−i** (interactive) option is in effect, *rm* asks whether to delete each file, and, under **−r**, whether to examine each directory.

Rmdir removes entries for the named directories, which must be empty.

SEE ALSO

unlink(2)

DIAGNOSTICS

Generally self-explanatory. It is forbidden to remove the file '..' merely to avoid the antisocial consequences of inadvertently doing something like 'rm −r .*'.

NAME

roff − format text

SYNOPSIS

roff [+n] [−n] [−s] [−h] file ...

nroff −**mr** [option] ... file ...
troff −**mr** [option] ... file ...

DESCRIPTION

Roff formats text according to control lines embedded in the text in the given files. Encountering a nonexistent file terminates printing. Incoming inter-terminal messages are turned off during printing. The optional flag arguments mean:

+n Start printing at the first page with number *n*.

−n Stop printing at the first page numbered higher than *n*.

−s Stop before each page (including the first) to allow paper manipulation; resume on receipt of an interrupt signal.

−h Insert tabs in the output stream to replace spaces whenever appropriate.

Input consists of intermixed *text lines*, which contain information to be formatted, and *request lines*, which contain instructions about how to format it. Request lines begin with a distinguished *control character*, normally a period.

Output lines may be *filled* as nearly as possible with words without regard to input lineation. Line *breaks* may be caused at specified places by certain commands, or by the appearance of an empty input line or an input line beginning with a space.

The capabilities of *roff* are specified in the attached Request Summary. Numerical values are denoted there by n or +n, titles by t, and single characters by c. Numbers denoted +n may be signed + or −, in which case they signify relative changes to a quantity, otherwise they signify an absolute resetting. Missing n fields are ordinarily taken to be 1, missing t fields to be empty, and c fields to shut off the appropriate special interpretation.

Running titles usually appear at top and bottom of every page. They are set by requests like

.he 'part1'part2'part3'

Part1 is left justified, part2 is centered, and part3 is right justified on the page. Any % sign in a title is replaced by the current page number. Any nonblank may serve as a quote.

ASCII tab characters are replaced in the input by a *replacement character*, normally a space, according to the column settings given by a .ta command. (See .tr for how to convert this character on output.)

Automatic hyphenation of filled output is done under control of .hy. When a word contains a designated *hyphenation character*, that character disappears from the output and hyphens can be introduced into the word at the marked places only.

The −**mr** option of *nroff* or *troff*(1) simulates *roff* to the greatest extent possible.

FILES

/usr/lib/suftab suffix hyphenation tables
/tmp/rtm?   temporary

BUGS

Roff is the simplest of the text formatting programs, and is utterly frozen.

REQUEST SUMMARY

Request Break Initial Meaning
the current line is stopped.

NAME
     sa, accton — system accounting

SYNOPSIS
     sa [**−abcjlnrstuv**] [file]

     /etc/accton [file]

DESCRIPTION
     With an argument naming an existing *file, accton* causes system accounting information for
     every process executed to be placed at the end of the file. If no arguemnt is given, accounting
     is turned off.

     Sa reports on, cleans up, and generally maintains accounting files.

     Sa is able to condense the information in */usr/adm/acct* into a summary file */usr/adm/savacct*
     which contains a count of the number of times each command was called and the time
     resources consumed. This condensation is desirable because on a large system *acct* can grow by
     100 blocks per day. The summary file is read before the accounting file, so the reports include
     all available information.

     If a file name is given as the last argument, that file will be treated as the accounting file; *sha* is
     the default. There are zillions of options:

     a   Place all command names containing unprintable characters and those used only once
             under the name '***other.'

     b   Sort output by sum of user and system time divided by number of calls. Default sort is
             by sum of user and system times.

     c   Besides total user, system, and real time for each command print percentage of total
             time over all commands.

     j   Instead of total minutes time for each category, give seconds per call.

     l   Separate system and user time; normally they are combined.

     m   Print number of processes and number of CPU minutes for each user.

     n   Sort by number of calls.

     r   Reverse order of sort.

     s   Merge accounting file into summary file */usr/adm/savacct* when done.

     t   For each command report ratio of real time to the sum of user and system times.

     u   Superseding all other flags, print for each command in the accounting file the user ID
             and command name.

     v   If the next character is a digit *n,* then type the name of each command used *n* times or
             fewer. Await a reply from the typewriter; if it begins with 'y', add the command to the
             category '**junk**.' This is used to strip out garbage.

FILES
     /usr/adm/acct   raw accounting
     /usr/adm/savacct   summary
     /usr/adm/usracct   per-user summary

SEE ALSO
     ac(1), acct(2)

NAME

sed — stream editor

SYNOPSIS

sed [−**n**] [−**e** script] [−**f** sfile] [file] ...

DESCRIPTION

Sed copies the named *files* (standard input default) to the standard output, edited according to a script of commands. The −**f** option causes the script to be taken from file *sfile*; these options accumulate. If there is just one −**e** option and no −**f**'s, the flag −**e** may be omitted. The −**n** option suppresses the default output.

A script consists of editing commands, one per line, of the following form:

[address [, address]] function [arguments]

In normal operation *sed* cyclically copies a line of input into a *pattern space* (unless there is something left after a 'D' command), applies in sequence all commands whose *addresses* select that pattern space, and at the end of the script copies the pattern space to the standard output (except under −**n**) and deletes the pattern space.

An *address* is either a decimal number that counts input lines cumulatively across files, a '$' that addresses the last line of input, or a context address, '/regular expression/', in the style of *ed*(1) modified thus:

The escape sequence '\n' matches a newline embedded in the pattern space.

A command line with no addresses selects every pattern space.

A command line with one address selects each pattern space that matches the address.

A command line with two addresses selects the inclusive range from the first pattern space that matches the first address through the next pattern space that matches the second. (If the second address is a number less than or equal to the line number first selected, only one line is selected.) Thereafter the process is repeated, looking again for the first address.

Editing commands can be applied only to non-selected pattern spaces by use of the negation function '!' (below).

In the following list of functions the maximum number of permissible addresses for each function is indicated in parentheses.

An argument denoted *text* consists of one or more lines, all but the last of which end with '\' to hide the newline. Backslashes in text are treated like backslashes in the replacement string of an 's' command, and may be used to protect initial blanks and tabs against the stripping that is done on every script line.

An argument denoted *rfile* or *wfile* must terminate the command line and must be preceded by exactly one blank. Each *wfile* is created before processing begins. There can be at most 10 distinct *wfile* arguments.

(1) a\
text

Append. Place *text* on the output before reading the next input line.

(2) b *label*

Branch to the ':' command bearing the *label*. If *label* is empty, branch to the end of the script.

(2) c\
text

Change. Delete the pattern space. With 0 or 1 address or at the end of a 2-address range, place *text* on the output. Start the next cycle.

(2) d　　Delete the pattern space. Start the next cycle.

(2) D　　Delete the initial segment of the pattern space through the first newline. Start the next cycle.

(2) g　　Replace the contents of the pattern space by the contents of the hold space.

(2) G　　Append the contents of the hold space to the pattern space.

(2) h　　Replace the contents of the hold space by the contents of the pattern space.

(2) H　　Append the contents of the pattern space to the hold space.

(1) i\
text　　Insert. Place *text* on the standard output.

(2) l　　List the pattern space on the standard output in an unambiguous form. Non-printing characters are spelled in two digit ascii, and long lines are folded.

(2) n　　Copy the pattern space to the standard output. Replace the pattern space with the next line of input.

(2) N　　Append the next line of input to the pattern space with an embedded newline. (The current line number changes.)

(2) p　　Print. Copy the pattern space to the standard output.

(2) P　　Copy the initial segment of the pattern space through the first newline to the standard output.

(1) q　　Quit. Branch to the end of the script. Do not start a new cycle.

(2) r *rfile*
　　　　　Read the contents of *rfile*. Place them on the output before reading the next input line.

(2) s/*regular expression*/*replacement*/*flags*
　　　　　Substitute the *replacement* string for instances of the *regular expression* in the pattern space. Any character may be used instead of '/'. For a fuller description see *ed*(1). *Flags* is zero or more of

　　　　　g　　　　Global. Substitute for all nonoverlapping instances of the *regular expression* rather than just the first one.

　　　　　p　　　　Print the pattern space if a replacement was made.

　　　　　w *wfile*　Write. Append the pattern space to *wfile* if a replacement was made.

(2) t *label*
　　　　　Test. Branch to the ':' command bearing the *label* if any substitutions have been made since the most recent reading of an input line or execution of a 't'. If *label* is empty, branch to the end of the script.

(2) w *wfile*
　　　　　Write. Append the pattern space to *wfile*.

(2) x　　Exchange the contents of the pattern and hold spaces.

(2) y/*string1*/*string2*/
　　　　　Transform. Replace all occurrences of characters in *string1* with the corresponding character in *string2*. The lengths of *string1* and *string2* must be equal.

(2)! *function*
　　　　　Don't. Apply the *function* (or group, if *function* is '{') only to lines *not* selected by the address(es).

(0) : *label*
　　　　　This command does nothing; it bears a *label* for 'b' and 't' commands to branch to.

(1) =   Place the current line number on the standard output as a line.

(2) {   Execute the following commands through a matching '}' only when the pattern space is selected.

(0)   An empty command is ignored.

SEE ALSO

ed(1), grep(1), awk(1)

NAME

sh, for, case, if, while, :, ., break, continue, cd, eval, exec, exit, export, login, newgrp, read, readonly, set, shift, times, trap, umask, wait — command language

SYNOPSIS

sh [**−ceiknrstuvx**] [arg] ...

DESCRIPTION

Sh is a command programming language that executes commands read from a terminal or a file. See **invocation** for the meaning of arguments to the shell.

Commands.

A *simple-command* is a sequence of non blank *words* separated by blanks (a blank is a **tab** or a **space**). The first word specifies the name of the command to be executed. Except as specified below the remaining words are passed as arguments to the invoked command. The command name is passed as argument 0 (see *exec*(2)). The *value* of a simple-command is its exit status if it terminates normally or 200+*status* if it terminates abnormally (see *signal*(2) for a list of status values).

A *pipeline* is a sequence of one or more *commands* separated by I. The standard output of each command but the last is connected by a *pipe*(2) to the standard input of the next command. Each command is run as a separate process; the shell waits for the last command to terminate.

A *list* is a sequence of one or more *pipelines* separated by ;, &, && or II and optionally terminated by ; or &. ; and & have equal precedence which is lower than that of && and II, && and II also have equal precedence. A semicolon causes sequential execution; an ampersand causes the preceding *pipeline* to be executed without waiting for it to finish. The symbol && (II) causes the *list* following to be executed only if the preceding *pipeline* returns a zero (non zero) value. Newlines may appear in a *list,* instead of semicolons, to delimit commands.

A *command* is either a simple-command or one of the following. The value returned by a command is that of the last simple-command executed in the command.

for *name* [**in** *word* ...] **do** *list* **done**
> Each time a **for** command is executed *name* is set to the next word in the **for** word list If **in** *word* ... is omitted then **in** "**$@**" is assumed. Execution ends when there are no more words in the list.

case *word* **in** [*pattern* [I *pattern*] ...) *list* ;;] ... **esac**
> A **case** command executes the *list* associated with the first pattern that matches *word*. The form of the patterns is the same as that used for file name generation.

if *list* **then** *list* [**elif** *list* **then** *list*] ... [**else** *list*] **fi**
> The *list* following **if** is executed and if it returns zero the *list* following **then** is executed. Otherwise, the *list* following **elif** is executed and if its value is zero the *list* following **then** is executed. Failing that the **else** *list* is executed.

while *list* [**do** *list*] **done**
> A **while** command repeatedly executes the **while** *list* and if its value is zero executes the **do** *list;* otherwise the loop terminates. The value returned by a **while** command is that of the last executed command in the **do** *list*. **until** may be used in place of **while** to negate the loop termination test.

(*list*)   Execute *list* in a subshell.

{ *list* }   *list* is simply executed.

The following words are only recognized as the first word of a command and when not quoted.

> **if then else elif fi case in esac for while until do done { }**

Command substitution.
The standard output from a command enclosed in a pair of grave accents (` `` `) may be used as part or all of a word; newlines becoming spaces na trailing newlines are removed.

Parameter substitution.
The character **$** is used to introduce substitutable parameters. Positional parameters may be assigned values by **set**. Variables may be set by writing

> *name* = *value* [*name* = *value*] ...

$ {*parameter*}

> A *parameter* is a sequence of letters, digits or underscores (a *name*), a digit, or any of the characters *** @ # ? − $!**. The value, if any, of the parameter is substituted. The braces are required only when *parameter* is followed by a letter, digit, or underscore that is not to be interpreted as part of its name. If *parameter* is a digit then it is a positional parameter. If *parameter* is ***** or **@** then all the positional parameters, starting with **$1**, are substituted separated by spaces. **$0** is set from argument zero when the shell is invoked.

$ {*parameter* − *word*}

> If *parameter* is set then substitute its value; otherwise substitute *word*.

$ {*parameter* = *word*}

> If *parameter* is not set then set it to *word;* the value of the parameter is then substituted. Positional parameters may not be assigned to in this way.

$ {*parameter* ? *word*}

> If *parameter* is set then substitute its value; otherwise, print *word* and exit from the shell. If *word* is omitted then a standard message is printed.

$ {*parameter* + *word*}

> If *parameter* is set then substitute *word;* otherwise substitute nothing.

In the above *word* is not evaluated unless it is to be used as the substituted string. (So that, for example, echo ${d−`pwd`} will only execute *pwd* if *d* is unset.)

The following *parameters* are automatically set by the shell.

#	The number of positional parameters in decimal.
−	Options supplied to the shell on invocation or by **set**.
?	The value returned by the last executed command in decimal.
$	The process number of this shell.
!	The process number of the last background command invoked.

The following *parameters* are used but not set by the shell.

HOME	The default argument (home directory) for the **cd** command.
PATH	The search path for commands (see **execution**).
MAIL	If this variable is set to the name of a mail file then the shell informs the user of the arrival of mail in the specified file.
PS1	Primary prompt string, by default '$ '.
PS2	Secondary prompt string, by default '> '.
IFS	Internal field separators, normally **space**, **tab**, and **newline**.

Blank interpretation.
After parameter and command substitution, any results of substitution are scanned for internal field separator characters (those found in **$IFS**) and split into distinct arguments where such characters are found. Explicit null arguments ("" or ``) are retained. Implicit null arguments (those resulting from *parameters* that have no values) are removed.

File name generation.

Following substitution, each command word is scanned for the characters *, ? and [. If one of these characters appears then the word is regarded as a pattern. The word is replaced with alphabetically sorted file names that match the pattern. If no file name is found that matches the pattern then the word is left unchanged. The character . at the start of a file name or immediately following a /, and the character /, must be matched explicitly.

*   Matches any string, including the null string.
?   Matches any single character.
[...]   Matches any one of the characters enclosed. A pair of characters separated by —
            matches any character lexically between the pair.

Quoting.

The following characters have a special meaning to the shell and cause termination of a word unless quoted.

            ; & ( ) | < > newline space tab

A character may be *quoted* by preceding it with a \. **\newline** is ignored. All characters enclosed between a pair of quote marks (` `), except a single quote, are quoted. Inside double quotes (" ") parameter and command substitution occurs and \ quotes the characters \ ` " and $.

"$*" is equivalent to "$1 $2 ..." whereas
"$@" is equivalent to "$1" "$2" ... .

Prompting.

When used interactively, the shell prompts with the value of PS1 before reading a command. If at any time a newline is typed and further input is needed to complete a command then the secondary prompt ($PS2) is issued.

Input output.

Before a command is executed its input and output may be redirected using a special notation interpreted by the shell. The following may appear anywhere in a simple-command or may precede or follow a *command* and are not passed on to the invoked command. Substitution occurs before *word* or *digit* is used.

<*word* Use file *word* as standard input (file descriptor 0).

>*word* Use file *word* as standard output (file descriptor 1). If the file does not exist then it is created; otherwise it is truncated to zero length.

>>*word*

            Use file *word* as standard output. If the file exists then output is appended (by seeking to the end); otherwise the file is created.

<<*word*

            The shell input is read up to a line the same as *word*, or end of file. The resulting document becomes the standard input. If any character of *word* is quoted then no interpretation is placed upon the characters of the document; otherwise, parameter and command substitution occurs, **\newline** is ignored, and \ is used to quote the characters \ $ ` and the first character of *word*.

<& *digit*

            The standard input is duplicated from file descriptor *digit;* see *dup*(2). Similarly for the standard output using >.

<& —   The standard input is closed. Similarly for the standard output using >.

If one of the above is preceded by a digit then the file descriptor created is that specified by the digit (instead of the default 0 or 1). For example,

        ... 2>&1

creates file descriptor 2 to be a duplicate of file descriptor 1.

If a command is followed by **&** then the default standard input for the command is the empty file (/dev/null). Otherwise, the environment for the execution of a command contains the file descriptors of the invoking shell as modified by input output specifications.

Environment.

The environment is a list of name-value pairs that is passed to an executed program in the same way as a normal argument list; see *exec*(2) and *environ*(5). The shell interacts with the environment in several ways. On invocation, the shell scans the environment and creates a *parameter* for each name found, giving it the corresponding value. Executed commands inherit the same environment. If the user modifies the values of these *parameters* or creates new ones, none of these affects the environment unless the **export** command is used to bind the shell's *parameter* to the environment. The environment seen by any executed command is thus composed of any unmodified name-value pairs originally inherited by the shell, plus any modifications or additions, all of which must be noted in **export** commands.

The environment for any *simple-command* may be augmented by prefixing it with one or more assignments to *parameters*. Thus these two lines are equivalent

        TERM=450 cmd args
        (export TERM; TERM=450; cmd args)

If the −**k** flag is set, *all* keyword arguments are placed in the environment, even if they occur after the command name. The following prints 'a=b c' and 'c':
echo a=b c
set −k
echo a=b c

Signals.

The INTERRUPT and QUIT signals for an invoked command are ignored if the command is followed by **&**; otherwise signals have the values inherited by the shell from its parent. (But see also **trap**.)

Execution.

Each time a command is executed the above substitutions are carried out. Except for the 'special commands' listed below a new process is created and an attempt is made to execute the command via an *exec*(2).

The shell parameter **$PATH** defines the search path for the directory containing the command. Each alternative directory name is separated by a colon (:). The default path is **:/bin:/usr/bin**. If the command name contains a / then the search path is not used. Otherwise, each directory in the path is searched for an executable file. If the file has execute permission but is not an *a.out* file, it is assumed to be a file containing shell commands. A subshell (i.e., a separate process) is invoked to read it. A parenthesized command is also executed in a subshell.

Special commands.

The following commands are executed in the shell process and except where specified no input output redirection is permitted for such commands.

:   No effect; the command does nothing.
. *file*   Read and execute commands from *file* and return. The search path **$PATH** is used to find the directory containing *file*.
break [*n*]
        Exit from the enclosing **for** or **while** loop, if any. If *n* is specified then break *n* levels.
continue [*n*]
        Resume the next iteration of the enclosing **for** or **while** loop. If *n* is specified then

resume at the *n*-th enclosing loop.

cd [*arg*]

Change the current directory to *arg*. The shell parameter **$HOME** is the default *arg*.

eval [*arg* ...]

The arguments are read as input to the shell and the resulting command(s) executed.

exec [*arg* ...]

The command specified by the arguments is executed in place of this shell without creating a new process. Input output arguments may appear and if no other arguments are given cause the shell input output to be modified.

exit [*n*]

Causes a non interactive shell to exit with the exit status specified by *n*. If *n* is omitted then the exit status is that of the last command executed. (An end of file will also exit from the shell.)

export [*name* ...]

The given names are marked for automatic export to the *environment* of subsequently-executed commands. If no arguments are given then a list of exportable names is printed.

login [*arg* ...]

Equivalent to 'exec login arg ...'.

newgrp [*arg* ...]

Equivalent to 'exec newgrp arg ...'.

read *name* ...

One line is read from the standard input; successive words of the input are assigned to the variables *name* in order, with leftover words to the last variable. The return code is 0 unless the end-of-file is encountered.

readonly [*name* ...]

The given names are marked readonly and the values of the these names may not be changed by subsequent assignment. If no arguments are given then a list of all readonly names is printed.

set [−eknptuvx [*arg* ...]]

−e   If non interactive then exit immediately if a command fails.

−k   All keyword arguments are placed in the environment for a command, not just those that precede the command name.

−n   Read commands but do not execute them.

−t   Exit after reading and executing one command.

−u   Treat unset variables as an error when substituting.

−v   Print shell input lines as they are read.

−x   Print commands and their arguments as they are executed.

−   Turn off the −x and −v options.

These flags can also be used upon invocation of the shell. The current set of flags may be found in **$−**.

Remaining arguments are positional parameters and are assigned, in order, to **$1, $2,** etc. If no arguments are given then the values of all names are printed.

shift   The positional parameters from **$2**... are renamed **$1**...

times   Print the accumulated user and system times for processes run from the shell.

trap [*arg*] [*n*] ...

Arg is a command to be read and executed when the shell receives signal(s) *n*. (Note that *arg* is scanned once when the trap is set and once when the trap is taken.) Trap commands are executed in order of signal number. If *arg* is absent then all trap(s) *n* are reset to their original values. If *arg* is the null string then this signal is ignored by the shell and by invoked commands. If *n* is 0 then the command *arg* is executed on exit from the shell, otherwise upon receipt of signal *n* as numbered in *signal*(2). *Trap* with no arguments prints a list of commands associated with each signal number.

umask [*nnn*]

The user file creation mask is set to the octal value *nnn* (see *umask*(2)). If *nnn* is omitted, the current value of the mask is printed.

wait [*n*]

Wait for the specified process and report its termination status. If *n* is not given then all currently active child processes are waited for. The return code from this command is that of the process waited for.

Invocation.

If the first character of argument zero is −, commands are first read from **$HOME/.profile**, if such a file exists. Commands are then read from the file named by the first argument of *sh* (standard input default). The following options are interpreted by the shell when it is invoked.

−**c** *string*   If the −**c** flag is present then commands are read from *string*.

−**s**   If the −**s** flag is present or if no arguments remain then commands are read from the standard input. Shell output is written to file descriptor 2.

−**i**   If the −**i** flag is present or if the shell input and output are attached to a terminal (as told by *gtty*) then this shell is *interactive*. In this case the terminate signal SIGTERM (see *signal*(2)) is ignored (so that 'kill 0' does not kill an interactive shell) and the interrupt signal SIGINT is caught and ignored (so that **wait** is interruptable). In all cases SIGQUIT is ignored by the shell.

Remaining arguments are treated as arguments to a set commnd. **set** command.

FILES

$HOME/.profile
/tmp/sh*
/dev/null

SEE ALSO

test(1), exec(2),

DIAGNOSTICS

Errors detected by the shell, such as syntax errors cause the shell to return a non zero exit status. If the shell is being used non interactively then execution of the shell file is abandoned. Otherwise, the shell returns the exit status of the last command executed (see also **exit**).

BUGS

If << is used to provide standard input to an asynchronous process invoked by &, the shell gets mixed up about naming the input document. A garbage file /tmp/sh* is created, and the shell complains about not being able to find the file by another name.

NAME

    size — size of an object file

SYNOPSIS

    size [object ...]

DESCRIPTION

    Size prints the (decimal) number of bytes required by the text, data, and bss portions, and their sum in octal and decimal, of each object-file argument. If no file is specified, **a.out** is used.

SEE ALSO

    a.out(5)

NAME

      sleep — suspend execution for an interval

SYNOPSIS

      sleep time

DESCRIPTION

      Sleep suspends execution for *time* seconds. It is used to execute a command after a certain amount of time as in:

            (sleep 105; command)&

      or to execute a command every so often, as in:

            while true
            do
                    command
                    sleep 37
            done

SEE ALSO

      alarm(2), sleep(3)

BUGS

      Time must be less than 65536 seconds.

NAME

    sort − sort or merge files

SYNOPSIS

    sort [−**mubdfinrtx**] [+*pos1* [−*pos2*]] ... [−**o** name] [−**T** directory] [name]
    ...

DESCRIPTION

    Sort sorts lines of all the named files together and writes the result on the standard output. The name '−' means the standard input. If no input files are named, the standard input is sorted.

    The default sort key is an entire line. Default ordering is lexicographic by bytes in machine collating sequence. The ordering is affected globally by the following options, one or more of which may appear.

b   Ignore leading blanks (spaces and tabs) in field comparisons.

d   'Dictionary' order: only letters, digits and blanks are significant in comparisons.

f   Fold upper case letters onto lower case.

i   Ignore characters outside the ASCII range 040-0176 in nonnumeric comparisons.

n   An initial numeric string, consisting of optional blanks, optional minus sign, and zero or more digits with optional decimal point, is sorted by arithmetic value. Option **n** implies option **b.**

r   Reverse the sense of comparisons.

tx   'Tab character' separating fields is *x.*

    The notation +*pos1* −*pos2* restricts a sort key to a field beginning at *pos1* and ending just before *pos2*. *Pos1* and *pos2* each have the form *m.n*, optionally followed by one or more of the flags **bdfinr,** where *m* tells a number of fields to skip from the beginning of the line and *n* tells a number of characters to skip further. If any flags are present they override all the global ordering options for this key. If the **b** option is in effect *n* is counted from the first nonblank in the field; **b** is attached independently to *pos2*. A missing *.n* means .0; a missing −*pos2* means the end of the line. Under the −**tx** option, fields are strings separated by *x*; otherwise fields are nonempty nonblank strings separated by blanks.

    When there are multiple sort keys, later keys are compared only after all earlier keys compare equal. Lines that otherwise compare equal are ordered with all bytes significant.

    These option arguments are also understood:

c   Check that the input file is sorted according to the ordering rules; give no output unless the file is out of sort.

m   Merge only, the input files are already sorted.

o   The next argument is the name of an output file to use instead of the standard output. This file may be the same as one of the inputs.

T   The next argument is the name of a directory in which temporary files should be made.

u   Suppress all but one in each set of equal lines. Ignored bytes and bytes outside keys do not participate in this comparison.

    Examples. Print in alphabetical order all the unique spellings in a list of words. Capitalized words differ from uncapitalized.

               sort −u +0f +0 list

    Print the password file (*passwd*(5)) sorted by user id number (the 3rd colon-separated field).

> sort −t: +2n /etc/passwd

Print the first instance of each month in an already sorted file of (month day) entries. The options −**um** with just one input file make the choice of a unique representative from a set of equal lines predictable.

> sort −um +0 −1 dates

FILES

/usr/tmp/stm*, /tmp/*: first and second tries for temporary files

SEE ALSO

uniq(1), comm(1), rev(1), join(1)

DIAGNOSTICS

Comments and exits with nonzero status for various trouble conditions and for disorder discovered under option −**c**.

BUGS

Very long lines are silently truncated.

NAME
     spell, spellin, spellout — find spelling errors

SYNOPSIS
     spell [option] ... [file] ...

     /usr/src/cmd/spell/spellin [list]

     /usr/src/cmd/spell/spellout [**−d**] list

DESCRIPTION
     Spell collects words from the named documents, and looks them up in a spelling list. Words
     that neither occur among nor are derivable (by applying certain inflections, prefixes or suffixes)
     from words in the spelling list are printed on the standard output. If no files are named, words
     are collected from the standard input.

     Spell ignores most *troff, tbl* and *eqn*(1) constructions.

     Under the **−v** option, all words not literally in the spelling list are printed, and plausible deriva-
     tions from spelling list words are indicated.

     Under the **−b** option, British spelling is checked. Besides preferring *centre, colour, speciality,*
     travelled, etc., this option insists upon *-ise* in words like *standardise,* Fowler and the OED to the
     contrary notwithstanding.

     Under the **−x** option, every plausible stem is printed with '=' for each word.

     The spelling list is based on many sources, and while more haphazard than an ordinary diction-
     ary, is also more effective in respect to proper names and popular technical words. Coverage of
     the specialized vocabularies of biology, medicine and chemistry is light.

     Pertinent auxiliary files may be specified by name arguments, indicated below with their default
     settings. Copies of all output are accumulated in the history file. The stop list filters out
     misspellings (e.g. thier=thy−y+ier) that would otherwise pass.

     Two routines help maintain the hash lists used by *spell.* Both expect a list of words, one per
     line, from the standard input. *Spellin* adds the words on the standard input to the preexisting
     list and places a new list on the standard output. If no *list* is specified, the new list is created
     from scratch. *Spellout* looks up each word in the standard input and prints on the standard out-
     put those that are missing from (or present on, with option **−d**) the hash list.

FILES
     D=/usr/dict/hlist[ab]: hashed spelling lists, American & British
     S=/usr/dict/hstop: hashed stop list
     H=/usr/dict/spellhist: history file
     /usr/lib/spell
     deroff(1), sort(1), tee(1), sed(1)

BUGS
     The spelling list's coverage is uneven; new installations will probably wish to monitor the out-
     put for several months to gather local additions.
     British spelling was done by an American.

NAME

spline — interpolate smooth curve

SYNOPSIS

spline [option] ...

DESCRIPTION

Spline takes pairs of numbers from the standard input as abcissas and ordinates of a function. It produces a similar set, which is approximately equally spaced and includes the input set, on the standard output. The cubic spline output (R. W. Hamming, *Numerical Methods for Scientists and Engineers,* 2nd ed., 349ff) has two continuous derivatives, and sufficiently many points to look smooth when plotted, for example by *graph*(1).

The following options are recognized, each as a separate argument.

−**a** Supply abscissas automatically (they are missing from the input); spacing is given by the next argument, or is assumed to be 1 if next argument is not a number.

−**k** The constant *k* used in the boundary value computation

$$y_0'' = ky_1'', \quad y_n'' = ky_{n-1}''$$

is set by the next argument. By default $k = 0$.

−**n** Space output points so that approximately *n* intervals occur between the lower and upper *x* limits. (Default $n = 100$.)

−**p** Make output periodic, i.e. match derivatives at ends. First and last input values should normally agree.

−**x** Next 1 (or 2) arguments are lower (and upper) *x* limits. Normally these limits are calculated from the data. Automatic abcissas start at lower limit (default 0).

SEE ALSO

graph(1)

DIAGNOSTICS

When data is not strictly monotone in *x, spline* reproduces the input without interpolating extra points.

BUGS

A limit of 1000 input points is enforced silently.

NAME

   split — split a file into pieces

SYNOPSIS

   split [−*n*] [file [name]]

DESCRIPTION

   Split reads *file* and writes it in *n*-line pieces (default 1000), as many as necessary, onto a set of output files. The name of the first output file is *name* with **aa** appended, and so on lexicographically. If no output name is given, **x** is default.

   If no input file is given, or if − is given in its stead, then the standard input file is used.

NAME

strip — remove symbols and relocation bits

SYNOPSIS

strip name ...

DESCRIPTION

Strip removes the symbol table and relocation bits ordinarily attached to the output of the assembler and loader. This is useful to save space after a program has been debugged.

The effect of *strip* is the same as use of the −s option of *ld*.

FILES

/tmp/stm?   temporary file

SEE ALSO

ld(1)

NAME

struct − structure Fortran programs

SYNOPSIS

struct [option] ...   file

DESCRIPTION

Struct translates the Fortran program specified by *file* (standard input default) into a Ratfor program. Wherever possible, Ratfor control constructs replace the original Fortran. Statement numbers appear only where still necessary. Cosmetic changes are made, including changing Hollerith strings into quoted strings and relational operators into symbols (.e.g. '.GT.' into '>'). The output is appropriately indented.

The following options may occur in any order.

−s   Input is accepted in standard format, i.e. comments are specified by a c, C, or * in column 1, and continuation lines are specified by a nonzero, nonblank character in column 6. Normally, a statement whose first nonblank character is not alphanumeric is treated as a continuation.

−i   Do not turn computed goto statements into switches. (Ratfor does not turn switches back into computed goto statements.)

−a   Turn sequences of else ifs into a non-Ratfor switch of the form

```
switch {
            case pred1: code
            case pred2: code
            case pred3: code
            default: code
        }
```

The case predicates are tested in order; the code appropriate to only one case is executed. This generalized form of switch statement does not occur in Ratfor.

−b   Generate goto's instead of multilevel break statements.

−n   Generate goto's instead of multilevel next statements.

−e*n*   If *n* is 0 (default), place code within a loop only if it can lead to an iteration of the loop. If *n* is nonzero, admit code segments with fewer than *n* statements to a loop if otherwise the loop would have exits to several places including the segment, and the segment can be reached only from the loop.

FILES

/tmp/struct*
/usr/lib/struct/*

SEE ALSO

f77(1)

BUGS

Struct knows Fortran 66 syntax, but not full Fortran 77 (alternate returns, IF...THEN...ELSE, etc.)

If an input Fortran program contains identifiers which are reserved words in Ratfor, the structured version of the program will not be a valid Ratfor program.

Extended range DO's generate cryptic errors.

Columns 73-80 are not special even when −s is in effect.

Will not generate Ratfor FOR statements.

NAME

stty — set terminal options

SYNOPSIS

stty [option ...]

DESCRIPTION

Stty sets certain I/O options on the current output terminal. With no argument, it reports the current settings of the options. The option strings are selected from the following set:

even	allow even parity
—even	disallow even parity
odd	allow odd parity
—odd	disallow odd parity
raw	raw mode input (no erase, kill, interrupt, quit, EOT; parity bit passed back)
—raw	negate raw mode
cooked	same as '—raw'
cbreak	make each character available to *read*(2) as received; no erase and kill
—cbreak	
	make characters available to *read* only when newline is received
—nl	allow carriage return for new-line, and output CR-LF for carriage return or new-line
nl	accept only new-line to end lines
echo	echo back every character typed
—echo	do not echo characters
lcase	map upper case to lower case
—lcase	do not map case
—tabs	replace tabs by spaces when printing
tabs	preserve tabs
ek	reset erase and kill characters back to normal # and @
erase *c*	set erase character to *c*. *C* can be of the form '^X' which is interpreted as a 'control X'.
kill *c*	set kill character to *c*. '^X' works here also.
cr0 cr1 cr2 cr3	
	select style of delay for carriage return (see *ioctl*(2))
nl0 nl1 nl2 nl3	
	select style of delay for linefeed
tab0 tab1 tab2 tab3	
	select style of delay for tab
ff0 ff1	select style of delay for form feed
bs0 bs1	select style of delay for backspace
tty33	set all modes suitable for the Teletype Corporation Model 33 terminal.
tty37	set all modes suitable for the Teletype Corporation Model 37 terminal.
vt05	set all modes suitable for Digital Equipment Corp. VT05 terminal
tn300	set all modes suitable for a General Electric TermiNet 300
ti700	set all modes suitable for Texas Instruments 700 series terminal
tek	set all modes suitable for Tektronix 4014 terminal
hup	hang up dataphone on last close.
—hup	do not hang up dataphone on last close.
0	hang up phone line immediately
50 75 110 134 150 200 300 600 1200 1800 2400 4800 9600 exta extb	
	Set terminal baud rate to the number given, if possible. (These are the speeds supported by the DH-11 interface).

SEE ALSO

ioctl(2), tabs(1)

NAME

su — substitute user id temporarily

SYNOPSIS

su [userid]

DESCRIPTION

Su demands the password of the specified *userid,* and if it is given, changes to that *userid* and invokes the Shell *sh*(1) without changing the current directory or the user environment (see *environ*(5)). The new user ID stays in force until the Shell exits.

If no *userid* is specified, 'root' is assumed. To remind the super-user of his responsibilities, the Shell substitutes '#' for its usual prompt.

SEE ALSO

sh(1)

NAME

    sum — sum and count blocks in a file

SYNOPSIS

    sum file

DESCRIPTION

    Sum calculates and prints a 16-bit checksum for the named file, and also prints the number of blocks in the file. It is typically used to look for bad spots, or to validate a file communicated over some transmission line.

SEE ALSO

    wc(1)

DIAGNOSTICS

    'Read error' is indistinguishable from end of file on most devices; check the block count.

NAME

sync — update the super block

SYNOPSIS

sync

DESCRIPTION

Sync executes the *sync* system primitive. If the system is to be stopped, *sync* must be called to insure file system integrity. See *sync*(2) for details.

SEE ALSO

sync(2), update(8)

NAME

    tabs − set terminal tabs

SYNOPSIS

    tabs [−**n**] [terminal]

DESCRIPTION

    Tabs sets the tabs on a variety of terminals. Various of the terminal names given in *term*(7) are recognized; the default is, however, suitable for most 300 baud terminals. If the −**n** flag is present then the left margin is not indented as is normal.

SEE ALSO

    stty(1), term(7)

NAME

tail — deliver the last part of a file

SYNOPSIS

tail [±number[**lbc**]] [file]

DESCRIPTION

Tail copies the named file to the standard output beginning at a designated place. If no file is named, the standard input is used.

Copying begins at distance +*number* from the beginning, or −*number* from the end of the input. *Number* is counted in units of lines, blocks or characters, according to the appended option **l**, **b** or **c**. When no units are specified, counting is by lines.

SEE ALSO

dd(1)

BUGS

Tails relative to the end of the file are treasured up in a buffer, and thus are limited in length. Various kinds of anomalous behavior may happen with character special files.

NAME

tar — tape archiver

SYNOPSIS

tar [key] [name ...]

DESCRIPTION

Tar saves and restores files on magtape. Its actions are controlled by the *key* argument. The *key* is a string of characters containing at most one function letter and possibly one or more function modifiers. Other arguments to the command are file or directory names specifying which files are to be dumped or restored. In all cases, appearance of a directory name refers to the files and (recursively) subdirectories of that directory.

The function portion of the key is specified by one of the following letters:

r   The named files are written on the end of the tape. The **c** function implies this.

x   The named files are extracted from the tape. If the named file matches a directory whose contents had been written onto the tape, this directory is (recursively) extracted. The owner, modification time, and mode are restored (if possible). If no file argument is given, the entire content of the tape is extracted. Note that if multiple entries specifying the same file are on the tape, the last one overwrites all earlier.

t   The names of the specified files are listed each time they occur on the tape. If no file argument is given, all of the names on the tape are listed.

u   The named files are added to the tape if either they are not already there or have been modified since last put on the tape.

c   Create a new tape; writing begins on the beginning of the tape instead of after the last file. This command implies **r**.

The following characters may be used in addition to the letter which selects the function desired.

0,...,7   This modifier selects the drive on which the tape is mounted. The default is **1**.

v   Normally *tar* does its work silently. The **v** (verbose) option causes it to type the name of each file it treats preceded by the function letter. With the **t** function, **v** gives more information about the tape entries than just the name.

w   causes *tar* to print the action to be taken followed by file name, then wait for user confirmation. If a word beginning with 'y' is given, the action is performed. Any other input means don't do it.

f   causes *tar* to use the next argument as the name of the archive instead of /dev/mt?. If the name of the file is '—', tar writes to standard output or reads from standard input, whichever is appropriate. Thus, *tar* can be used as the head or tail of a filter chain *Tar* can also be used to move hierarchies with the command

            cd fromdir; tar cf - . | (cd todir; tar xf -)

b   causes *tar* to use the next argument as the blocking factor for tape records. The default is 1, the maximum is 20. This option should only be used with raw magnetic tape archives (See **f** above). The block size is determined automatically when reading tapes (key letters 'x' and 't').

l   tells *tar* to complain if it cannot resolve all of the links to the files dumped. If this is not specified, no error messages are printed.

m   tells *tar* to not restore the modification times. The mod time will be the time of extraction.

FILES

> /dev/mt?
> /tmp/tar*

DIAGNOSTICS

> Complaints about bad key characters and tape read/write errors.
> Complaints if enough memory is not available to hold the link tables.

BUGS

> There is no way to ask for the *n*-th occurrence of a file.
> Tape errors are handled ungracefully.
> The **u** option can be slow.
> The **b** option should not be used with archives that are going to be updated. The current
> magtape driver cannot backspace raw magtape. If the archive is on a disk file the **b** option
> should not be used at all, as updating an archive stored in this manner can destroy it.
> The current limit on file name length is 100 characters.

NAME

    tbl — format tables for nroff or troff

SYNOPSIS

    tbl [files] ...

DESCRIPTION

    Tbl is a preprocessor for formatting tables for *nroff* or *troff*(1). The input files are copied to the standard output, except for lines between .TS and .TE command lines, which are assumed to describe tables and reformatted. Details are given in the reference manual.

    As an example, letting \t represent a tab (which should be typed as a genuine tab) the input

```
.TS
c s s
c c s
c c c
l n n.
Household Population
Town\tHouseholds
\tNumber\tSize
Bedminster\t789\t3.26
Bernards Twp.\t3087\t3.74
Bernardsville\t2018\t3.30
Bound Brook\t3425\t3.04
Branchburg\t1644\t3.49
Bridgewater\t7897\t3.81
Far Hills\t240\t3.19
.TE
```

yields

Household Population		
Town	Households	
	Number	Size
Bedminster	789	3.26
Bernards Twp.	3087	3.74
Bernardsville	2018	3.30
Bound Brook	3425	3.04
Branchburg	1644	3.49
Bridgewater	7897	3.81
Far Hills	240	3.19

    If no arguments are given, *tbl* reads the standard input, so it may be used as a filter. When it is used with *eqn* or *neqn* the *tbl* command should be first, to minimize the volume of data passed through pipes.

SEE ALSO

    troff(1), eqn(1)

    M. E. Lesk, *TBL*.

NAME

tc — photypesetter simulator

SYNOPSIS

tc [−t] [−sN] [−pL] [file]

DESCRIPTION

Tc interprets its input (standard input default) as device codes for a Graphic Systems photo-typesetter (cat). The standard output of *tc* is intended for a Tektronix 4015 (a 4014 teminal with ASCII and APL character sets). The sixteen typesetter sizes are mapped into the 4014's four sizes; the entire TROFF character set is drawn using the 4014's character generator, using overstruck combinations where necessary. Typical usage:

troff −t file | tc

At the end of each page *tc* waits for a newline (empty line) from the keyboard before continuing on to the next page. In this wait state, the command **e** will suppress the screen erase before the next page; **s**N will cause the next N pages to be skipped; and **!**line will send line to the shell.

The command line options are:

−t   Don't wait between pages; for directing output into a file.

−sN   Skip the first N pages.

−pL   Set page length to L. L may include the scale factors **p** (points), **i** (inches), **c** (centimeters), and **P** (picas); default is picas.

'−*l w*' Multiply the default aspect ratio, 1.5, of a displayed page by *l/w*.

SEE ALSO

troff(1), plot(1)

BUGS

Font distinctions are lost.
The aspect ratio option is unbelievable.

NAME
        tee — pipe fitting
SYNOPSIS
        tee [−i] [−a] [file] ...
DESCRIPTION
        Tee transcribes the standard input to the standard output and makes copies in the *files*. Option
        −i ignores interrupts; option −a causes the output to be appended to the *files* rather than
        overwriting them.

NAME

test − condition command

SYNOPSIS

test expr

DESCRIPTION

test evaluates the expression *expr*, and if its value is true then returns zero exit status; other-wise, a non zero exit status is returned. *test* returns a non zero exit if there are no arguments.

The following primitives are used to construct *expr*.

−**r** file   true if the file exists and is readable.

−**w** file   true if the file exists and is writable.

−**f** file   true if the file exists and is not a directory.

−**d** file   true if the file exists and is a directory.

−**s** file   true if the file exists and has a size greater than zero.

−**t** [fildes]

        true if the open file whose file descriptor number is *fildes* (1 by default) is associated with a terminal device.

−**z** s1   true if the length of string *s1* is zero.

−**n** s1   true if the length of the string *s1* is nonzero.

s1 = s2   true if the strings *s1* and *s2* are equal.

s1 != s2 true if the strings *s1* and *s2* are not equal.

s1   true if *s1* is not the null string.

n1 −**eq** n2

        true if the integers *n1* and *n2* are algebraically equal. Any of the comparisons −**ne**, −**gt**, −**ge**, −**lt**, or −**le** may be used in place of −**eq**.

These primaries may be combined with the following operators:

!   unary negation operator

−**a**   binary *and* operator

−**o**   binary *or* operator

(expr)

       parentheses for grouping.

−**a** has higher precedence than −**o**. Notice that all the operators and flags are separate argu-ments to *test*. Notice also that parentheses are meaningful to the Shell and must be escaped.

SEE ALSO

sh(1), find(1)

NAME

time — time a command

SYNOPSIS

time command

DESCRIPTION

The given command is executed; after it is complete, *time* prints the elapsed time during the command, the time spent in the system, and the time spent in execution of the command. Times are reported in seconds.

The execution time can depend on what kind of memory the program happens to land in; the user time in MOS is often half what it is in core.

The times are printed on the diagnostic output stream.

BUGS

Elapsed time is accurate to the second, while the CPU times are measured to the 60th second. Thus the sum of the CPU times can be up to a second larger than the elapsed time.

NAME

      tk — paginator for the Tektronix 4014

SYNOPSIS

      tk [−**t**] [−*N*] [−**p***L*] [file]

DESCRIPTION

      The output of *tk* is intended for a Tektronix 4014 terminal. *Tk* arranges for 66 lines to fit on the screen, divides the screen into *N* columns, and contributes an eight space page offset in the (default) single-column case. Tabs, spaces, and backspaces are collected and plotted when necessary. Teletype Model 37 half- and reverse-line sequences are interpreted and plotted. At the end of each page *tk* waits for a newline (empty line) from the keyboard before continuing on to the next page. In this wait state, the command !*command* will send the *command* to the shell.

      The command line options are:

      −**t**   Don't wait between pages; for directing output into a file.

      −*N*   Divide the screen into *N* columns and wait after the last column.

      −**p***L*   Set page length to *L* lines.

SEE ALSO

      pr(1)

NAME
　　　　touch − update date last modified of a file

SYNOPSIS
　　　　touch [−c] file ...

DESCRIPTION
　　　　Touch attempts to set the modified date of each *file*. This is done by reading a character from
　　　　the file and writing it back.

　　　　If a *file* does not exist, an attempt will be made to create it unless the −c option is specified.

NAME

tp — manipulate tape archive

SYNOPSIS

tp [key] [name ...]

DESCRIPTION

Tp saves and restores files on DECtape or magtape. Its actions are controlled by the *key* argument. The key is a string of characters containing at most one function letter and possibly one or more function modifiers. Other arguments to the command are file or directory names specifying which files are to be dumped, restored, or listed. In all cases, appearance of a directory name refers to the files and (recursively) subdirectories of that directory.

The function portion of the key is specified by one of the following letters:

r   The named files are written on the tape. If files with the same names already exist, they are replaced. 'Same' is determined by string comparison, so './abc' can never be the same as '/usr/dmr/abc' even if '/usr/dmr' is the current directory. If no file argument is given, '.' is the default.

u   updates the tape. **u** is like **r,** but a file is replaced only if its modification date is later than the date stored on the tape; that is to say, if it has changed since it was dumped. **u** is the default command if none is given.

d   deletes the named files from the tape. At least one name argument must be given. This function is not permitted on magtapes.

x   extracts the named files from the tape to the file system. The owner and mode are restored. If no file argument is given, the entire contents of the tape are extracted.

t   lists the names of the specified files. If no file argument is given, the entire contents of the tape is listed.

The following characters may be used in addition to the letter which selects the function desired.

m   Specifies magtape as opposed to DECtape.

0,...,7 This modifier selects the drive on which the tape is mounted. For DECtape, **x** is default; for magtape '0' is the default.

v   Normally *tp* does its work silently. The **v** (verbose) option causes it to type the name of each file it treats preceded by the function letter. With the **t** function, **v** gives more information about the tape entries than just the name.

c   means a fresh dump is being created; the tape directory is cleared before beginning. Usable only with **r** and **u.** This option is assumed with magtape since it is impossible to selectively overwrite magtape.

i   Errors reading and writing the tape are noted, but no action is taken. Normally, errors cause a return to the command level.

f   Use the first named file, rather than a tape, as the archive. This option is known to work only with **x.**

w   causes *tp* to pause before treating each file, type the indicative letter and the file name (as with **v**) and await the user's response. Response **y** means 'yes', so the file is treated. Null response means 'no', and the file does not take part in whatever is being done. Response **x** means 'exit'; the *tp* command terminates immediately. In the **x** function, files previously asked about have been extracted already. With **r, u,** and **d** no change has been made to the tape.

FILES

/dev/tap?

/dev/mt?

SEE ALSO

ar(1), tar(1)

DIAGNOSTICS

Several; the non-obvious one is 'Phase error', which means the file changed after it was selected for dumping but before it was dumped.

BUGS

A single file with several links to it is treated like several files.

Binary-coded control information makes magnetic tapes written by *tp* difficult to carry to other machines; *tar*(1) avoids the problem.

NAME

tr — translate characters

SYNOPSIS

tr [**−cds**] [string1 [string2]]

DESCRIPTION

Tr copies the standard input to the standard output with substitution or deletion of selected characters. Input characters found in *string1* are mapped into the corresponding characters of *string2*. When *string2* is short it is padded to the length of *string1* by duplicating its last character. Any combination of the options **−cds** may be used: **−c** complements the set of characters in *string1* with respect to the universe of characters whose ASCII codes are 01 through 0377 octal; **−d** deletes all input characters in *string1;* **−s** squeezes all strings of repeated output characters that are in *string2* to single characters.

In either string the notation *a−b* means a range of characters from *a* to *b* in increasing ASCII order. The character '\' followed by 1, 2 or 3 octal digits stands for the character whose ASCII code is given by those digits. A '\' followed by any other character stands for that character.

The following example creates a list of all the words in 'file1' one per line in 'file2', where a word is taken to be a maximal string of alphabetics. The second string is quoted to protect '\' from the Shell. 012 is the ASCII code for newline.

        tr −cs A−Za−z '\012' <file1 >file2

SEE ALSO

ed(1), ascii(7)

BUGS

Won't handle ASCII NUL in *string1* or *string2;* always deletes NUL from input.

NAME

troff, nroff — text formatting and typesetting

SYNOPSIS

troff [option] ... [file] ...

nroff [option] ... [file] ...

DESCRIPTION

Troff formats text in the named *files* for printing on a Graphic Systems C/A/T phototypesetter; *nroff* for typewriter-like devices. Their capabilities are described in the *Nroff/Troff user's manual*.

If no *file* argument is present, the standard input is read. An argument consisting of a single minus (−) is taken to be a file name corresponding to the standard input. The options, which may appear in any order so long as they appear before the files, are:

- **−o***list* Print only pages whose page numbers appear in the comma-separated *list* of numbers and ranges. A range *N−M* means pages *N* through *M*; an initial *−N* means from the beginning to page *N*; and a final *N−* means from *N* to the end.

- **−n***N* Number first generated page *N*.

- **−s***N* Stop every *N* pages. *Nroff* will halt prior to every *N* pages (default *N*=1) to allow paper loading or changing, and will resume upon receipt of a newline. *Troff* will stop the phototypesetter every *N* pages, produce a trailer to allow changing cassettes, and resume when the typesetter's start button is pressed.

- **−m***name* Prepend the macro file **/usr/lib/tmac/tmac.***name* to the input *files*.

- **−r***aN* Set register *a* (one-character) to *N*.

- **−i** Read standard input after the input files are exhausted.

- **−q** Invoke the simultaneous input-output mode of the **rd** request.

Nroff only

- **−T***name* Prepare output for specified terminal. Known *names* are **37** for the (default) Teletype Corporation Model 37 terminal, **tn300** for the GE TermiNet 300 (or any terminal without half-line capability), **300S** for the DASI-300S, **300** for the DASI-300, and **450** for the DASI-450 (Diablo Hyterm).

- **−e** Produce equally-spaced words in adjusted lines, using full terminal resolution.

- **−h** Use output tabs during horizontal spacing to speed output and reduce output character count. Tab settings are assumed to be every 8 nominal character widths.

Troff only

- **−t** Direct output to the standard output instead of the phototypesetter.

- **−f** Refrain from feeding out paper and stopping phototypesetter at the end of the run.

- **−w** Wait until phototypesetter is available, if currently busy.

- **−b** Report whether the phototypesetter is busy or available. No text processing is done.

- **−a** Send a printable ASCII approximation of the results to the standard output.

- **−p***N* Print all characters in point size *N* while retaining all prescribed spacings and motions, to reduce phototypesetter elapsed time.

- **−g** Prepare output for a GCOS phototypesetter and direct it to the standard output (see *gcat*(1)).

If the file */usr/adm/tracct* is writable, *troff* keeps phototypesetter accounting records there. The integrity of that file may be secured by making *troff* a 'set user-id' program.

FILES

/usr/lib/suftab	suffix hyphenation tables
/tmp/ta*	temporary file
/usr/lib/tmac/tmac.*	standard macro files
/usr/lib/term/*	terminal driving tables for *nroff*
/usr/lib/font/*	font width tables for *troff*
/dev/cat	phototypesetter
/usr/adm/tracct	accounting statistics for /dev/cat

SEE ALSO

J. F. Ossanna, *Nroff/Troff user's manual*

B. W. Kernighan, *A TROFF Tutorial*

eqn(1), tbl(1)

col(1), tk(1) (*nroff* only)

tc(1), gcat(1) (*troff* only)

NAME

true, false — provide truth values

SYNOPSIS

true

false

DESCRIPTION

True does nothing, successfully. *False* does nothing, unsuccessfully. They are typically used in input to *sh*(1) such as:

```
while true
do
          command
done
```

SEE ALSO

sh(1)

DIAGNOSTICS

True has exit status zero, *false* nonzero.

NAME

tsort — topological sort

SYNOPSIS

tsort [file]

DESCRIPTION

Tsort produces on the standard output a totally ordered list of items consistent with a partial ordering of items mentioned in the input *file*. If no *file* is specified, the standard input is understood.

The input consists of pairs of items (nonempty strings) separated by blanks. Pairs of different items indicate ordering. Pairs of identical items indicate presence, but not ordering.

SEE ALSO

lorder(1)

DIAGNOSTICS

Odd data: there is an odd number of fields in the input file.

BUGS

Uses a quadratic algorithm; not worth fixing for the typical use of ordering a library archive file.

NAME

    tty — get terminal name

SYNOPSIS

    tty

DESCRIPTION

    Tty prints the pathname of the user's terminal.

DIAGNOSTICS

    'not a tty' if the standard input file is not a terminal.

NAME

uniq — report repeated lines in a file

SYNOPSIS

uniq [**−udc** [+n] [−n]] [input [output]]

DESCRIPTION

Uniq reads the input file comparing adjacent lines. In the normal case, the second and succeeding copies of repeated lines are removed; the remainder is written on the output file. Note that repeated lines must be adjacent in order to be found; see *sort*(1). If the **−u** flag is used, just the lines that are not repeated in the original file are output. The **−d** option specifies that one copy of just the repeated lines is to be written. The normal mode output is the union of the **−u** and **−d** mode outputs.

The **−c** option supersedes **−u** and **−d** and generates an output report in default style but with each line preceded by a count of the number of times it occurred.

The *n* arguments specify skipping an initial portion of each line in the comparison:

−n   The first *n* fields together with any blanks before each are ignored. A field is defined as a string of non-space, non-tab characters separated by tabs and spaces from its neighbors.

+n   The first *n* characters are ignored. Fields are skipped before characters.

SEE ALSO

sort(1), comm(1)

NAME

    units — conversion program

SYNOPSIS

    units

DESCRIPTION

    Units converts quantities expressed in various standard scales to their equivalents in other scales. It works interactively in this fashion:

        You have: inch
        You want: cm
            * 2.54000e+00
            / 3.93701e−01

    A quantity is specified as a multiplicative combination of units optionally preceded by a numeric multiplier. Powers are indicated by suffixed positive integers, division by the usual sign:

        You have: 15 pounds force/in2
        You want: atm
            * 1.02069e+00
            / 9.79730e−01

    Units only does multiplicative scale changes. Thus it can convert Kelvin to Rankine, but not Centigrade to Fahrenheit. Most familiar units, abbreviations, and metric prefixes are recognized, together with a generous leavening of exotica and a few constants of nature including:

pi	ratio of circumference to diameter
c	speed of light
e	charge on an electron
g	acceleration of gravity
force	same as g
mole	Avogadro's number
water	pressure head per unit height of water
au	astronomical unit

    'Pound' is a unit of mass. Compound names are run together, e.g. 'lightyear'. British units that differ from their US counterparts are prefixed thus: 'brgallon'. Currency is denoted 'belgiumfranc', 'britainpound', ...

    For a complete list of units, 'cat /usr/lib/units'.

FILES

    /usr/lib/units

BUGS

    Don't base your financial plans on the currency conversions.

NAME

uucp, uulog — unix to unix copy

SYNOPSIS

uucp [option] ...   source-file ...   destination-file

uulog [option] ...

DESCRIPTION

Uucp copies files named by the source-file arguments to the destination-file argument. A file name may be a path name on your machine, or may have the form

> system-name!pathname

where 'system-name' is taken from a list of system names which *uucp* knows about. Shell metacharacters ?*[] appearing in the pathname part will be expanded on the appropriate system.

Pathnames may be one of

(1)   a full pathname;

(2)   a pathname preceded by ~*user*; where *user* is a userid on the specified system and is replaced by that user's login directory;

(3)   anything else is prefixed by the current directory.

If the result is an erroneous pathname for the remote system the copy will fail. If the destination-file is a directory, the last part of the source-file name is used.

Uucp preserves execute permissions across the transmission and gives 0666 read and write permissions (see *chmod*(2)).

The following options are interpreted by *uucp*.

−**d**   Make all necessary directories for the file copy.

−**c**   Use the source file when copying out rather than copying the file to the spool directory.

−**m**   Send mail to the requester when the copy is complete.

Uulog maintains a summary log of *uucp* and *uux*(1) transactions in the file '/usr/spool/uucp/LOGFILE' by gathering information from partial log files named '/usr/spool/uucp/LOG.*.?'. It removes the partial log files.

The options cause *uulog* to print logging information:

−s*sys*   Print information about work involving system *sys*.

−u*user*
        Print information about work done for the specified *user*.

FILES

/usr/spool/uucp - spool directory
/usr/lib/uucp/* - other data and program files

SEE ALSO

uux(1), mail(1)
D. A. Nowitz, *Uucp Implementation Description*

WARNING

The domain of remotely accessible files can (and for obvious security reasons, usually should) be severely restricted. You will very likely not be able to fetch files by pathname; ask a responsible person on the remote system to send them to you. For the same reasons you will probably not be able to send files to arbitrary pathnames.

BUGS

All files received by *uucp* will be owned by uucp.

The −m option will only work sending files or receiving a single file. (Receiving multiple files specified by special shell characters ?*[] will not activate the −m option.)

NAME

uux — unix to unix command execution

SYNOPSIS

uux [—] command-string

DESCRIPTION

Uux will gather 0 or more files from various systems, execute a command on a specified system and send standard output to a file on a specified system.

The command-string is made up of one or more arguments that look like a shell command line, except that the command and file names may be prefixed by system-name!. A null system-name is interpreted as the local system.

File names may be one of

(1) a full pathname;

(2) a pathname preceded by ˜*xxx*; where *xxx* is a userid on the specified system and is replaced by that user's login directory;

(3) anything else is prefixed by the current directory.

The '—' option will cause the standard input to the *uux* command to be the standard input to the command-string.

For example, the command

uux "!diff usg!/usr/dan/f1 pwba!/a4/dan/f1 > !fi.diff"

will get the f1 files from the usg and pwba machines, execute a *diff* command and put the results in f1.diff in the local directory.

Any special shell characters such as <>;| should be quoted either by quoting the entire command-string, or quoting the special characters as individual arguments.

FILES

/usr/uucp/spool - spool directory
/usr/uucp/* - other data and programs

SEE ALSO

uucp(1)

D. A. Nowitz, *Uucp implementation description*

WARNING

An installation may, and for security reasons generally will, limit the list of commands executable on behalf of an incoming request from *uux*. Typically, a restricted site will permit little other than the receipt of mail via *uux*.

BUGS

Only the first command of a shell pipeline may have a system-name!. All other commands are executed on the system of the first command.

The use of the shell metacharacter * will probably not do what you want it to do.

The shell tokens << and >> are not implemented.

There is no notification of denial of execution on the remote machine.

NAME

wait − await completion of process

SYNOPSIS

wait

DESCRIPTION

Wait until all processes started with **&** have completed, and report on abnormal terminations.

Because the *wait* (2) system call must be executed in the parent process, the Shell itself executes *wait,* without creating a new process.

SEE ALSO

sh(1)

BUGS

Not all the processes of a 3- or more-stage pipeline are children of the Shell, and thus can't be waited for.

NAME

wall − write to all users

SYNOPSIS

/etc/**wall**

DESCRIPTION

Wall reads its standard input until an end-of-file. It then sends this message, preceded by 'Broadcast Message ...', to all logged in users.

The sender should be super-user to override any protections the users may have invoked.

FILES

/dev/tty?
/etc/utmp

SEE ALSO

mesg(1), write(1)

DIAGNOSTICS

'Cannot send to ...' when the open on a user's tty file fails.

NAME

    wc — word count

SYNOPSIS

    wc [−lwc] [name ...]

DESCRIPTION

    Wc counts lines, words and characters in the named files, or in the standard input if no name
    appears. A word is a maximal string of characters delimited by spaces, tabs or newlines.

    If the optional argument is present, just the specified counts (lines, words or characters) are
    selected by the letters **l**, **w**, or **c**.

NAME

who — who is on the system

SYNOPSIS

who [who-file] [**am I**]

DESCRIPTION

Who, without an argument, lists the login name, terminal name, and login time for each current UNIX user.

Without an argument, *who* examines the /etc/utmp file to obtain its information. If a file is given, that file is examined. Typically the given file will be /usr/adm/wtmp, which contains a record of all the logins since it was created. Then *who* lists logins, logouts, and crashes since the creation of the wtmp file. Each login is listed with user name, terminal name (with '/dev/' suppressed), and date and time. When an argument is given, logouts produce a similar line without a user name. Reboots produce a line with 'x' in the place of the device name, and a fossil time indicative of when the system went down.

With two arguments, as in 'who am I' (and also 'who are you'), *who* tells who you are logged in as.

FILES

/etc/utmp

SEE ALSO

getuid(2), utmp(5)

NAME

write − write to another user

SYNOPSIS

write user [ttyname]

DESCRIPTION

Write copies lines from your terminal to that of another user. When first called, it sends the message

Message from yourname yourttyname...

The recipient of the message should write back at this point. Communication continues until an end of file is read from the terminal or an interrupt is sent. At that point *write* writes 'EOT' on the other terminal and exits.

If you want to write to a user who is logged in more than once, the *ttyname* argument may be used to indicate the appropriate terminal name.

Permission to write may be denied or granted by use of the *mesg* command. At the outset writing is allowed. Certain commands, in particular *nroff* and *pr*(1) disallow messages in order to prevent messy output.

If the character '!' is found at the beginning of a line, *write* calls the shell to execute the rest of the line as a command.

The following protocol is suggested for using *write*: when you first write to another user, wait for him to write back before starting to send. Each party should end each message with a distinctive signal—(**o**) for 'over' is conventional—that the other may reply. (**oo**) for 'over and out' is suggested when conversation is about to be terminated.

FILES

/etc/utmp   to find user
/bin/sh   to execute '!'

SEE ALSO

mesg(1), who(1), mail(1)

NAME

yacc — yet another compiler-compiler

SYNOPSIS

yacc [−**vd**] grammar

DESCRIPTION

Yacc converts a context-free grammar into a set of tables for a simple automaton which executes an LR(1) parsing algorithm. The grammar may be ambiguous; specified precedence rules are used to break ambiguities.

The output file, *y.tab.c*, must be compiled by the C compiler to produce a program *yyparse*. This program must be loaded with the lexical analyzer program, *yylex*, as well as *main* and *yyerror*, an error handling routine. These routines must be supplied by the user; *Lex*(1) is useful for creating lexical analyzers usable by *yacc*.

If the −**v** flag is given, the file *y.output* is prepared, which contains a description of the parsing tables and a report on conflicts generated by ambiguities in the grammar.

If the −**d** flag is used, the file *y.tab.h* is generated with the *define* statements that associate the *yacc*-assigned 'token codes' with the user-declared 'token names'. This allows source files other than *y.tab.c* to access the token codes.

FILES

```
y.output
y.tab.c
y.tab.h                 defines for token names
yacc.tmp, yacc.acts     temporary files
/usr/lib/yaccpar        parser prototype for C programs
/lib/liby.a             library with default 'main' and 'yyerror'
```

SEE ALSO

lex(1)

LR Parsing by A. V. Aho and S. C. Johnson, Computing Surveys, June, 1974.

YACC − Yet Another Compiler Compiler by S. C. Johnson.

DIAGNOSTICS

The number of reduce-reduce and shift-reduce conflicts is reported on the standard output; a more detailed report is found in the *y.output* file. Similarly, if some rules are not reachable from the start symbol, this is also reported.

BUGS

Because file names are fixed, at most one *yacc* process can be active in a given directory at a time.

Section 2
SYSTEM CALLS

NAME

intro, errno — introduction to system calls and error numbers

SYNOPSIS

#include <errno.h>

DESCRIPTION

Section 2 of this manual lists all the entries into the system. Most of these calls have an error return. An error condition is indicated by an otherwise impossible returned value. Almost always this is −1; the individual sections specify the details. An error number is also made available in the external variable *errno*. *Errno* is not cleared on successful calls, so it should be tested only after an error has occurred.

There is a table of messages associated with each error, and a routine for printing the message; See *perror*(3). The possible error numbers are not recited with each writeup in section 2, since many errors are possible for most of the calls. Here is a list of the error numbers, their names as defined in <errno.h>, and the messages available using *perror*.

0　　　Error 0
　　　　Unused.

1　EPERM　Not owner
　　　　Typically this error indicates an attempt to modify a file in some way forbidden except to its owner or super-user. It is also returned for attempts by ordinary users to do things allowed only to the super-user.

2　ENOENT　No such file or directory
　　　　This error occurs when a file name is specified and the file should exist but doesn't, or when one of the directories in a path name does not exist.

3　ESRCH　No such process
　　　　The process whose number was given to *signal* and *ptrace* does not exist, or is already dead.

4　EINTR　Interrupted system call
　　　　An asynchronous signal (such as interrupt or quit), which the user has elected to catch, occurred during a system call. If execution is resumed after processing the signal, it will appear as if the interrupted system call returned this error condition.

5　EIO　I/O error
　　　　Some physical I/O error occurred during a *read* or *write*. This error may in some cases occur on a call following the one to which it actually applies.

6　ENXIO　No such device or address
　　　　I/O on a special file refers to a subdevice that does not exist, or beyond the limits of the device. It may also occur when, for example, a tape drive is not dialled in or no disk pack is loaded on a drive.

7　E2BIG　Arg list too long
　　　　An argument list longer than 5120 bytes is presented to *exec*.

8　ENOEXEC　Exec format error
　　　　A request is made to execute a file which, although it has the appropriate permissions, does not start with a valid magic number, see *a.out*(5).

9　EBADF　Bad file number
　　　　Either a file descriptor refers to no open file, or a read (resp. write) request is made to a file that is open only for writing (resp. reading).

10　ECHILD　No children
　　　　Wait and the process has no living or unwaited-for children.

11 EAGAIN No more processes
    In a *fork*, the system's process table is full or the user is not allowed to create any more processes.

12 ENOMEM Not enough core
    During an *exec* or *break*, a program asks for more core than the system is able to supply. This is not a temporary condition; the maximum core size is a system parameter. The error may also occur if the arrangement of text, data, and stack segments requires too many segmentation registers.

13 EACCES Permission denied
    An attempt was made to access a file in a way forbidden by the protection system.

14 EFAULT Bad address
    The system encountered a hardware fault in attempting to access the arguments of a system call.

15 ENOTBLK Block device required
    A plain file was mentioned where a block device was required, e.g. in *mount*.

16 EBUSY Mount device busy
    An attempt to mount a device that was already mounted or an attempt was made to dismount a device on which there is an active file (open file, current directory, mounted-on file, active text segment).

17 EEXIST File exists
    An existing file was mentioned in an inappropriate context, e.g. *link*.

18 EXDEV Cross-device link
    A link to a file on another device was attempted.

19 ENODEV No such device
    An attempt was made to apply an inappropriate system call to a device; e.g. read a write-only device.

20 ENOTDIR Not a directory
    A non-directory was specified where a directory is required, for example in a path name or as an argument to *chdir*.

21 EISDIR Is a directory
    An attempt to write on a directory.

22 EINVAL Invalid argument
    Some invalid argument: dismounting a non-mounted device, mentioning an unknown signal in *signal*, reading or writing a file for which *seek* has generated a negative pointer. Also set by math functions, see *intro*(3).

23 ENFILE File table overflow
    The system's table of open files is full, and temporarily no more *opens* can be accepted.

24 EMFILE Too many open files
    Customary configuration limit is 20 per process.

25 ENOTTY Not a typewriter
    The file mentioned in *stty* or *gtty* is not a terminal or one of the other devices to which these calls apply.

26 ETXTBSY Text file busy
    An attempt to execute a pure-procedure program that is currently open for writing (or reading!). Also an attempt to open for writing a pure-procedure program that is being executed.

27 EFBIG File too large
   The size of a file exceeded the maximum (about 10^9 bytes).

28 ENOSPC No space left on device
   During a *write* to an ordinary file, there is no free space left on the device.

29 ESPIPE Illegal seek
   An *lseek* was issued to a pipe. This error should also be issued for other non-seekable devices.

30 EROFS Read-only file system
   An attempt to modify a file or directory was made on a device mounted read-only.

31 EMLINK Too many links
   An attempt to make more than 32767 links to a file.

32 EPIPE Broken pipe
   A write on a pipe for which there is no process to read the data. This condition normally generates a signal; the error is returned if the signal is ignored.

33 EDOM Math argument
   The argument of a function in the math package (3M) is out of the domain of the function.

34 ERANGE Result too large
   The value of a function in the math package (3M) is unrepresentable within machine precision.

SEE ALSO
   intro(3)

ASSEMBLER
   as /usr/include/sys.s file ...

The PDP11 assembly language interface is given for each system call. The assembler symbols are defined in '/usr/include/sys.s'.

Return values appear in registers r0 and r1; it is unwise to count on these registers being preserved when no value is expected. An erroneous call is always indicated by turning on the c-bit of the condition codes. The error number is returned in r0. The presence of an error is most easily tested by the instructions *bes* and *bec* ('branch on error set (or clear)'). These are synonyms for the *bcs* and *bcc* instructions.

On the Interdata 8/32, the system call arguments correspond well to the arguments of the C routines. The sequence is:

```
la      %2,errno
l       %0,&callno
svc     0,args
```

Thus register 2 points to a word into which the error number will be stored as needed; it is cleared if no error occurs. Register 0 contains the system call number; the nomenclature is identical to that on the PDP11. The argument of the *svc* is the address of the arguments, laid out in storage as in the C calling sequence. The return value is in register 2 (possibly 3 also, as in *pipe*) and is −1 in case of error. The overflow bit in the program status word is also set when errors occur.

NAME

access − determine accessibility of file

SYNOPSIS

access(name, mode)
char *name;

DESCRIPTION

Access checks the given file *name* for accessibility according to *mode*, which is 4 (read), 2 (write) or 1 (execute) or a combination thereof. Specifying mode 0 tests whether the directories leading to the file can be searched and the file exists.

An appropriate error indication is returned if *name* cannot be found or if any of the desired access modes would not be granted. On disallowed accesses −1 is returned and the error code is in *errno*. 0 is returned from successful tests.

The user and group IDs with respect to which permission is checked are the real UID and GID of the process, so this call is useful to set-UID programs.

Notice that it is only access bits that are checked. A directory may be announced as writable by *access,* but an attempt to open it for writing will fail (although files may be created there); a file may look executable, but *exec* will fail unless it is in proper format.

SEE ALSO

stat(2)

ASSEMBLER

(access = 33.)
sys access; name; mode

NAME

acct — turn accounting on or off

SYNOPSIS

acct(file)
char *file;

DESCRIPTION

The system is prepared to write a record in an accounting *file* for each process as it terminates. This call, with a null-terminated string naming an existing file as argument, turns on accounting; records for each terminating process are appended to *file*. An argument of 0 causes accounting to be turned off.

The accounting file format is given in *acct*(5).

SEE ALSO

acct(5), sa(1)

DIAGNOSTICS

On error −1 is returned. The file must exist and the call may be exercised only by the super-user. It is erroneous to try to turn on accounting when it is already on.

BUGS

No accounting is produced for programs running when a crash occurs. In particular nonterminating programs are never accounted for.

ASSEMBLER

(acct = 51.)
sys acct; file

NAME

  alarm − schedule signal after specified time

SYNOPSIS

  alarm(seconds)
  unsigned seconds;

DESCRIPTION

  Alarm causes signal SIGALRM, see *signal*(2), to be sent to the invoking process in a number of seconds given by the argument. Unless caught or ignored, the signal terminates the process.

  Alarm requests are not stacked; successive calls reset the alarm clock. If the argument is 0, any alarm request is cancelled. Because the clock has a 1-second resolution, the signal may occur up to one second early; because of scheduling delays, resumption of execution of when the signal is caught may be delayed an arbitrary amount. The longest specifiable delay time is 65535 seconds.

  The return value is the amount of time previously remaining in the alarm clock.

SEE ALSO

  pause(2), signal(2), sleep(3)

ASSEMBLER

  (alarm = 27.)
  (seconds in r0)
  sys alarm
  (previous amount in r0)

NAME

brk, sbrk, break — change core allocation

SYNOPSIS

char *brk(addr)

char *sbrk(incr)

DESCRIPTION

Brk sets the system's idea of the lowest location not used by the program (called the break) to *addr* (rounded up to the next multiple of 64 bytes on the PDP11, 256 bytes on the Interdata 8/32, 512 bytes on the VAX-11/780). Locations not less than *addr* and below the stack pointer are not in the address space and will thus cause a memory violation if accessed.

In the alternate function *sbrk, incr* more bytes are added to the program's data space and a pointer to the start of the new area is returned.

When a program begins execution via *exec* the break is set at the highest location defined by the program and data storage areas. Ordinarily, therefore, only programs with growing data areas need to use *break*.

SEE ALSO

exec(2), malloc(3), end(3)

DIAGNOSTICS

Zero is returned if the break could be set; −1 if the program requests more memory than the system limit or if too many segmentation registers would be required to implement the break.

BUGS

Setting the break in the range 0177701 to 0177777 (on the PDP11) is the same as setting it to zero.

ASSEMBLER

(break = 17.)
sys break; addr

Break performs the function of *brk*. The name of the routine differs from that in C for historical reasons.

NAME

chdir, chroot — change default directory

SYNOPSIS

chdir(dirname)
char *dirname;

chroot(dirname)
char *dirname;

DESCRIPTION

Dirname is the address of the pathname of a directory, terminated by a null byte. *Chdir* causes this directory to become the current working directory, the starting point for path names not beginning with '/'.

Chroot sets the root directory, the starting point for path names beginning with '/'. The call is restricted to the super-user.

SEE ALSO

cd(1)

DIAGNOSTICS

Zero is returned if the directory is changed; −1 is returned if the given name is not that of a directory or is not searchable.

ASSEMBLER

(chdir = 12.)
sys chdir; dirname

(chroot = 61.)
sys chroot; dirname

NAME
     chmod — change mode of file

SYNOPSIS
     chmod(name, mode)
     char *name;

DESCRIPTION
     The file whose name is given as the null-terminated string pointed to by *name* has its mode
     changed to *mode*. Modes are constructed by ORing together some combination of the follow-
     ing:

          04000 set user ID on execution
          02000 set group ID on execution
          01000 save text image after execution
          00400 read by owner
          00200 write by owner
          00100 execute (search on directory) by owner
          00070 read, write, execute (search) by group
          00007 read, write, execute (search) by others

     If an executable file is set up for sharing (−n or −i option of *ld*(1)) then mode 1000 prevents
     the system from abandoning the swap-space image of the program-text portion of the file when
     its last user terminates. Thus when the next user of the file executes it, the text need not be
     read from the file system but can simply be swapped in, saving time. Ability to set this bit is
     restricted to the super-user since swap space is consumed by the images; it is only worth while
     for heavily used commands.

     Only the owner of a file (or the super-user) may change the mode. Only the super-user can set
     the 1000 mode.

SEE ALSO
     chmod(1)

DIAGNOSTIC
     Zero is returned if the mode is changed; −1 is returned if *name* cannot be found or if current
     user is neither the owner of the file nor the super-user.

ASSEMBLER
     (chmod = 15.)
     sys chmod; name; mode

NAME

    chown — change owner and group of a file

SYNOPSIS

    chown(name, owner, group)

    char *name;

DESCRIPTION

    The file whose name is given by the null-terminated string pointed to by *name* has its *owner* and *group* changed as specified. Only the super-user may execute this call, because if users were able to give files away, they could defeat the (nonexistent) file-space accounting procedures.

SEE ALSO

    chown(1), passwd(5)

DIAGNOSTICS

    Zero is returned if the owner is changed; −1 is returned on illegal owner changes.

ASSEMBLER

    (chown = 16.)

    sys chown; name; owner; group

NAME

 close − close a file

SYNOPSIS

 close(fildes)

DESCRIPTION

 Given a file descriptor such as returned from an *open, creat, dup* or *pipe*(2) call, *close* closes the associated file. A close of all files is automatic on *exit,* but since there is a limit on the number of open files per process, *close* is necessary for programs which deal with many files.

 Files are closed upon termination of a process, and certain file descriptors may be closed by *exec*(2) (see *ioctl*(2)).

SEE ALSO

 creat(2), open(2), pipe(2), exec(2), ioctl(2)

DIAGNOSTICS

 Zero is returned if a file is closed; −1 is returned for an unknown file descriptor.

ASSEMBLER

 (close = 6.)
 (file descriptor in r0)
 sys close

NAME
　　　creat − create a new file

SYNOPSIS
　　　creat(name, mode)
　　　char *name;

DESCRIPTION
　　　Creat creates a new file or prepares to rewrite an existing file called *name*, given as the address of a null-terminated string. If the file did not exist, it is given mode *mode*, as modified by the process's mode mask (see *umask*(2)). Also see *chmod*(2) for the construction of the *mode* argument.

　　　If the file did exist, its mode and owner remain unchanged but it is truncated to 0 length.

　　　The file is also opened for writing, and its file descriptor is returned.

　　　The *mode* given is arbitrary; it need not allow writing. This feature is used by programs which deal with temporary files of fixed names. The creation is done with a mode that forbids writing. Then if a second instance of the program attempts a *creat*, an error is returned and the program knows that the name is unusable for the moment.

SEE ALSO
　　　write(2), close(2), chmod(2), umask (2)

DIAGNOSTICS
　　　The value −1 is returned if: a needed directory is not searchable; the file does not exist and the directory in which it is to be created is not writable; the file does exist and is unwritable; the file is a directory; there are already too many files open.

ASSEMBLER
　　　(creat = 8.)
　　　sys creat; name; mode
　　　(file descriptor in r0)

NAME

dup, dup2 — duplicate an open file descriptor

SYNOPSIS

dup(fildes)
int fildes;

dup2(fildes, fildes2)
int fildes, fildes2;

DESCRIPTION

Given a file descriptor returned from an *open, pipe,* or *creat* call, *dup* allocates another file descriptor synonymous with the original. The new file descriptor is returned.

In the second form of the call, *fildes* is a file descriptor referring to an open file, and *fildes2* is a non-negative integer less than the maximum value allowed for file descriptors (approximately 19). *Dup2* causes *fildes2* to refer to the same file as *fildes*. If *fildes2* already referred to an open file, it is closed first.

SEE ALSO

creat(2), open(2), close(2), pipe(2)

DIAGNOSTICS

The value −1 is returned if: the given file descriptor is invalid; there are already too many open files.

ASSEMBLER

(dup = 41.)
(file descriptor in r0)
(new file descriptor in r1)
sys dup
(file descriptor in r0)

The *dup2* entry is implemented by adding 0100 to *fildes*.

NAME

execl, execv, execle, execve, execlp, execvp, exec, exece, environ − execute a file

SYNOPSIS

execl(name, arg0, arg1, ..., argn, 0)
char *name, *arg0, *arg1, ..., *argn;

execv(name, argv)
char *name, *argv[ ];

execle(name, arg0, arg1, ..., argn, 0, envp)
char *name, *arg0, *arg1, ..., *argn, *envp[ ];

execve(name, argv, envp);
char *name, *argv[ ], *envp[ ];

extern char **environ;

DESCRIPTION

Exec in all its forms overlays the calling process with the named file, then transfers to the entry point of the core image of the file. There can be no return from a successful exec; the calling core image is lost.

Files remain open across *exec* unless explicit arrangement has been made; see *ioctl*(2). Ignored signals remain ignored across these calls, but signals that are caught (see *signal*(2)) are reset to their default values.

Each user has a *real* user ID and group ID and an *effective* user ID and group ID. The real ID identifies the person using the system; the effective ID determines his access privileges. *Exec* changes the effective user and group ID to the owner of the executed file if the file has the 'set-user-ID' or 'set-group-ID' modes. The real user ID is not affected.

The *name* argument is a pointer to the name of the file to be executed. The pointers $arg[0]$, $arg[1]$ ... address null-terminated strings. Conventionally $arg[0]$ is the name of the file.

From C, two interfaces are available. *Execl* is useful when a known file with known arguments is being called; the arguments to *execl* are the character strings constituting the file and the arguments; the first argument is conventionally the same as the file name (or its last component). A 0 argument must end the argument list.

The *execv* version is useful when the number of arguments is unknown in advance; the arguments to *execv* are the name of the file to be executed and a vector of strings containing the arguments. The last argument string must be followed by a 0 pointer.

When a C program is executed, it is called as follows:

        main(argc, argv, envp)
        int argc;
        char **argv, **envp;

where *argc* is the argument count and *argv* is an array of character pointers to the arguments themselves. As indicated, *argc* is conventionally at least one and the first member of the array points to a string containing the name of the file.

Argv is directly usable in another *execv* because $argv[argc]$ is 0.

Envp is a pointer to an array of strings that constitute the *environment* of the process. Each string consists of a name, an "=", and a null-terminated value. The array of pointers is terminated by a null pointer. The shell *sh*(1) passes an environment entry for each global shell variable defined when the program is called. See *environ*(5) for some conventionally used names. The C run-time start-off routine places a copy of *envp* in the global cell *environ,* which is used by *execv* and *execl* to pass the environment to any subprograms executed by the current program. The *exec* routines use lower-level routines as follows to pass an environment explicitly:

execle(file, arg0, arg1, . . . , argn, 0, environ);
execve(file, argv, environ);

Execlp and *execvp* are called with the same arguments as *execl* and *execv*, but duplicate the shell's actions in searching for an executable file in a list of directories. The directory list is obtained from the environment.

FILES

/bin/sh shell, invoked if command file found by *execlp* or *execvp*

SEE ALSO

fork(2), environ(5)

DIAGNOSTICS

If the file cannot be found, if it is not executable, if it does not start with a valid magic number (see *a.out*(5)), if maximum memory is exceeded, or if the arguments require too much space, a return constitutes the diagnostic; the return value is −1. Even for the super-user, at least one of the execute-permission bits must be set for a file to be executed.

BUGS

If *execvp* is called to execute a file that turns out to be a shell command file, and if it is impossible to execute the shell, the values of *argv[0]* and *argv[−1]* will be modified before return.

ASSEMBLER

(exec = 11.)

sys exec; name; argv

(exece = 59.)

sys exece; name; argv; envp

Plain *exec* is obsoleted by *exece*, but remains for historical reasons.

When the called file starts execution on the PDP11, the stack pointer points to a word containing the number of arguments. Just above this number is a list of pointers to the argument strings, followed by a null pointer, followed by the pointers to the environment strings and then another null pointer. The strings themselves follow; a 0 word is left at the very top of memory.

```
sp→    nargs
       arg0
       ...
       argn
       0
       env0
       ...
       envm
       0
arg0:  <arg0\0>
       ...
env0:  <env0\0>
       0
```

On the Interdata 8/32, the stack begins at a conventional place (currently 0xD0000) and grows upwards. After *exec*, the layout of data on the stack is as follows.

```
        int     0
arg0:   byte    ...
        ...
argp0:  int     arg0
```

```
                ...
        int     0
envp0:  int     env0
                ...
        int     0
%2→     space   40
        int     nargs
        int     argp0
        int     envp0
%3→
```

This arrangement happens to conform well to C calling conventions.

NAME

exit − terminate process

SYNOPSIS

exit(status)
int status;

_exit(status)
int status;

DESCRIPTION

Exit is the normal means of terminating a process. *Exit* closes all the process's files and notifies the parent process if it is executing a *wait*. The low-order 8 bits of *status* are available to the parent process.

This call can never return.

The C function *exit* may cause cleanup actions before the final 'sys exit'. The function *_exit* circumvents all cleanup.

SEE ALSO

wait(2)

ASSEMBLER

(exit = 1.)
(status in r0)
sys exit

NAME

fork — spawn new process

SYNOPSIS

fork( )

DESCRIPTION

Fork is the only way new processes are created. The new process's core image is a copy of that of the caller of *fork*. The only distinction is the fact that the value returned in the old (parent) process contains the process ID of the new (child) process, while the value returned in the child is 0. Process ID's range from 1 to 30,000. This process ID is used by *wait*(2).

Files open before the fork are shared, and have a common read-write pointer. In particular, this is the way that standard input and output files are passed and also how pipes are set up.

SEE ALSO

wait(2), exec(2)

DIAGNOSTICS

Returns −1 and fails to create a process if: there is inadequate swap space, the user is not super-user and has too many processes, or the system's process table is full. Only the super-user can take the last process-table slot.

ASSEMBLER

(fork = 2.)

sys fork

(new process return)

(old process return, new process ID in r0)

The return locations in the old and new process differ by one word. The C-bit is set in the old process if a new process could not be created.

NAME
>   getpid − get process identification

SYNOPSIS
>   **getpid( )**

DESCRIPTION
>   *Getpid* returns the process ID of the current process. Most often it is used to generate uniquely-named temporary files.

SEE ALSO
>   mktemp(3)

ASSEMBLER
>   (getpid = 20.)
>   **sys getpid**
>   (pid in r0)

NAME

getuid, getgid, geteuid, getegid — get user and group identity

SYNOPSIS

getuid( )

geteuid( )

getgid( )

getegid( )

DESCRIPTION

Getuid returns the real user ID of the current process, *geteuid* the effective user ID. The real user ID identifies the person who is logged in, in contradistinction to the effective user ID, which determines his access permission at the moment. It is thus useful to programs which operate using the 'set user ID' mode, to find out who invoked them.

Getgid returns the real group ID, *getegid* the effective group ID.

SEE ALSO

setuid(2)

ASSEMBLER

(getuid = 24.)

sys getuid

(real user ID in r0, effective user ID in r1)

(getgid = 47.)

sys getgid

(real group ID in r0, effective group ID in r1)

NAME

      indir — indirect system call

ASSEMBLER

      (indir = 0.)

      sys indir; call

      The system call at the location *call* is executed. Execution resumes after the *indir* call.

      The main purpose of *indir* is to allow a program to store arguments in system calls and execute them out of line in the data segment. This preserves the purity of the text segment.

      If *indir* is executed indirectly, it is a no-op. If the instruction at the indirect location is not a system call, *indir* returns error code EINVAL; see *intro*(2).

NAME

ioctl, stty, gtty — control device

SYNOPSIS

#include <sgtty.h>

ioctl(fildes, request, argp)
struct sgttyb *argp;

stty(fildes, argp)
struct sgttyb *argp;

gtty(fildes, argp)
struct sgttyb *argp;

DESCRIPTION

Ioctl performs a variety of functions on character special files (devices). The writeups of various devices in section 4 discuss how *ioctl* applies to them.

For certain status setting and status inquiries about terminal devices, the functions *stty* and *gtty* are equivalent to

        ioctl(fildes, TIOCSETP, argp)
        ioctl(fildes, TIOCGETP, argp)

respectively; see *tty*(4).

The following two calls, however, apply to any open file:

        ioctl(fildes, FIOCLEX, NULL);
        ioctl(fildes, FIONCLEX, NULL);

The first causes the file to be closed automatically during a successful *exec* operation; the second reverses the effect of the first.

SEE ALSO

stty(1), tty(4), exec(2)

DIAGNOSTICS

Zero is returned if the call was successful; −1 if the file descriptor does not refer to the kind of file for which it was intended.

BUGS

Strictly speaking, since *ioctl* may be extended in different ways to devices with different properties, *argp* should have an open-ended declaration like

        union { struct sgttyb ...; ... } *argp;

The important thing is that the size is fixed by 'struct sgttyb'.

ASSEMBLER

(ioctl = 54.)
sys ioctl; fildes; request; argp

(stty = 31.)
(file descriptor in r0)
stty; argp

(gtty = 32.)
(file descriptor in r0)
sys gtty; argp

NAME

kill — send signal to a process

SYNOPSIS

kill(pid, sig);

DESCRIPTION

Kill sends the signal *sig* to the process specified by the process number in r0. See *signal*(2) for a list of signals.

The sending and receiving processes must have the same effective user ID, otherwise this call is restricted to the super-user.

If the process number is 0, the signal is sent to all other processes in the sender's process group; see *tty*(4).

If the process number is −1, and the user is the super-user, the signal is broadcast universally except to processes 0 and 1, the scheduler and initialization processes, see *init*(8).

Processes may send signals to themselves.

SEE ALSO

signal(2), kill(1)

DIAGNOSTICS

Zero is returned if the process is killed; −1 is returned if the process does not have the same effective user ID and the user is not super-user, or if the process does not exist.

ASSEMBLER

(kill = 37.)
(process number in r0)
sys kill; sig

NAME

link — link to a file

SYNOPSIS

link(name1, name2)
char *name1, *name2;

DESCRIPTION

A link to *name1* is created; the link has the name *name2*. Either name may be an arbitrary path name.

SEE ALSO

ln(1), unlink(2)

DIAGNOSTICS

Zero is returned when a link is made; −1 is returned when *name1* cannot be found; when *name2* already exists; when the directory of *name2* cannot be written; when an attempt is made to link to a directory by a user other than the super-user; when an attempt is made to link to a file on another file system; when a file has too many links.

ASSEMBLER

(link = 9.)
sys link; name1; name2

NAME

lock — lock a process in primary memory

SYNOPSIS

lock(flag)

DESCRIPTION

If the *flag* argument is non-zero, the process executing this call will not be swapped except if it is required to grow. If the argument is zero, the process is un*lock*ed. This call may only be executed by the super-user.

BUGS

*Lock*ed processes interfere with the compaction of primary memory and can cause deadlock. This system call is not considered a permanent part of the system.

ASSEMBLER

(lock = 53.)

sys lock; flag

NAME
lseek, tell — move read/write pointer

SYNOPSIS
long lseek(fildes, offset, whence)
long offset;

long tell(fildes)

DESCRIPTION
The file descriptor refers to a file open for reading or writing. The read (resp. write) pointer for the file is set as follows:

If *whence* is 0, the pointer is set to *offset* bytes.

If *whence* is 1, the pointer is set to its current location plus *offset*.

If *whence* is 2, the pointer is set to the size of the file plus *offset*.

The returned value is the resulting pointer location.

The obsolete function *tell* (*fildes*) is identical to *lseek* (*fildes, 0L, 1*).

Seeking far beyond the end of a file, then writing, creates a gap or 'hole', which occupies no physical space and reads as zeros.

SEE ALSO
open(2), creat(2), fseek(3)

DIAGNOSTICS
−1 is returned for an undefined file descriptor, seek on a pipe, or seek to a position before the beginning of file.

BUGS
Lseek is a no-op on character special files.

ASSEMBLER
(lseek = 19.)
(file descriptor in r0)
sys lseek; offset1; offset2; whence

Offset1 and *offset2* are the high and low words of *offset*; r0 and r1 contain the pointer upon return.

NAME

mknod — make a directory or a special file

SYNOPSIS

mknod(name, mode, addr)
char *name;

DESCRIPTION

Mknod creates a new file whose name is the null-terminated string pointed to by *name*. The mode of the new file (including directory and special file bits) is initialized from *mode*. (The protection part of the mode is modified by the process's mode mask; see *umask*(2)). The first block pointer of the i-node is initialized from *addr*. For ordinary files and directories *addr* is normally zero. In the case of a special file, *addr* specifies which special file.

Mknod may be invoked only by the super-user.

SEE ALSO

mkdir(1), mknod(1), filsys(5)

DIAGNOSTICS

Zero is returned if the file has been made; −1 if the file already exists or if the user is not the super-user.

ASSEMBLER

(mknod = 14.)
sys mknod; name; mode; addr

NAME

mount, umount — mount or remove file system

SYNOPSIS

mount(special, name, rwflag)
char *special, *name;

umount(special)
char *special;

DESCRIPTION

Mount announces to the system that a removable file system has been mounted on the block-structured special file *special;* from now on, references to file *name* will refer to the root file on the newly mounted file system. *Special* and *name* are pointers to null-terminated strings containing the appropriate path names.

Name must exist already. *Name* must be a directory (unless the root of the mounted file system is not a directory). Its old contents are inaccessible while the file system is mounted.

The *rwflag* argument determines whether the file system can be written on; if it is 0 writing is allowed, if non-zero no writing is done. Physically write-protected and magnetic tape file systems must be mounted read-only or errors will occur when access times are updated, whether or not any explicit write is attempted.

Umount announces to the system that the *special* file is no longer to contain a removable file system. The associated file reverts to its ordinary interpretation.

SEE ALSO

mount(1)

DIAGNOSTICS

Mount returns 0 if the action occurred; −1 if *special* is inaccessible or not an appropriate file; if *name* does not exist; if *special* is already mounted; if *name* is in use; or if there are already too many file systems mounted.

Umount returns 0 if the action occurred; −1 if if the special file is inaccessible or does not have a mounted file system, or if there are active files in the mounted file system.

ASSEMBLER

(mount = 21.)
sys mount; special; name; rwflag

(umount = 22.)
sys umount; special

NAME

mpx — create and manipulate multiplexed files

SYNOPSIS

mpx(name, access) char *name;

join(fd, xd)

chan(xd)

extract(i, xd)

attach(i, xd)

detach(i, xd)

connect(fd, cd, end)

npgrp(i, xd, pgrp)

ckill(i, xd, signal)

#include <sys/mx.h>
mpxcall(cmd, vec)
int *vec;

DESCRIPTION

mpxcall(cmd, vec) is the system call shared by the library routines described below. *Cmd* selects a command using values defined in *<sys/mx.h>*. *Vec* is the address of a structure containing the arguments for the command.

mpx(name, access)

Mpx creates and opens the file *name* with access permission *access* (see *creat*(2)) and returns a file descriptor available for reading and writing. A -1 is returned if the file cannot be created, if *name* already exists, or if the file table or other operating system data structures are full. The file descriptor is required for use with other routines.

If *name* designates a null string, a file descriptor is returned as described but no entry is created in the file system.

Once created an mpx file may be opened (see *open*(2)) by any process. This provides a form of interprocess communication whereby a process B can 'call' process A by opening an mpx file created by A. To B, the file is ordinary with one exception: the *connect* primitive could be applied to it. Otherwise the functions described below are used only in process A and descendants that inherit the open mpx file.

When a process opens an mpx file, the owner of the file receives a control message when the file is next read. The method for 'answering' this kind of call involves using *attach* and *detach* as described in more detail below.

Once B has opened A's mpx file it is said to have a *channel* to A. A channel is a pair of data streams: in this case, one from B to A and the other from A to B. Several processes may open the same mpx file yielding multiple channels within the one mpx file. By accessing the appropriate channel, A can communicate with B and any others. When A reads (see *read*(2)) from the mpx file data written to A by the other processes appears in A's buffer using a record format described in *mpxio*(5). When A writes (see *write*(2)) on its mpx file the data must be formatted in a similar way.

The following commands are used to manipulate mpx files and channels.

    join — adds a new channel on an mpx file to an open file F. I/O on the new channel is I/O on F.
    chan — creates a new channel.

extract — file descriptor maintenance.

connect — similar to join except that the open file F is connected to an existing channel.

attach and *detach* — used with call protocol.

npgrp — manipulates process group numbers so that a channel can act as a control terminal (see *tty*(4)).

ckill — send signal (see *signal*(2)) to process group through channel.

A maximum of 15 channels may be connected to an mpx file. They are numbered 0 through 14. *Join* may be used to make one mpx file appear as a channel on another mpx file. A hierarchy or tree of mpx files may be set up in this way. In this case one of the mpx files must be the root of a tree where the other mpx files are interior nodes. The maximum depth of such a tree is 4.

An *index* is a 16-bit value that denotes a location in an mpx tree other than the root: the path through mpx 'nodes' from the root to the location is expressed as a sequence of 4-bit nibbles. The branch taken at the root is represented by the low-order 4-bits of an index. Each succeeding branch is specified by the next higher-order nibble. If the length of a path to be expressed is less than 4, then the illegal channel number, 15, must be used to terminate the sequence. This is not strictly necessary for the simple case of a tree consisting of only a root node: its channels can be expressed by the numbers 0 through 14. An index *i* and file descriptor *xd* for the root of an mpx tree are required as arguments to most of the commands described below. Indices also serve as channel identifiers in the record formats given in *mpxio*(5). Since -1 is not a valid index, it can be returned as a error indication by subroutines that normally return indices.

The operating system informs the process managing an mpx file of changes in the status of channels attached to the file by generating messages that are read along with data from the channels. The form and content of these messages is described in *mpxio*(5).

join(fd, xd) establishes a connection (channel) between an mpx file and another object. *Fd* is an open file descriptor for a character device or an mpx file and *xd* is the file descriptor of an mpx file. *Join* returns the index for the new channel if the operation succeeds and −1 if it does not.

Following join, *fd* may still be used in any system call that would have been meaningful before the join operation. Thus a process can read and write directly to *fd* as well as access it via *xd*. If the number of channels required for a tree of mpx files exceeds the number of open files permitted a process by the operating system, some of the file descriptors can be released using the standard *close*(2) call. Following a close on an active file descriptor for a channel or internal mpx node, that object may still be accessed through the root of the tree.

chan(xd) allocates a channel and connects one end of it to the mpx file represented by file descriptor *xd*. *Chan* returns the index of the new channel or a −1 indicating failure. The *extract* primitive can be used to get a non-multiplexed file descriptor for the free end of a channel created by *chan*.

Both *chan* and *join* operate on the mpx file specified by *xd*. File descriptors for interior nodes of an mpx tree must be preserved or reconstructed with *extract* for use with *join* or *chan*. For the remaining commands described here, *xd* denotes the file descriptor for the root of an mpx tree.

Extract(i, xd) returns a file descriptor for the object with index *i* on the mpx tree with root file descriptor *xd*. A −1 is returned by extract if a file descriptor is not available or if the arguments do not refer to an existing channel and mpx file.

attach(i, xd)

detach(i, xd). If a process A has created an mpx file represented by file descriptor *xd*, then a process B can open (see *open*(2)) the mpx file. The purpose is to establish a channel between

A and B through the mpx file. *Attach* and *Detach* are used by A to respond to such opens.

An open request by B fails immediately if a new channel cannot be allocated on the mpx file, if the mpx file does not exist, or if it does exist but there is no process (A) with a multiplexed file descriptor for the mpx file (i.e. *xd* as returned by *mpx*(2)). Otherwise a channel with index number *i* is allocated. The next time A reads on file descriptor *xd*, the WATCH control message (see *mpxio*(5)) will be delivered on channel *i*. A responds to this message with *attach* or *detach*. The former causes the open to complete and return a file descriptor to B. The latter deallocates channel *i* and causes the open to fail.

One mpx file may be placed in 'listener' mode. This is done by writing *ioctl(xd, MXLSTN, 0)* where *xd* is an mpx file descriptor and MXLSTN is defined in */usr/include/sgtty.h*. The semantics of listener mode are that all file names discovered by *open*(2) to have the syntax *system!pathname* (see *uucp*(1)) are treated as opens on the mpx file. The operating system sends the listener process an OPEN message (see *mpxio*(5)) which includes the file name being opened. *Attach* and *detach* then apply as described above.

Detach has two other uses: it closes and releases the resources of any active channel it is applied to, and should be used to respond to a CLOSE message (see *mpxio*(5)) on a channel so the channel may be reused.

connect(fd, cd, end). *Fd* is a character file descriptor and *cd* is a file descriptor for a channel, such as might be obtained via *extract(chan(xd), xd)* or by *open*(2) followed by *attach*. *Connect* splices the two streams together. If *end* is negative, only the output of *fd* is spliced to the input of *cd*. If *end* is positive, the output of *cd* is spliced to the input of *fd*. If *end* is zero, then both splices are made.

npgrp(i, xd, pgrp). If *xd* is negative *npgrp* applies to the process executing it, otherwise *i* and *xd* are interpreted as a channel index and mpx file descriptor and *npgrp* is applied to the process on the non-multiplexed end of the channel. If *pgrp* is zero, the process group number of the indicated process is set to the process number of that process, otherwise the value of *pgrp* is used as the process group number.

Npgrp normally returns the new process group number. If *i* and *xd* specify a nonexistant channel, *npgrp* returns −1.

ckill(i, xd, signal) sends the specified signal (see *signal*(2)) through the channel specified by *i* and *xd*. If the channel is connected to anything other than a process, *ckill* is a null operation. If there is a process at the other end of the channel, the process group will be interrupted (see *signal*(2), *kill*(2)). *Ckill* normally returns *signal*. If *ch* and *xd* specify a nonexistent channel, *ckill* returns −1.

FILES

    /usr/include/sys/mx.h
    /usr/include/sgtty.h

SEE ALSO

    mpxio(5)

BUGS

    Mpx files are an experimental part of the operating system more subject to change and prone to bugs than other parts. Maintenance programs, e.g. *icheck*(1), diagnose mpx files as an illegal mode. Channels may only be connected to objects in the operating system that are accessible through the line discipline mechanism. Higher performace line disciplines are needed. The maximum tree depth restriction is not really checked. A non-destructive *disconnect* primitive (inverse of *connect*) is not provided. A non-blocking flow control strategy based on messages defined in *mpxio*(5) should not be attempted by novices; the enabling *ioctl* command should be protected. The *join* operation could be subsumed by *connect*. A mechanism is needed for moving a channel from one location in an mpx tree to another.

NAME

    mpxcall — multiplexor and channel interface

SYNOPSIS

    mpxcall(arg1, arg2, arg3, cmd)

DESCRIPTION

    Mpxcall supplies a primitive interface to the kernel used by the routines listed below. Each routine that uses *mpxcall* passes an integer *cmd* as the fourth argument. These are defined in */usr/include/mx.h*. *Mpxcall* always returns an integer which is to be interpreted in accordance with the definition of *cmd*.

SEE ALSO

    group(2), join(2), extract(2), connect(2), chan(2), attach(2), detach(2)

DIAGNOSTICS

    The value −1 is returned on error.

NAME

  nice − set program priority

SYNOPSIS

  nice(incr)

DESCRIPTION

  The scheduling priority of the process is augmented by *incr*. Positive priorities get less service than normal. Priority 10 is recommended to users who wish to execute long-running programs without flak from the administration.

  Negative increments are ignored except on behalf of the super-user. The priority is limited to the range −20 (most urgent) to 20 (least).

  The priority of a process is passed to a child process by *fork*(2). For a privileged process to return to normal priority from an unknown state, *nice* should be called successively with arguments −40 (goes to priority −20 because of truncation), 20 (to get to 0), then 0 (to maintain compatibility with previous versions of this call).

SEE ALSO

  nice(1)

ASSEMBLER

  (nice = 34.)
  (priority in r0)
  sys nice

NAME

open — open for reading or writing

SYNOPSIS

open(name, mode)
char *name;

DESCRIPTION

Open opens the file *name* for reading (if *mode* is 0), writing (if *mode* is 1) or for both reading and writing (if *mode* is 2). *Name* is the address of a string of ASCII characters representing a path name, terminated by a null character.

The file is positioned at the beginning (byte 0). The returned file descriptor must be used for subsequent calls for other input-output functions on the file.

SEE ALSO

creat(2), read(2), write(2), dup(2), close(2)

DIAGNOSTICS

The value −1 is returned if the file does not exist, if one of the necessary directories does not exist or is unreadable, if the file is not readable (resp. writable), or if too many files are open.

ASSEMBLER

(open = 5.)
sys open; name; mode
(file descriptor in r0)

NAME

      pause − stop until signal

SYNOPSIS

      pause( )

DESCRIPTION

      Pause never returns normally. It is used to give up control while waiting for a signal from *kill*(2) or *alarm*(2).

SEE ALSO

      kill(1), kill(2), alarm(2), signal(2), setjmp(3)

ASSEMBLER

      (pause = 29.)

      sys pause

NAME

phys — allow a process to access physical addresses

SYNOPSIS

phys(segreg, size, physadr)

DESCRIPTION

The argument *segreg* specifies a process virtual (data-space) address range of 8K bytes starting at virtual address *segreg*×8K bytes. This address range is mapped into physical address *physadr*×64 bytes. Only the first *size*×64 bytes of this mapping is addressable. If *size* is zero, any previous mapping of this virtual address range is nullified. For example, the call

phys(6, 1, 0177775);

will map virtual addresses 0160000-0160077 into physical addresses 017777500-017777577. In particular, virtual address 0160060 is the PDP-11 console located at physical address 017777560.

This call may only be executed by the super-user.

SEE ALSO

PDP-11 segmentation hardware

DIAGNOSTICS

The function value zero is returned if the physical mapping is in effect. The value −1 is returned if not super-user, if *segreg* is not in the range 0-7, if *size* is not in the range 0-127, or if the specified *segreg* is already used for other than a previous call to *phys*.

BUGS

This system call is obviously very machine dependent and very dangerous. This system call is not considered a permanent part of the system.

ASSEMBLER

(phys = 52.)

sys phys; segreg; size; physadr

NAME

pipe — create an interprocess channel

SYNOPSIS

pipe(fildes)
int fildes[2];

DESCRIPTION

The *pipe* system call creates an I/O mechanism called a pipe. The file descriptors returned can be used in read and write operations. When the pipe is written using the descriptor *fildes*[1] up to 4096 bytes of data are buffered before the writing process is suspended. A read using the descriptor *fildes*[0] will pick up the data. Writes with a count of 4096 bytes or less are atomic; no other process can intersperse data.

It is assumed that after the pipe has been set up, two (or more) cooperating processes (created by subsequent *fork* calls) will pass data through the pipe with *read* and *write* calls.

The Shell has a syntax to set up a linear array of processes connected by pipes.

Read calls on an empty pipe (no buffered data) with only one end (all write file descriptors closed) returns an end-of-file.

SEE ALSO

sh(1), read(2), write(2), fork(2)

DIAGNOSTICS

The function value zero is returned if the pipe was created; -1 if too many files are already open. A signal is generated if a write on a pipe with only one end is attempted.

BUGS

Should more than 4096 bytes be necessary in any pipe among a loop of processes, deadlock will occur.

ASSEMBLER

(pipe = 42.)
sys pipe
(read file descriptor in r0)
(write file descriptor in r1)

NAME

pkon, pkoff — establish packet protocol

SYNOPSIS

pkon(fd, size)

pkoff(fd)

DESCRIPTION

Pkon establishes packet protocol (see *pk*(4)) on the open character special file whose file descriptor is *fd*. *Size* is a desired packet size, a power of 2 in the range $32 \leq size \leq 4096$. The size is negotiated with a remote packet driver, and a possibly smaller actual packet size is returned.

An asynchronous line used for packet communication should be in raw mode; see *tty*(4).

Pkoff turns off the packet driver on the channel whose file descriptor is *fd*.

SEE ALSO

pk(4), pkopen(3), tty(4), signal(2)

DIAGNOSTICS

Pkon returns -1 if *fd* does not describe an open file, or if packet communication cannot be established.

Pkoff returns -1 for an unknown file descriptor.

Writing on a packet driver link that has been shut down by *close* or *pkoff* at the other end raises signal SIGPIPE in the writing process.

NAME

    profil — execution time profile

SYNOPSIS

    profil(buff, bufsiz, offset, scale)
    char *buff;
    int bufsiz, offset, scale;

DESCRIPTION

    Buff points to an area of core whose length (in bytes) is given by *bufsiz*. After this call, the user's program counter (pc) is examined each clock tick (60th second); *offset* is subtracted from it, and the result multiplied by *scale*. If the resulting number corresponds to a word inside *buff*, that word is incremented.

    The scale is interpreted as an unsigned, fixed-point fraction with binary point at the left: 0177777(8) gives a 1-1 mapping of pc's to words in *buff*; 077777(8) maps each pair of instruction words together. 02(8) maps all instructions onto the beginning of *buff* (producing a non-interrupting core clock).

    Profiling is turned off by giving a *scale* of 0 or 1. It is rendered ineffective by giving a *bufsiz* of 0. Profiling is turned off when an *exec* is executed, but remains on in child and parent both after a *fork*. Profiling may be turned off if an update in *buff* would cause a memory fault.

SEE ALSO

    monitor(3), prof(1)

ASSEMBLER

    (profil = 44.)
    sys profil; buff; bufsiz; offset; scale

NAME

ptrace — process trace

SYNOPSIS

#include <signal.h>

ptrace(request, pid, addr, data)
int *addr;

DESCRIPTION

Ptrace provides a means by which a parent process may control the execution of a child process, and examine and change its core image. Its primary use is for the implementation of break-point debugging. There are four arguments whose interpretation depends on a *request* argument. Generally, *pid* is the process ID of the traced process, which must be a child (no more distant descendant) of the tracing process. A process being traced behaves normally until it encounters some signal whether internally generated like 'illegal instruction' or externally generated like 'interrupt.' See *signal*(2) for the list. Then the traced process enters a stopped state and its parent is notified via *wait*(2). When the child is in the stopped state, its core image can be examined and modified using *ptrace*. If desired, another *ptrace* request can then cause the child either to terminate or to continue, possibly ignoring the signal.

The value of the *request* argument determines the precise action of the call:

0　　This request is the only one used by the child process; it declares that the process is to be traced by its parent. All the other arguments are ignored. Peculiar results will ensue if the parent does not expect to trace the child.

1,2　The word in the child process's address space at *addr* is returned. If I and D space are separated, request 1 indicates I space, 2 D space. *Addr* must be even. The child must be stopped. The input *data* is ignored.

3　　The word of the system's per-process data area corresponding to *addr* is returned. *Addr* must be even and less than 512. This space contains the registers and other information about the process; its layout corresponds to the *user* structure in the system.

4,5　The given *data* is written at the word in the process's address space corresponding to *addr*, which must be even. No useful value is returned. If I and D space are separated, request 4 indicates I space, 5 D space. Attempts to write in pure procedure fail if another process is executing the same file.

6　　The process's system data is written, as it is read with request 3. Only a few locations can be written in this way: the general registers, the floating point status and registers, and certain bits of the processor status word.

7　　The *data* argument is taken as a signal number and the child's execution continues at location *addr* as if it had incurred that signal. Normally the signal number will be either 0 to indicate that the signal that caused the stop should be ignored, or that value fetched out of the process's image indicating which signal caused the stop. If *addr* is (int *)1 then execution continues from where it stopped.

8　　The traced process terminates.

9　　Execution continues as in request 7; however, as soon as possible after execution of at least one instruction, execution stops again. The signal number from the stop is SIGTRAP. (On the PDP-11 the T-bit is used and just one instruction is executed; on the Interdata the stop does not take place until a store instruction is executed.) This is part of the mechanism for implementing breakpoints.

As indicated, these calls (except for request 0) can be used only when the subject process has stopped. The *wait* call is used to determine when a process stops; in such a case the 'termination' status returned by *wait* has the value 0177 to indicate stoppage rather than genuine termination.

To forestall possible fraud, *ptrace* inhibits the set-user-id facility on subsequent *exec*(2) calls. If a traced process calls *exec*, it will stop before executing the first instruction of the new image showing signal SIGTRAP.

On the Interdata 8/32, 'word' means a 32-bit word and 'even' means 0 mod 4.

SEE ALSO

wait(2), signal(2), adb(1)

DIAGNOSTICS

The value −1 is returned if *request* is invalid, *pid* is not a traceable process, *addr* is out of bounds, or *data* specifies an illegal signal number.

BUGS

On the Interdata 8/32, 'as soon as possible' (request 7) means 'as soon as a store instruction has been executed.'

The request 0 call should be able to specify signals which are to be treated normally and not cause a stop. In this way, for example, programs with simulated floating point (which use 'illegal instruction' signals at a very high rate) could be efficiently debugged.

The error indication, −1, is a legitimate function value; *errno,* see *intro*(2), can be used to disambiguate.

It should be possible to stop a process on occurrence of a system call; in this way a completely controlled environment could be provided.

ASSEMBLER

(ptrace = 26.)
(data in r0)
sys ptrace; pid; addr; request
(value in r0)

NAME

read — read from file

SYNOPSIS

read(fildes, buffer, nbytes)
char *buffer;

DESCRIPTION

A file descriptor is a word returned from a successful *open, creat, dup,* or *pipe* call. *Buffer* is the location of *nbytes* contiguous bytes into which the input will be placed. It is not guaranteed that all *nbytes* bytes will be read; for example if the file refers to a typewriter at most one line will be returned. In any event the number of characters read is returned.

If the returned value is 0, then end-of-file has been reached.

SEE ALSO

open(2), creat(2), dup(2), pipe(2)

DIAGNOSTICS

As mentioned, 0 is returned when the end of the file has been reached. If the read was otherwise unsuccessful the return value is −1. Many conditions can generate an error: physical I/O errors, bad buffer address, preposterous *nbytes,* file descriptor not that of an input file.

ASSEMBLER

(read = 3.)
(file descriptor in r0)
sys read; buffer; nbytes
(byte count in r0)

NAME

setuid, setgid — set user and group ID

SYNOPSIS

setuid(uid)

setgid(gid)

DESCRIPTION

The user ID (group ID) of the current process is set to the argument. Both the effective and the real ID are set. These calls are only permitted to the super-user or if the argument is the real ID.

SEE ALSO

getuid(2)

DIAGNOSTICS

Zero is returned if the user (group) ID is set; −1 is returned otherwise.

ASSEMBLER

(setuid = 23.)
(user ID in r0)
sys setuid

(setgid = 46.)
(group ID in r0)
sys setgid

NAME

signal − catch or ignore signals

SYNOPSIS

#include <signal.h>

(*signal(sig, func))()
(*func)();

DESCRIPTION

A signal is generated by some abnormal event, initiated either by user at a typewriter (quit, interrupt), by a program error (bus error, etc.), or by request of another program (kill). Normally all signals cause termination of the receiving process, but a *signal* call allows them either to be ignored or to cause an interrupt to a specified location. Here is the list of signals with names as in the include file.

SIGHUP	1	hangup
SIGINT	2	interrupt
SIGQUIT	3*	quit
SIGILL	4*	illegal instruction (not reset when caught)
SIGTRAP	5*	trace trap (not reset when caught)
SIGIOT	6*	IOT instruction
SIGEMT	7*	EMT instruction
SIGFPE	8*	floating point exception
SIGKILL	9	kill (cannot be caught or ignored)
SIGBUS	10*	bus error
SIGSEGV	11*	segmentation violation
SIGSYS	12*	bad argument to system call
SIGPIPE	13	write on a pipe or link with no one to read it
SIGALRM	14	alarm clock
SIGTERM	15	software termination signal
	16	unassigned

The starred signals in the list above cause a core image if not caught or ignored.

If *func* is SIG_DFL, the default action for signal *sig* is reinstated; this default is termination, sometimes with a core image. If *func* is SIG_IGN the signal is ignored. Otherwise when the signal occurs *func* will be called with the signal number as argument. A return from the function will continue the process at the point it was interrupted. Except as indicated, a signal is reset to SIG_DFL after being caught. Thus if it is desired to catch every such signal, the catching routine must issue another *signal* call.

When a caught signal occurs during certain system calls, the call terminates prematurely. In particular this can occur during a *read* or *write*(2) on a slow device (like a typewriter; but not a file); and during *pause* or *wait*(2). When such a signal occurs, the saved user status is arranged in such a way that when return from the signal-catching takes place, it will appear that the system call returned an error status. The user's program may then, if it wishes, re-execute the call.

The value of *signal* is the previous (or initial) value of *func* for the particular signal.

After a *fork*(2) the child inherits all signals. *Exec*(2) resets all caught signals to default action.

SEE ALSO

kill(1), kill(2), ptrace(2), setjmp(3)

DIAGNOSTICS

The value (int)−1 is returned if the given signal is out of range.

BUGS

If a repeated signal arrives before the last one can be reset, there is no chance to catch it.

The type specification of the routine and its *func* argument are problematical.

ASSEMBLER

(signal = 48.)

sys signal; sig; label

(old label in r0)

If *label* is 0, default action is reinstated. If *label* is odd, the signal is ignored. Any other even *label* specifies an address in the process where an interrupt is simulated. An RTI or RTT instruction will return from the interrupt.

NAME

stat, fstat − get file status

SYNOPSIS

#include <sys/types.h>
#include <sys/stat.h>

stat(name, buf)
char *name;
struct stat *buf;

fstat(fildes, buf)
struct stat *buf;

DESCRIPTION

Stat obtains detailed information about a named file. *Fstat* obtains the same information about an open file known by the file descriptor from a successful *open, creat, dup* or *pipe*(2) call.

Name points to a null-terminated string naming a file; *buf* is the address of a buffer into which information is placed concerning the file. It is unnecessary to have any permissions at all with respect to the file, but all directories leading to the file must be searchable. The layout of the structure pointed to by buf as defined in *<stat.h>* is given below. *St_mode* is encoded according to the '#define' statements.

```
struct     stat
{
           dev_t      st_dev;
           ino_t      st_ino;
           unsigned   short st_mode;
           short      st_nlink;
           short      st_uid;
           short      st_gid;
           dev_t      st_rdev;
           off_t      st_size;
           time_t     st_atime;
           time_t     st_mtime;
           time_t     st_ctime;
};


#define  S_IFMT     0170000  /* type of file */
#define  S_IFDIR    0040000  /* directory */
#define  S_IFCHR    0020000  /* character special */
#define  S_IFBLK    0060000  /* block special */
#define  S_IFREG    0100000  /* regular */
#define  S_IFMPC    0030000  /* multiplexed char special */
#define  S_IFMPB    0070000  /* multiplexed block special */
#define  S_ISUID    0004000  /* set user id on execution */
#define  S_ISGID    0002000  /* set group id on execution */
#define  S_ISVTX    0001000  /* save swapped text even after use */
#define  S_IREAD    0000400  /* read permission, owner */
#define  S_IWRITE   0000200  /* write permission, owner */
#define  S_IEXEC    0000100  /* execute/search permission, owner */
```

The mode bits 0000070 and 0000007 encode group and others permissions (see *chmod*(2)). The defined types, *ino_t, off_t, time_t,* name various width integer values; *dev_t* encodes major and minor device numbers; their exact definitions are in the include file *<sys/types.h>* (see *types*(5).

When *fildes* is associated with a pipe, *fstat* reports an ordinary file with restricted permissions. The size is the number of bytes queued in the pipe.

st_atime is the file was last read. For reasons of efficiency, it is not set when a directory is searched, although this would be more logical. *st_mtime* is the time the file was last written or created. It is not set by changes of owner, group, link count, or mode. *st_ctime* is set both both by writing and changing the i-node.

SEE ALSO

　　ls(1), filsys(5)

DIAGNOSTICS

　　Zero is returned if a status is available; −1 if the file cannot be found.

ASSEMBLER

　　(stat = 18.)

　　sys stat; name; buf

　　(fstat = 28.)

　　(file descriptor in r0)

　　sys fstat; buf

NAME

    stime − set time

SYNOPSIS

    stime(tp)
    long *tp;

DESCRIPTION

    Stime sets the system's idea of the time and date. Time, pointed to by *tp*, is measured in seconds from 0000 GMT Jan 1, 1970. Only the super-user may use this call.

SEE ALSO

    date(1), time(2), ctime(3)

DIAGNOSTICS

    Zero is returned if the time was set; −1 if user is not the super-user.

ASSEMBLER

    (stime = 25.)
    (time in r0-r1)
    sys stime

NAME

        sync — update super-block

SYNOPSIS

        sync( )

DESCRIPTION

        Sync causes all information in core memory that should be on disk to be written out. This
        includes modified super blocks, modified i-nodes, and delayed block I/O.

        It should be used by programs which examine a file system, for example *icheck, df,* etc. It is
        mandatory before a boot.

SEE ALSO

        sync(1), update(8)

BUGS

        The writing, although scheduled, is not necessarily complete upon return from *sync*.

ASSEMBLER

        (sync = 36.)
        sys sync

NAME

  time, ftime — get date and time

SYNOPSIS

  long time(0)

  long time(tloc)
  long *tloc;

  #include <sys/types.h>
  #include <sys/timeb.h>
  ftime(tp)
  struct timeb *tp;

DESCRIPTION

  Time returns the time since 00:00:00 GMT, Jan. 1, 1970, measured in seconds.

  If *tloc* is nonnull, the return value is also stored in the place to which *tloc* points.

  The *ftime* entry fills in a structure pointed to by its argument, as defined by *<sys/timeb.h>*:

NAME

      times − get process times

SYNOPSIS

      times(buffer)
      struct tbuffer *buffer;

DESCRIPTION

      Times returns time-accounting information for the current process and for the terminated child processes of the current process. All times are in 1/HZ seconds, where HZ=60 in North America.

      After the call, the buffer will appear as follows:

      struct tbuffer {
               long   proc_user_time;
               long   proc_system_time;
               long   child_user_time;
               long   child_system_time;
      };

      The children times are the sum of the children's process times and their children's times.

SEE ALSO

      time(1), time(2)

ASSEMBLER

      (times = 43.)
      sys times; buffer

NAME

umask — set file creation mode mask

SYNOPSIS

umask(complmode)

DESCRIPTION

Umask sets a mask used whenever a file is created by *creat*(2) or *mknod*(2): the actual mode
(see *chmod*(2)) of the newly-created file is the logical **and** of the given mode and the complement of the argument. Only the low-order 9 bits of the mask (the protection bits) participate.
In other words, the mask shows the bits to be turned off when files are created.

The previous value of the mask is returned by the call. The value is initially 0 (no restrictions). The mask is inherited by child processes.

SEE ALSO

creat(2), mknod(2), chmod(2)

ASSEMBLER

(umask = 60.)

sys umask; complmode

NAME

unlink — remove directory entry

SYNOPSIS

unlink(name)
char *name;

DESCRIPTION

Name points to a null-terminated string. *Unlink* removes the entry for the file pointed to by *name* from its directory. If this entry was the last link to the file, the contents of the file are freed and the file is destroyed. If, however, the file was open in any process, the actual destruction is delayed until it is closed, even though the directory entry has disappeared.

SEE ALSO

rm(1), link(2)

DIAGNOSTICS

Zero is normally returned; −1 indicates that the file does not exist, that its directory cannot be written, or that the file contains pure procedure text that is currently in use. Write permission is not required on the file itself. It is also illegal to unlink a directory (except for the super-user).

ASSEMBLER

(unlink = 10.)
sys unlink; name

NAME

        utime − set file times

SYNOPSIS

        #include <sys/types.h>
        utime(file, timep)
        char *file;
        time_t timep[2];

DESCRIPTION

        The *utime* call uses the 'accessed' and 'updated' times in that order from the *timep* vector to set
        the corresponding recorded times for *file*.

        The caller must be the owner of the file or the super-user. The 'inode-changed' time of the file
        is set to the current time.

SEE ALSO

        stat (2)

ASSEMBLER

        (utime = 30.)
        sys utime; file; timep

NAME

wait — wait for process to terminate

SYNOPSIS

wait(status)
int *status;

wait(0)

DESCRIPTION

Wait causes its caller to delay until a signal is received or one of its child processes terminates. If any child has died since the last *wait*, return is immediate; if there are no children, return is immediate with the error bit set (resp. with a value of −1 returned). The normal return yields the process ID of the terminated child. In the case of several children several *wait* calls are needed to learn of all the deaths.

If (int)*status* is nonzero, the high byte of the word pointed to receives the low byte of the argument of *exit* when the child terminated. The low byte receives the termination status of the process. See *signal*(2) for a list of termination statuses (signals); 0 status indicates normal termination. A special status (0177) is returned for a stopped process which has not terminated and can be restarted. See *ptrace*(2). If the 0200 bit of the termination status is set, a core image of the process was produced by the system.

If the parent process terminates without waiting on its children, the initialization process (process ID = 1) inherits the children.

SEE ALSO

exit(2), fork(2), signal(2)

DIAGNOSTICS

Returns −1 if there are no children not previously waited for.

ASSEMBLER

(wait = 7.)
sys wait
(process ID in r0)
(status in r1)

The high byte of the status is the low byte of r0 in the child at termination.

NAME

write — write on a file

SYNOPSIS

write(fildes, buffer, nbytes)
char *buffer;

DESCRIPTION

A file descriptor is a word returned from a successful *open, creat, dup,* or *pipe*(2) call.

Buffer is the address of *nbytes* contiguous bytes which are written on the output file. The number of characters actually written is returned. It should be regarded as an error if this is not the same as requested.

Writes which are multiples of 512 characters long and begin on a 512-byte boundary in the file are more efficient than any others.

SEE ALSO

creat(2), open(2), pipe(2)

DIAGNOSTICS

Returns −1 on error: bad descriptor, buffer address, or count; physical I/O errors.

ASSEMBLER

(write = 4.)
(file descriptor in r0)
sys write; buffer; nbytes
(byte count in r0)

Section 3
SUBROUTINES

NAME
intro − introduction to library functions

SYNOPSIS
#include <stdio.h>

#include <math.h>

DESCRIPTION
This section describes functions that may be found in various libraries, other than those functions that directly invoke UNIX system primitives, which are described in section 2. Functions are divided into various libraries distinguished by the section number at the top of the page:

(3)   These functions, together with those of section 2 and those marked (3S), constitute library *libc,* which is automatically loaded by the C compiler *cc*(1) and the Fortran compiler *f77*(1). The link editor *ld*(1) searches this library under the '−lc' option. Declarations for some of these functions may be obtained from include files indicated on the appropriate pages.

(3M)   These functions constitute the math library, *libm.* They are automatically loaded as needed by the Fortran compiler *f77*(1). The link editor searches this library under the '−lm' option. Declarations for these functions may be obtained from the include file <math.h>.

(3S)   These functions constitute the 'standard I/O package', see *stdio*(3). These functions are in the library *libc* already mentioned. Declarations for these functions may be obtained from the include file <stdio.h>.

(3X)   Various specialized libraries have not been given distinctive captions. The files in which these libraries are found are named on the appropriate pages.

FILES
/lib/libc.a

/lib/libm.a, /usr/lib/libm.a (one or the other)

SEE ALSO
stdio(3), nm(1), ld(1), cc(1), f77(1), intro(2)

DIAGNOSTICS
Functions in the math library (3M) may return conventional values when the function is undefined for the given arguments or when the value is not representable. In these cases the external variable *errno* (see *intro*(2)) is set to the value EDOM or ERANGE. The values of EDOM and ERANGE are defined in the include file <*math.h*>.

ASSEMBLER
In assembly language these functions may be accessed by simulating the C calling sequence. For example, *ecvt*(3) might be called this way:

```
        setd
        mov     $sign,−(sp)
        mov     $decpt,−(sp)
        mov     ndigit,−(sp)
        movf    value,−(sp)
        jsr     pc,_ecvt
        add     $14.,sp
```

NAME
     abort — generate IOT fault

DESCRIPTION
     Abort executes the PDP11 IOT instruction. This causes a signal that normally terminates the
     process with a core dump, which may be used for debugging.

SEE ALSO
     adb(1), signal(2), exit(2)

DIAGNOSTICS
     Usually 'IOT trap — core dumped' from the shell.

NAME

    abs − integer absolute value

SYNOPSIS

    abs(i)

DESCRIPTION

    Abs returns the absolute value of its integer operand.

SEE ALSO

    floor(3) for *fabs*

BUGS

    You get what the hardware gives on the largest negative integer.

NAME
        assert − program verification

SYNOPSIS
        #include <assert.h>

        assert (expression)

DESCRIPTION
        Assert is a macro that indicates *expression* is expected to be true at this point in the program. It
        causes an *exit*(2) with a diagnostic comment on the standard output when *expression* is false (0).
        Compiling with the *cc*(1) option −DNDEBUG effectively deletes *assert* from the program.

DIAGNOSTICS
        'Assertion failed: file *f* line *n*.' *F* is the source file and *n* the source line number of the *assert*
        statement.

NAME

  atof, atoi, atol − convert ASCII to numbers

SYNOPSIS

  double atof(nptr)
  char *nptr;

  atoi(nptr)
  char *nptr;

  long atol(nptr)
  char *nptr;

DESCRIPTION

  These functions convert a string pointed to by *nptr* to floating, integer, and long integer representation respectively. The first unrecognized character ends the string.

  Atof recognizes an optional string of tabs and spaces, then an optional sign, then a string of digits optionally containing a decimal point, then an optional 'e' or 'E' followed by an optionally signed integer.

  Atoi and *atol* recognize an optional string of tabs and spaces, then an optional sign, then a string of digits.

SEE ALSO

  scanf(3)

BUGS

  There are no provisions for overflow.

NAME

crypt, setkey, encrypt — DES encryption

SYNOPSIS

char *crypt(key, salt)
char *key, *salt;

setkey(key)
char *key;

encrypt(block, edflag)
char *block;

DESCRIPTION

Crypt is the password encryption routine. It is based on the NBS Data Encryption Standard, with variations intended (among other things) to frustrate use of hardware implementations of the DES for key search.

The first argument to *crypt* is a user's typed password. The second is a 2-character string chosen from the set [a-zA-Z0-9./]. The *salt* string is used to perturb the DES algorithm in one of 4096 different ways, after which the password is used as the key to encrypt repeatedly a constant string. The returned value points to the encrypted password, in the same alphabet as the salt. The first two characters are the salt itself.

The other entries provide (rather primitive) access to the actual DES algorithm. The argument of *setkey* is a character array of length 64 containing only the characters with numerical value 0 and 1. If this string is divided into groups of 8, the low-order bit in each group is ignored, leading to a 56-bit key which is set into the machine.

The argument to the *encrypt* entry is likewise a character array of length 64 containing 0's and 1's. The argument array is modified in place to a similar array representing the bits of the argument after having been subjected to the DES algorithm using the key set by *setkey*. If *edflag* is 0, the argument is encrypted; if non-zero, it is decrypted.

SEE ALSO

passwd(1), passwd(5), login(1), getpass(3)

BUGS

The return value points to static data whose content is overwritten by each call.

NAME

    ctime, localtime, gmtime, asctime, timezone — convert date and time to ASCII

SYNOPSIS

    char *ctime(clock)
    long *clock;

    #include <time.h>

    struct tm *localtime(clock)
    long *clock;

    struct tm *gmtime(clock)
    long *clock;

    char *asctime(tm)
    struct tm *tm;

    char *timezone(zone, dst)

DESCRIPTION

Ctime converts a time pointed to by *clock* such as returned by *time*(2) into ASCII and returns a pointer to a 26-character string in the following form. All the fields have constant width.

    Sun Sep 16 01:03:52 1973\n\0

Localtime and *gmtime* return pointers to structures containing the broken-down time. *Localtime* corrects for the time zone and possible daylight savings time; *gmtime* converts directly to GMT, which is the time UNIX uses. *Asctime* converts a broken-down time to ASCII and returns a pointer to a 26-character string.

The structure declaration from the include file is:

    struct   tm {   /* see ctime(3) */
             int   tm_sec;
             int   tm_min;
             int   tm_hour;
             int   tm_mday;
             int   tm_mon;
             int   tm_year;
             int   tm_wday;
             int   tm_yday;
             int   tm_isdst;
    };

These quantities give the time on a 24-hour clock, day of month (1-31), month of year (0-11), day of week (Sunday = 0), year — 1900, day of year (0-365), and a flag that is nonzero if daylight saving time is in effect.

When local time is called for, the program consults the system to determine the time zone and whether the standard U.S.A. daylight saving time adjustment is appropriate. The program knows about the peculiarities of this conversion in 1974 and 1975; if necessary, a table for these years can be extended.

Timezone returns the name of the time zone associated with its first argument, which is measured in minutes westward from Greenwich. If the second argument is 0, the standard name is used, otherwise the Daylight Saving version. If the required name does not appear in a table built into the routine, the difference from GMT is produced; e.g. in Afghanistan *timezone(—(60*4+30), 0)* is appropriate because it is 4:30 ahead of GMT and the string **GMT+4:30** is produced.

SEE ALSO

time(2)

BUGS

The return values point to static data whose content is overwritten by each call.

NAME

isalpha, isupper, islower, isdigit, isalnum, isspace, ispunct, isprint, iscntrl, isascii — character classification

SYNOPSIS

#include <ctype.h>

isalpha(c)

. . .

DESCRIPTION

These macros classify ASCII-coded integer values by table lookup. Each is a predicate returning nonzero for true, zero for false. *Isascii* is defined on all integer values; the rest are defined only where *isascii* is true and on the single non-ASCII value EOF (see *stdio*(3)).

isalpha	*c* is a letter
isupper	*c* is an upper case letter
islower	*c* is a lower case letter
isdigit	*c* is a digit
isalnum	*c* is an alphanumeric character
isspace	*c* is a space, tab, carriage return, newline, or formfeed
ispunct	*c* is a punctuation character (neither control nor alphanumeric)
isprint	*c* is a printing character, code 040(8) (space) through 0176 (tilde)
iscntrl	*c* is a delete character (0177) or ordinary control character (less than 040).
isascii	*c* is an ASCII character, code less than 0200

SEE ALSO

ascii(7)

NAME

dbminit, fetch, store, delete, firstkey, nextkey — data base subroutines

SYNOPSIS

typedef struct { char *dptr; int dsize; } datum;

dbminit(file)
char *file;

datum fetch(key)
datum key;

store(key, content)
datum key, content;

delete(key)
datum key;

datum firstkey();

datum nextkey(key);
datum key;

DESCRIPTION

These functions maintain key/content pairs in a data base. The functions will handle very large (a billion blocks) databases and will access a keyed item in one or two filesystem accesses. The functions are obtained with the loader option **−ldbm**.

*Key*s and *content*s are described by the *datum* typedef. A *datum* specifies a string of *dsize* bytes pointed to by *dptr*. Arbitrary binary data, as well as normal ASCII strings, are allowed. The data base is stored in two files. One file is a directory containing a bit map and has '.dir' as its suffix. The second file contains all data and has '.pag' as its suffix.

Before a database can be accessed, it must be opened by *dbminit*. At the time of this call, the files *file*.**dir** and *file*.**pag** must exist. (An empty database is created by creating zero-length '.dir' and '.pag' files.)

Once open, the data stored under a key is accessed by *fetch* and data is placed under a key by *store*. A key (and its associated contents) is deleted by *delete*. A linear pass through all keys in a database may be made, in an (apparently) random order, by use of *firstkey* and *nextkey*. *First-key* will return the first key in the database. With any key *nextkey* will return the next key in the database. This code will traverse the data base:

        for(key=firstkey(); key.dptr!=NULL; key=nextkey(key))

DIAGNOSTICS

All functions that return an *int* indicate errors with negative values. A zero return indicates ok. Routines that return a *datum* indicate errors with a null (0) *dptr*.

BUGS

The '.pag' file will contain holes so that its apparent size is about four times its actual content. Older UNIX systems may create real file blocks for these holes when touched. These files cannot be copied by normal means (cp, cat, tp, tar, ar) without filling in the holes.

Dptr pointers returned by these subroutines point into static storage that is changed by subsequent calls.

The sum of the sizes of a key/content pair must not exceed the internal block size (currently 512 bytes). Moreover all key/content pairs that hash together must fit on a single block. *Store* will return an error in the event that a disk block fills with inseparable data.

Delete does not physically reclaim file space, although it does make it available for reuse.

The order of keys presented by *firstkey* and *nextkey* depends on a hashing function, not on anything interesting.

NAME
        ecvt, fcvt, gcvt — output conversion

SYNOPSIS
        char *ecvt(value, ndigit, decpt, sign)
        double value;
        int ndigit, *decpt, *sign;

        char *fcvt(value, ndigit, decpt, sign)
        double value;
        int ndigit, *decpt, *sign;

        char *gcvt(value, ndigit, buf)
        double value;
        char *buf;

DESCRIPTION
        Ecvt converts the *value* to a null-terminated string of *ndigit* ASCII digits and returns a pointer
        thereto. The position of the decimal point relative to the beginning of the string is stored
        indirectly through *decpt* (negative means to the left of the returned digits). If the sign of the
        result is negative, the word pointed to by *sign* is non-zero, otherwise it is zero. The low-order
        digit is rounded.

        Fcvt is identical to *ecvt*, except that the correct digit has been rounded for Fortran F-format out-
        put of the number of digits specified by *ndigits*.

        Gcvt converts the *value* to a null-terminated ASCII string in *buf* and returns a pointer to *buf*. It
        attempts to produce *ndigit* significant digits in Fortran F format if possible, otherwise E format,
        ready for printing. Trailing zeros may be suppressed.

SEE ALSO
        printf(3)

BUGS
        The return values point to static data whose content is overwritten by each call.

NAME

    end, etext, edata — last locations in program

SYNOPSIS

    extern end;

    extern etext;

    extern edata;

DESCRIPTION

    These names refer neither to routines nor to locations with interesting contents. The address of *etext* is the first address above the program text, *edata* above the initialized data region, and *end* above the uninitialized data region.

    When execution begins, the program break coincides with *end,* but many functions reset the program break, among them the routines of *brk*(2), *malloc*(3), standard input/output (*stdio*(3)), the profile (−**p**) option of *cc*(1), etc. The current value of the program break is reliably returned by 'sbrk(0)', see *brk*(2).

SEE ALSO

    brk(2), malloc(3)

NAME

exp, log, log10, pow, sqrt — exponential, logarithm, power, square root

SYNOPSIS

#include <math.h>

double exp(x)
double x;

double log(x)
double x;

double log10(x)
double x;

double pow(x, y)
double x, y;

double sqrt(x)
double x;

DESCRIPTION

Exp returns the exponential function of *x*.

Log returns the natural logarithm of *x*; *log10* returns the base 10 logarithm.

Pow returns x^y.

Sqrt returns the square root of *x*.

SEE ALSO

hypot(3), sinh(3), intro(2)

DIAGNOSTICS

Exp and *pow* return a huge value when the correct value would overflow; *errno* is set to ERANGE. *Pow* returns 0 and sets *errno* to EDOM when the second argument is negative and non-integral and when both arguments are 0.

Log returns 0 when *x* is zero or negative; *errno* is set to EDOM.

Sqrt returns 0 when *x* is negative; *errno* is set to EDOM.

NAME

fclose, fflush — close or flush a stream

SYNOPSIS

#include <stdio.h>

fclose(stream)
FILE *stream;

fflush(stream)
FILE *stream;

DESCRIPTION

Fclose causes any buffers for the named *stream* to be emptied, and the file to be closed. Buffers allocated by the standard input/output system are freed.

Fclose is performed automatically upon calling *exit*(2).

Fflush causes any buffered data for the named output *stream* to be written to that file. The stream remains open.

SEE ALSO

close(2), fopen(3), setbuf(3)

DIAGNOSTICS

These routines return **EOF** if *stream* is not associated with an output file, or if buffered data cannot be transferred to that file.

NAME
　　　feof, ferror, clearerr, fileno — stream status inquiries

SYNOPSIS
　　　#include <stdio.h>

　　　feof(stream)
　　　FILE *stream;

　　　ferror(stream)
　　　FILE *stream

　　　clearerr(stream)
　　　FILE *stream

　　　fileno(stream)
　　　FILE *stream;

DESCRIPTION
　　　Feof returns non-zero when end of file is read on the named input *stream,* otherwise zero.

　　　Ferror returns non-zero when an error has occurred reading or writing the named *stream,* otherwise zero. Unless cleared by *clearerr,* the error indication lasts until the stream is closed.

　　　Clrerr resets the error indication on the named *stream.*

　　　Fileno returns the integer file descriptor associated with the *stream,* see *open*(2).

　　　These functions are implemented as macros; they cannot be redeclared.

SEE ALSO
　　　fopen(3), open(2)

NAME
　　　　fabs, floor, ceil — absolute value, floor, ceiling functions

SYNOPSIS
　　　　#include <math.h>

　　　　double floor(x)
　　　　double x;

　　　　double ceil(x)
　　　　double x;

　　　　double fabs(x)
　　　　double(x);

DESCRIPTION
　　　　Fabs returns the absolute value $|x|$.

　　　　Floor returns the largest integer not greater than x.

　　　　Ceil returns the smallest integer not less than x.

SEE ALSO
　　　　abs(3)

NAME

fopen, freopen, fdopen — open a stream

SYNOPSIS

#include <stdio.h>

FILE *fopen(filename, type)
char *filename, *type;

FILE *freopen(filename, type, stream)
char *filename, *type;
FILE *stream;

FILE *fdopen(fildes, type)
char *type;

DESCRIPTION

Fopen opens the file named by *filename* and associates a stream with it. *Fopen* returns a pointer to be used to identify the stream in subsequent operations.

Type is a character string having one of the following values:

"r"   open for reading

"w"   create for writing

"a"   append: open for writing at end of file, or create for writing

Freopen substitutes the named file in place of the open *stream*. It returns the original value of *stream*. The original stream is closed.

Freopen is typically used to attach the preopened constant names, **stdin, stdout, stderr,** to specified files.

Fdopen associates a stream with a file descriptor obtained from *open, dup, creat,* or *pipe*(2). The *type* of the stream must agree with the mode of the open file.

SEE ALSO

open(2), fclose(3)

DIAGNOSTICS

Fopen and *freopen* return the pointer **NULL** if *filename* cannot be accessed.

BUGS

Fdopen is not portable to systems other than UNIX.

NAME

  fread, fwrite — buffered binary input/output

SYNOPSIS

  #include <stdio.h>

  fread(ptr, sizeof(*ptr), nitems, stream)
  FILE *stream;

  fwrite(ptr, sizeof(*ptr), nitems, stream)
  FILE *stream;

DESCRIPTION

  Fread reads, into a block beginning at *ptr, nitems* of data of the type of **ptr* from the named input *stream*. It returns the number of items actually read.

  Fwrite appends at most *nitems* of data of the type of **ptr* beginning at *ptr* to the named output *stream*. It returns the number of items actually written.

SEE ALSO

  read(2), write(2), fopen(3), getc(3), putc(3), gets(3), puts(3), printf(3), scanf(3)

DIAGNOSTICS

  Fread and *fwrite* return 0 upon end of file or error.

NAME

frexp, ldexp, modf — split into mantissa and exponent

SYNOPSIS

        double frexp(value, eptr)
        double value;
        int *eptr;

        double ldexp(value, exp)
        double value;

        double modf(value, iptr)
        double value, *iptr;

DESCRIPTION

Frexp returns the mantissa of a double *value* as a double quantity, *x*, of magnitude less than 1 and stores an integer *n* such that *value* = $x*2**n$ indirectly through *eptr*.

Ldexp returns the quantity $value*2**exp$.

Modf returns the positive fractional part of *value* and stores the integer part indirectly through *iptr*.

NAME

fseek, ftell, rewind — reposition a stream

SYNOPSIS

#include <stdio.h>

fseek(stream, offset, ptrname)
FILE *stream;
long offset;

long ftell(stream)
FILE *stream;

rewind(stream)

DESCRIPTION

Fseek sets the position of the next input or output operation on the *stream*. The new position is at the signed distance *offset* bytes from the beginning, the current position, or the end of the file, according as *ptrname* has the value 0, 1, or 2.

Fseek undoes any effects of *ungetc*(3).

Ftell returns the current value of the offset relative to the beginning of the file associated with the named *stream*. It is measured in bytes on UNIX; on some other systems it is a magic cookie, and the only foolproof way to obtain an *offset* for *fseek*.

Rewind(stream) is equivalent to *fseek(stream, 0L, 0)*.

SEE ALSO

lseek(2), fopen(3)

DIAGNOSTICS

Fseek returns −1 for improper seeks.

NAME

getc, getchar, fgetc, getw — get character or word from stream

SYNOPSIS

#include <stdio.h>

int getc(stream)
FILE *stream;

int getchar()

int fgetc(stream)
FILE *stream;

int getw(stream)
FILE *stream;

DESCRIPTION

Getc returns the next character from the named input *stream*.

Getchar() is identical to *getc(stdin)*.

Fgetc behaves like *getc,* but is a genuine function, not a macro; it may be used to save object text.

Getw returns the next word from the named input *stream*. It returns the constant **EOF** upon end of file or error, but since that is a good integer value, *feof* and *ferror*(3) should be used to check the success of *getw*. *Getw* assumes no special alignment in the file.

SEE ALSO

fopen(3), putc(3), gets(3), scanf(3), fread(3), ungetc(3)

DIAGNOSTICS

These functions return the integer constant **EOF** at end of file or upon read error.

A stop with message, 'Reading bad file', means an attempt has been made to read from a stream that has not been opened for reading by *fopen*.

BUGS

The end-of-file return from *getchar* is incompatible with that in UNIX editions 1-6.

Because it is implemented as a macro, *getc* treats a *stream* argument with side effects incorrectly. In particular, 'getc(*f++);' doesn't work sensibly.

NAME

gets, fgets — get a string from a stream

SYNOPSIS

#include <stdio.h>

char *gets(s)
char *s;

char *fgets(s, n, stream)
char *s;
FILE *stream;

DESCRIPTION

Gets reads a string into *s* from the standard input stream **stdin.** The string is terminated by a newline character, which is replaced in *s* by a null character. *Gets* returns its argument.

Fgets reads $n-1$ characters, or up to a newline character, whichever comes first, from the *stream* into the string *s*. The last character read into *s* is followed by a null character. *Fgets* returns its first argument.

SEE ALSO

puts(3), getc(3), scanf(3), fread(3), ferror(3)

DIAGNOSTICS

Gets and *fgets* return the constant pointer NULL upon end of file or error.

BUGS

Gets deletes a newline, *fgets* keeps it, all in the name of backward compatibility.

NAME

      getenv − value for environment name

SYNOPSIS

      char *getenv(name)

      char *name;

DESCRIPTION

      Getenv searches the environment list (see *environ*(5)) for a string of the form *name* = *value* and returns *value* if such a string is present, otherwise 0 (NULL).

SEE ALSO

      environ(5), exec(2)

NAME

getgrent, getgrgid, getgrnam, setgrent, endgrent − get group file entry

SYNOPSIS

#include <grp.h>

struct group *getgrent();

struct group *getgrgid(gid) int gid;

struct group *getgrnam(name) char *name;

int setgrent();

int endgrent();

DESCRIPTION

Getgrent, *getgrgid* and *getgrnam* each return pointers to an object with the following structure containing the broken-out fields of a line in the group file.

```
struct   group { /* see getgrent(3) */
         char    *gr_name;
         char    *gr_passwd;
         int     gr_gid;
         char    **gr_mem;
};
```

The members of this structure are:

gr_name

The name of the group.

gr_passwd

The encrypted password of the group.

gr_gid   The numerical group-ID.

gr_mem

Null-terminated vector of pointers to the individual member names.

Getgrent simply reads the next line while *getgrgid* and *getgrnam* search until a matching *gid* or *name* is found (or until EOF is encountered). Each routine picks up where the others leave off so successive calls may be used to search the entire file.

A call to *setgrent* has the effect of rewinding the group file to allow repeated searches. *Endgrent* may be called to close the group file when processing is complete.

FILES

/etc/group

SEE ALSO

getlogin(3), getpwent(3), group(5)

DIAGNOSTICS

A null pointer (0) is returned on EOF or error.

BUGS

All information is contained in a static area so it must be copied if it is to be saved.

NAME

getlogin — get login name

SYNOPSIS

char *getlogin();

DESCRIPTION

Getlogin returns a pointer to the login name as found in */etc/utmp*. It may be used in conjunction with *getpwnam* to locate the correct password file entry when the same userid is shared by several login names.

If *getlogin* is called within a process that is not attached to a typewriter, it returns NULL. The correct procedure for determining the login name is to first call *getlogin* and if it fails, to call *getpwuid*.

FILES

/etc/utmp

SEE ALSO

getpwent(3), getgrent(3), utmp(5)

DIAGNOSTICS

Returns NULL (0) if name not found.

BUGS

The return values point to static data whose content is overwritten by each call.

NAME

getpass — read a password

SYNOPSIS

char *getpass(prompt)

char *prompt;

DESCRIPTION

Getpass reads a password from the file */dev/tty*, or if that cannot be opened, from the standard input, after prompting with the null-terminated string *prompt* and disabling echoing. A pointer is returned to a null-terminated string of at most 8 characters.

FILES

/dev/tty

SEE ALSO

crypt(3)

BUGS

The return value points to static data whose content is overwritten by each call.

NAME

        getpw — get name from UID

SYNOPSIS

        getpw(uid, buf)
        char *buf;

DESCRIPTION

        Getpw searches the password file for the (numerical) *uid*, and fills in *buf* with the corresponding
        line; it returns non-zero if *uid* could not be found. The line is null-terminated.

FILES

        /etc/passwd

SEE ALSO

        getpwent(3), passwd(5)

DIAGNOSTICS

        Non-zero return on error.

NAME

getpwent, getpwuid, getpwnam, setpwent, endpwent − get password file entry

SYNOPSIS

#include <pwd.h>

struct passwd *getpwent();

struct passwd *getpwuid(uid) int uid;

struct passwd *getpwnam(name) char *name;

int setpwent();

int endpwent();

DESCRIPTION

Getpwent, getpwuid and *getpwnam* each return a pointer to an object with the following structure containing the broken-out fields of a line in the password file.

```
struct   passwd {
         char    *pw_name;
         char    *pw_passwd;
         int     pw_uid;
         int     pw_gid;
         char    *pw_age;
         char    *pw_comment;
         char    *pw_gecos;
         char    *pw_dir;
         char    *pw_shell;
};
struct comment {
         char *c_dept;
         char *c_name;
         char *c_acct;
         char *c_bin;
};
```

The fields *pw_quota* and *pw_comment* are unused; the others have meanings described in *passwd*(5).

Getpwent reads the next line (opening the file if necessary); *setpwent* rewinds the file; *endpwent* closes it.

Getpwuid and *getpwnam* search from the beginning until a matching *uid* or *name* is found (or until EOF is encountered).

FILES

/etc/passwd

SEE ALSO

getlogin(3), getgrent(3), passwd(5)

DIAGNOSTICS

Null pointer (0) returned on EOF or error.

BUGS

All information is contained in a static area so it must be copied if it is to be saved.

NAME
        hypot, cabs — euclidean distance

SYNOPSIS
        #include <math.h>

        double hypot(x, y)
        double x, y;

        double cabs(z)
        struct { double x, y;} z;

DESCRIPTION
        Hypot and *cabs* return

$$sqrt(x*x + y*y),$$

        taking precautions against unwarranted overflows.

SEE ALSO
        exp(3) for *sqrt*

NAME

j0, j1, jn, y0, y1, yn — bessel functions

SYNOPSIS

#include <math.h>

double j0(x)
double x;

double j1(x)
double x;

double jn(n, x);
double x;

double y0(x)
double x;

double y1(x)
double x;

double yn(n, x)
double x;

DESCRIPTION

These functions calculate Bessel functions of the first and second kinds for real arguments and integer orders.

DIAGNOSTICS

Negative arguments cause *y0, y1,* and *yn* to return a huge negative value and set *errno* to EDOM.

NAME

　　l3tol, ltol3 — convert between 3-byte integers and long integers

SYNOPSIS

　　l3tol(lp, cp, n)
　　long *lp;
　　char *cp;

　　ltol3(cp, lp, n)
　　char *cp;
　　long *lp;

DESCRIPTION

　　L3tol converts a list of *n* three-byte integers packed into a character string pointed to by *cp* into a list of long integers pointed to by *lp*.

　　Ltol3 performs the reverse conversion from long integers (*lp*) to three-byte integers (*cp*).

　　These functions are useful for file-system maintenance; disk addresses are three bytes long.

SEE ALSO

　　filsys(5)

NAME

malloc, free, realloc, calloc — main memory allocator

SYNOPSIS

char *malloc(size)
unsigned size;

free(ptr)
char *ptr;

char *realloc(ptr, size)
char *ptr;
unsigned size;

char *calloc(nelem, elsize)
unsigned nelem, elsize;

DESCRIPTION

Malloc and *free* provide a simple general-purpose memory allocation package. *Malloc* returns a pointer to a block of at least *size* bytes beginning on a word boundary.

The argument to *free* is a pointer to a block previously allocated by *malloc*; this space is made available for further allocation, but its contents are left undisturbed.

Needless to say, grave disorder will result if the space assigned by *malloc* is overrun or if some random number is handed to *free*.

Malloc allocates the first big enough contiguous reach of free space found in a circular search from the last block allocated or freed, coalescing adjacent free blocks as it searches. It calls *sbrk* (see *break*(2)) to get more memory from the system when there is no suitable space already free.

Realloc changes the size of the block pointed to by *ptr* to *size* bytes and returns a pointer to the (possibly moved) block. The contents will be unchanged up to the lesser of the new and old sizes.

Realloc also works if *ptr* points to a block freed since the last call of *malloc, realloc* or *calloc*; thus sequences of *free, malloc* and *realloc* can exploit the search strategy of *malloc* to do storage compaction.

Calloc allocates space for an array of *nelem* elements of size *elsize*. The space is initialized to zeros.

Each of the allocation routines returns a pointer to space suitably aligned (after possible pointer coercion) for storage of any type of object.

DIAGNOSTICS

Malloc, realloc and *calloc* return a null pointer (0) if there is no available memory or if the arena has been detectably corrupted by storing outside the bounds of a block. *Malloc* may be recompiled to check the arena very stringently on every transaction; see the source code.

BUGS

When *realloc* returns 0, the block pointed to by *ptr* may be destroyed.

NAME
     mktemp — make a unique file name

SYNOPSIS
     char *mktemp(template)
     char *template;

DESCRIPTION
     Mktemp replaces *template* by a unique file name, and returns the address of the template. The template should look like a file name with six trailing X's, which will be replaced with the current process id and a unique letter.

SEE ALSO
     getpid(2)

NAME

monitor − prepare execution profile

SYNOPSIS

monitor(lowpc, highpc, buffer, bufsize, nfunc)
int (*lowpc)( ), (*highpc)( );
short buffer[ ];

DESCRIPTION

An executable program created by 'cc −p' automatically includes calls for *monitor* with default parameters; *monitor* needn't be called explicitly except to gain fine control over profiling.

Monitor is an interface to *profil*(2). *Lowpc* and *highpc* are the addresses of two functions; *buffer* is the address of a (user supplied) array of *bufsize* short integers. *Monitor* arranges to record a histogram of periodically sampled values of the program counter, and of counts of calls of certain functions, in the buffer. The lowest address sampled is that of *lowpc* and the highest is just below *highpc*. At most *nfunc* call counts can be kept; only calls of functions compiled with the profiling option −**p** of *cc*(1) are recorded. For the results to be significant, especially where there are small, heavily used routines, it is suggested that the buffer be no more than a few times smaller than the range of locations sampled.

To profile the entire program, it is sufficient to use

        extern etext();
        ...
        monitor((int)2, etext, buf, bufsize, nfunc);

Etext lies just above all the program text, see *end*(3).

To stop execution monitoring and write the results on the file *mon.out,* use

        monitor(0);

then *prof*(1) can be used to examine the results.

FILES

mon.out

SEE ALSO

prof(1), profil(2), cc(1)

NAME

itom, madd, msub, mult, mdiv, min, mout, pow, gcd, rpow — multiple precision integer arithmetic

SYNOPSIS

typedef struct { int len; short *val; } mint;

madd(a, b, c)
msub(a, b, c)
mult(a, b, c)
mdiv(a, b, q, r)
min(a)
mout(a)
pow(a, b, m, c)
gcd(a, b, c)
rpow(a, b, c)
msqrt(a, b, r)
mint *a, *b, *c, *m, *q, *r;

sdiv(a, n, q, r)
mint *a, *q;
short *r;

mint *itom(n)

DESCRIPTION

These routines perform arithmetic on integers of arbitrary length. The integers are stored using the defined type *mint*. Pointers to a *mint* should be initialized using the function *itom*, which sets the initial value to *n*. After that space is managed automatically by the routines.

madd, *msub*, *mult*, assign to their third arguments the sum, difference, and product, respectively, of their first two arguments. *mdiv* assigns the quotient and remainder, respectively, to its third and fourth arguments. *sdiv* is like *mdiv* except that the divisor is an ordinary integer. *msqrt* produces the square root and remainder of its first argument. *rpow* calculates *a* raised to the power *b*, while *pow* calculates this reduced modulo *m*. *min* and *mout* do decimal input and output.

The functions are obtained with the loader option *-lmp*.

DIAGNOSTICS

Illegal operations and running out of memory produce messages and core images.

NAME

        nlist − get entries from name list

SYNOPSIS

        #include <a.out.h>
        nlist(filename, nl)
        char *filename;
        struct nlist nl[ ];

DESCRIPTION

        Nlist examines the name list in the given executable output file and selectively extracts a list of values. The name list consists of an array of structures containing names, types and values. The list is terminated with a null name. Each name is looked up in the name list of the file. If the name is found, the type and value of the name are inserted in the next two fields. If the name is not found, both entries are set to 0. See *a.out*(5) for the structure declaration.

        This subroutine is useful for examining the system name list kept in the file **/unix**. In this way programs can obtain system addresses that are up to date.

SEE ALSO

        a.out(5)

DIAGNOSTICS

        All type entries are set to 0 if the file cannot be found or if it is not a valid namelist.

NAME

    perror, sys_errlist, sys_nerr — system error messages

SYNOPSIS

    perror(s)
    char *s;

    int sys_nerr;
    char *sys_errlist[];

DESCRIPTION

    Perror produces a short error message on the standard error file describing the last error
    encountered during a call to the system from a C program. First the argument string *s* is
    printed, then a colon, then the message and a new-line. Most usefully, the argument string is
    the name of the program which incurred the error. The error number is taken from the exter-
    nal variable *errno* (see *intro*(2)), which is set when errors occur but not cleared when non-
    erroneous calls are made.

    To simplify variant formatting of messages, the vector of message strings *sys_errlist* is provided;
    errno can be used as an index in this table to get the message string without the newline.
    Sys_nerr is the number of messages provided for in the table; it should be checked because new
    error codes may be added to the system before they are added to the table.

SEE ALSO

    intro(2)

NAME

pkopen, pkclose, pkread, pkwrite, pkfail — packet driver simulator

SYNOPSIS

char *pkopen(fd)

pkclose(ptr)
char *ptr;

pkread(ptr, buffer, count)
char *ptr, *buffer;

pkwrite(ptr, buffer, count)
char *ptr, *buffer;

pkfail( )

DESCRIPTION

These routines are a user-level implementation of the full-duplex end-to-end communication protocol described in *pk*(4). If *fd* is a file descriptor open for reading and writing, *pkopen* carries out the initial synchronization and returns an identifying pointer. The pointer is used as the first parameter to *pkread, pkwrite,* and *pkclose.*

Pkread, pkwrite and *pkclose* behave analogously to *read, write* and *close*(2). However, a write of zero bytes is meaningful and will produce a corresponding read of zero bytes.

SEE ALSO

pk(4), pkon(2)

DIAGNOSTICS

Pkfail is called upon persistent breakdown of communication. *Pkfail* must be supplied by the user.

Pkopen returns a null (0) pointer if packet protocol can not be established.

Pkread returns −1 on end of file, 0 in correspondence with a 0-length write.

BUGS

This simulation of *pk*(4) leaves something to be desired in needing special read and write routines, and in not being inheritable across calls of *exec*(2). Its prime use is on systems that lack *pk.*

These functions use *alarm*(2); simultaneous use of *alarm* for other puposes may cause trouble.

NAME

plot: openpl et al. — graphics interface

SYNOPSIS

openpl( )

erase( )

label(s) char s[ ];

line(x1, y1, x2, y2)

circle(x, y, r)

arc(x, y, x0, y0, x1, y1)

move(x, y)

cont(x, y)

point(x, y)

linemod(s) char s[ ];

space(x0, y0, x1, y1)

closepl( )

DESCRIPTION

These subroutines generate graphic output in a relatively device-independent manner. See *plot*(5) for a description of their effect. *Openpl* must be used before any of the others to open the device for writing. *Closepl* flushes the output.

String arguments to *label* and *linemod* are null-terminated, and do not contain newlines.

Various flavors of these functions exist for different output devices. They are obtained by the following *ld*(1) options:

−lplot   device-independent graphics stream on standard output for *plot*(1) filters
−l300   GSI 300 terminal
−l300s GSI 300S terminal
−l450   DASI 450 terminal
−l4014 Tektronix 4014 terminal

SEE ALSO

plot(5), plot(1), graph(1)

NAME

popen, pclose — initiate I/O to/from a process

SYNOPSIS

#include <stdio.h>

FILE *popen(command, type)
char *command, *type;

pclose(stream)
FILE *stream;

DESCRIPTION

The arguments to *popen* are pointers to null-terminated strings containing respectively a shell command line and an I/O mode, either "r" for reading or "w" for writing. It creates a pipe between the calling process and the command to be executed. The value returned is a stream pointer that can be used (as appropriate) to write to the standard input of the command or read from its standard output.

A stream opened by *popen* should be closed by *pclose*, which waits for the associated process to terminate and returns the exit status of the command.

Because open files are shared, a type "r" command may be used as an input filter, and a type "w" as an output filter.

SEE ALSO

pipe(2), fopen(3), fclose(3), system(3), wait(2)

DIAGNOSTICS

Popen returns a null pointer if files or processes cannot be created, or the Shell cannot be accessed.

Pclose returns −1 if *stream* is not associated with a 'popened' command.

BUGS

Buffered reading before opening an input filter may leave the standard input of that filter mispositioned. Similar problems with an output filter may be forestalled by careful buffer flushing, e.g. with *fflush*, see *fclose*(3).

NAME

printf, fprintf, sprintf — formatted output conversion

SYNOPSIS

#include <stdio.h>

printf(format [, arg] ...)
char *format;

fprintf(stream, format [, arg] ...)
FILE *stream;
char *format;

sprintf(s, format [, arg] ...)
char *s, format;

DESCRIPTION

Printf places output on the standard output stream *stdout*. *Fprintf* places output on the named output *stream*. *Sprintf* places 'output' in the string *s*, followed by the character '\0'.

Each of these functions converts, formats, and prints its arguments after the first under control of the first argument. The first argument is a character string which contains two types of objects: plain characters, which are simply copied to the output stream, and conversion specifications, each of which causes conversion and printing of the next successive *arg printf*.

Each conversion specification is introduced by the character %. Following the %, there may be

—   an optional minus sign '−' which specifies *left adjustment* of the converted value in the indicated field;

—   an optional digit string specifying a *field width;* if the converted value has fewer characters than the field width it will be blank-padded on the left (or right, if the left-adjustment indicator has been given) to make up the field width; if the field width begins with a zero, zero-padding will be done instead of blank-padding;

—   an optional period '.' which serves to separate the field width from the next digit string;

—   an optional digit string specifying a *precision* which specifies the number of digits to appear after the decimal point, for e- and f-conversion, or the maximum number of characters to be printed from a string;

—   the character **l** specifying that a following **d**, **o**, **x**, or **u** corresponds to a long integer *arg*. (A capitalized conversion code accomplishes the same thing.)

—   a character which indicates the type of conversion to be applied.

A field width or precision may be '*' instead of a digit string. In this case an integer *arg* supplies the field width or precision.

The conversion characters and their meanings are

dox   The integer *arg* is converted to decimal, octal, or hexadecimal notation respectively.

f   The float or double *arg* is converted to decimal notation in the style '[−]ddd.ddd' where the number of d's after the decimal point is equal to the precision specification for the argument. If the precision is missing, 6 digits are given; if the precision is explicitly 0, no digits and no decimal point are printed.

e   The float or double *arg* is converted in the style '[−]d.ddde±dd' where there is one digit before the decimal point and the number after is equal to the precision specification for the argument; when the precision is missing, 6 digits are produced.

g   The float or double *arg* is printed in style **d**, in style **f**, or in style **e**, whichever gives full precision in minimum space.

c   The character *arg* is printed. Null characters are ignored.

s   *Arg* is taken to be a string (character pointer) and characters from the string are printed until a null character or until the number of characters indicated by the precision specification is reached; however if the precision is 0 or missing all characters up to a null are printed.

u   The unsigned integer *arg* is converted to decimal and printed (the result will be in the range 0 to 65535).

%   Print a '%'; no argument is converted.

In no case does a non-existent or small field width cause truncation of a field; padding takes place only if the specified field width exceeds the actual width. Characters generated by *printf* are printed by *putc*(3).

Examples

To print a date and time in the form 'Sunday, July 3, 10:02', where *weekday* and *month* are pointers to null-terminated strings:

        printf("%s, %s %d, %02d:%02d", weekday, month, day, hour, min);

To print π to 5 decimals:

        printf("pi = %.5f", 4*atan(1.0));

SEE ALSO

        putc(3), scanf(3), ecvt(3)

BUGS

        Very wide fields (>128 characters) fail.

NAME
     putc, putchar, fputc, putw — put character or word on a stream

SYNOPSIS
     #include <stdio.h>

     int putc(c, stream)
     char c;
     FILE *stream;

     putchar(c)

     fputc(c, stream)
     FILE *stream;

     putw(w, stream)
     FILE *stream;

DESCRIPTION
     Putc appends the character *c* to the named output *stream*. It returns the character written.

     Putchar(c) is defined as *putc(c, stdout)*.

     Fputc behaves like *putc,* but is a genuine function rather than a macro. It may be used to save on object text.

     Putw appends word (i.e. **int**) *w* to the output *stream*. It returns the word written. *Putw* neither assumes nor causes special alignment in the file.

     The standard stream *stdout* is normally buffered if and only if the output does not refer to a terminal; this default may be changed by *setbuf*(3). The standard stream *stderr* is by default unbuffered unconditionally, but use of *freopen* (see *fopen*(3)) will cause it to become buffered; *setbuf*, again, will set the state to whatever is desired. When an output stream is unbuffered information appears on the destination file or terminal as soon as written; when it is buffered many characters are saved up and written as a block. *Fflush* (see *fclose*(3)) may be used to force the block out early.

SEE ALSO
     fopen(3), fclose(3), getc(3), puts(3), printf(3), fread(3)

DIAGNOSTICS
     These functions return the constant **EOF** upon error. Since this is a good integer, *ferror*(3) should be used to detect *putw* errors.

BUGS
     Because it is implemented as a macro, *putc* treats a *stream* argument with side effects improperly. In particular 'putc(c, *f++);' doesn't work sensibly.

NAME
        puts, fputs — put a string on a stream

SYNOPSIS
        #include <stdio.h>

        puts(s)
        char *s;

        fputs(s, stream)
        char *s;
        FILE *stream;

DESCRIPTION
        Puts copies the null-terminated string *s* to the standard output stream *stdout* and appends a new-
        line character.

        Fputs copies the null-terminated string *s* to the named output *stream*.

        Neither routine copies the terminal null character.

SEE ALSO
        fopen(3), gets(3), putc(3), printf(3), ferror(3)
        fread(3) for *fwrite*

BUGS
        Puts appends a newline, *fputs* does not, all in the name of backward compatibility.

NAME

 rand, srand — random number generator

SYNOPSIS

 srand(seed)
 int seed;

 rand( )

DESCRIPTION

 Rand uses a multiplicative congruential random number generator with period 2^{32} to return successive pseudo-random numbers in the range from 0 to $2^{15}-1$.

 The generator is reinitialized by calling *srand* with 1 as argument. It can be set to a random starting point by calling *srand* with whatever you like as argument.

NAME

qsort — quicker sort

SYNOPSIS

qsort(base, nel, width, compar)
char *base;
int (*compar)( );

DESCRIPTION

Qsort is an implementation of the quicker-sort algorithm. The first argument is a pointer to the base of the data; the second is the number of elements; the third is the width of an element in bytes; the last is the name of the comparison routine to be called with two arguments which are pointers to the elements being compared. The routine must return an integer less than, equal to, or greater than 0 according as the first argument is to be considered less than, equal to, or greater than the second.

SEE ALSO

sort(1)

NAME

scanf, fscanf, sscanf — formatted input conversion

SYNOPSIS

#include <stdio.h>

scanf(format [, pointer] . . .)
char *format;

fscanf(stream, format [, pointer] . . .)
FILE *stream;
char *format;

sscanf(s, format [, pointer] . . .)
char *s, *format;

DESCRIPTION

Scanf reads from the standard input stream *stdin*. *Fscanf* reads from the named input *stream*. *Sscanf* reads from the character string *s*. Each function reads characters, interprets them according to a format, and stores the results in its arguments. Each expects as arguments a control string *format,* described below, and a set of *pointer* arguments indicating where the converted input should be stored.

The control string usually contains conversion specifications, which are used to direct interpretation of input sequences. The control string may contain:

1. Blanks, tabs or newlines, which match optional white space in the input.

2. An ordinary character (not %) which must match the next character of the input stream.

3. Conversion specifications, consisting of the character %, an optional assignment suppressing character *, an optional numerical maximum field width, and a conversion character.

A conversion specification directs the conversion of the next input field; the result is placed in the variable pointed to by the corresponding argument, unless assignment suppression was indicated by *. An input field is defined as a string of non-space characters; it extends to the next inappropriate character or until the field width, if specified, is exhausted.

The conversion character indicates the interpretation of the input field; the corresponding pointer argument must usually be of a restricted type. The following conversion characters are legal:

%   a single '%' is expected in the input at this point; no assignment is done.

d   a decimal integer is expected; the corresponding argument should be an integer pointer.

o   an octal integer is expected; the corresponding argument should be a integer pointer.

x   a hexadecimal integer is expected; the corresponding argument should be an integer pointer.

s   a character string is expected; the corresponding argument should be a character pointer pointing to an array of characters large enough to accept the string and a terminating '\0', which will be added. The input field is terminated by a space character or a newline.

c   a character is expected; the corresponding argument should be a character pointer. The normal skip over space characters is suppressed in this case; to read the next non-space character, try '%1s'. If a field width is given, the corresponding argument should refer to a character array, and the indicated number of characters is read.

e   a floating point number is expected; the next field is converted accordingly and stored
f   through the corresponding argument, which should be a pointer to a *float*. The input format for floating point numbers is an optionally signed string of digits possibly containing a decimal point, followed by an optional exponent field consisting of an E or e followed by

an optionally signed integer.

[indicates a string not to be delimited by space characters. The left bracket is followed by a set of characters and a right bracket; the characters between the brackets define a set of characters making up the string. If the first character is not circumflex (ˆ), the input field is all characters until the first character not in the set between the brackets; if the first character after the left bracket is ˆ, the input field is all characters until the first character which is in the remaining set of characters between the brackets. The corresponding argument must point to a character array.

The conversion characters **d**, **o** and **x** may be capitalized or preceded by **l** to indicate that a pointer to **long** rather than to **int** is in the argument list. Similarly, the conversion characters **e** or **f** may be capitalized or preceded by **l** to indicate a pointer to **double** rather than to **float**. The conversion characters **d**, **o** and **x** may be preceeded by **h** to indicate a pointer to **short** rather than to **int**.

The *scanf* functions return the number of successfully matched and assigned input items. This can be used to decide how many input items were found. The constant **EOF** is returned upon end of input; note that this is different from 0, which means that no conversion was done; if conversion was intended, it was frustrated by an inappropriate character in the input.

For example, the call

```
int i; float x; char name[50];
scanf( "%d%f%s", &i, &x, name);
```

with the input line

```
25   54.32E−1  thompson
```

will assign to *i* the value 25, *x* the value 5.432, and *name* will contain *'thompson\0'*. Or,

```
int i; float x; char name[50];
scanf("%2d%f%*d%[1234567890]", &i, &x, name);
```

with input

```
56789 0123 56a72
```

will assign 56 to *i*, 789.0 to *x*, skip '0123', and place the string '56\0' in *name*. The next call to *getchar* will return 'a'.

SEE ALSO
atof(3), getc(3), printf(3)

DIAGNOSTICS
The *scanf* functions return **EOF** on end of input, and a short count for missing or illegal data items.

BUGS
The success of literal matches and suppressed assignments is not directly determinable.

NAME
     setbuf — assign buffering to a stream

SYNOPSIS
     #include <stdio.h>

     setbuf(stream, buf)
     FILE *stream;
     char *buf;

DESCRIPTION
     Setbuf is used after a stream has been opened but before it is read or written. It causes the character array *buf* to be used instead of an automatically allocated buffer. If *buf* is the constant pointer NULL, input/output will be completely unbuffered.

     A manifest constant BUFSIZ tells how big an array is needed:

                         char buf[BUFSIZ];

     A buffer is normally obtained from *malloc*(3) upon the first *getc* or *putc*(3) on the file, except that output streams directed to terminals, and the standard error stream *stderr* are normally not buffered.

SEE ALSO
     fopen(3), getc(3), putc(3), malloc(3)

NAME

setjmp, longjmp — non-local goto

SYNOPSIS

#include <setjmp.h>

setjmp(env)
jmp_buf env;

longjmp(env, val)
jmp_buf env;

DESCRIPTION

These routines are useful for dealing with errors and interrupts encountered in a low-level sub-routine of a program.

Setjmp saves its stack environment in *env* for later use by *longjmp*. It returns value 0.

Longjmp restores the environment saved by the last call of *setjmp*. It then returns in such a way that execution continues as if the call of *setjmp* had just returned the value *val* to the function that invoked *setjmp*, which must not itself have returned in the interim. All accessible data have values as of the time *longjmp* was called.

SEE ALSO

signal(2)

NAME

sin, cos, tan, asin, acos, atan, atan2 − trigonometric functions

SYNOPSIS

#include <math.h>

double sin(x)
double x;

double cos(x)
double x;

double asin(x)
double x;

double acos(x)
double x;

double atan(x)
double x;

double atan2(x, y)
double x, y;

DESCRIPTION

Sin, cos and *tan* return trigonometric functions of radian arguments. The magnitude of the argument should be checked by the caller to make sure the result is meaningful.

Asin returns the arc sin in the range $-\pi/2$ to $\pi/2$.

Acos returns the arc cosine in the range 0 to π.

Atan returns the arc tangent of x in the range $-\pi/2$ to $\pi/2$.

Atan2 returns the arc tangent of x/y in the range $-\pi$ to π.

DIAGNOSTICS

Arguments of magnitude greater than 1 cause *asin* and *acos* to return value 0; *errno* is set to EDOM. The value of *tan* at its singular points is a huge number, and *errno* is set to ERANGE.

BUGS

The value of *tan* for arguments greater than about 2**31 is garbage.

NAME

sinh, cosh, tanh − hyperbolic functions

SYNOPSIS

#include <math.h>

double sinh(x)
double x;

double cosh(x)
double x;

double tanh(x)
double x;

DESCRIPTION

These functions compute the designated hyperbolic functions for real arguments.

DIAGNOSTICS

Sinh and *cosh* return a huge value of appropriate sign when the correct value would overflow.

NAME

sleep — suspend execution for interval

SYNOPSIS

sleep(seconds)
unsigned seconds;

DESCRIPTION

The current process is suspended from execution for the number of seconds specified by the argument. The actual suspension time may be up to 1 second less than that requested, because scheduled wakeups occur at fixed 1-second intervals, and an arbitrary amount longer because of other activity in the system.

The routine is implemented by setting an alarm clock signal and pausing until it occurs. The previous state of this signal is saved and restored. If the sleep time exceeds the time to the alarm signal, the process sleeps only until the signal would have occurred, and the signal is sent 1 second later.

SEE ALSO

alarm(2), pause(2)

NAME

stdio — standard buffered input/output package

SYNOPSIS

include <stdio.h>

FILE *stdin;
FILE *stdout;
FILE *stderr;

DESCRIPTION

The functions described in Sections 3S constitute an efficient user-level buffering scheme. The in-line macros *getc* and *putc*(3) handle characters quickly. The higher level routines *gets, fgets, scanf, fscanf, fread, puts, fputs, printf, fprintf, fwrite* all use *getc* and *putc;* they can be freely inter-mixed.

A file with associated buffering is called a *stream*, and is declared to be a pointer to a defined type FILE. *Fopen*(3) creates certain descriptive data for a stream and returns a pointer to designate the stream in all further transactions. There are three normally open streams with constant pointers declared in the include file and associated with the standard open files:

stdin	standard input file
stdout	standard output file
stderr	standard error file

A constant 'pointer' NULL (0) designates no stream at all.

An integer constant EOF (−1) is returned upon end of file or error by integer functions that deal with streams.

Any routine that uses the standard input/output package must include the header file <stdio.h> of pertinent macro definitions. The functions and constants mentioned in sections labeled 3S are declared in the include file and need no further declaration. The constants, and the following 'functions' are implemented as macros; redeclaration of these names is perilous: *getc, getchar, putc, putchar, feof, ferror, fileno*.

SEE ALSO

open(2), close(2), read(2), write(2)

DIAGNOSTICS

The value EOF is returned uniformly to indicate that a FILE pointer has not been initialized with *fopen*, input (output) has been attempted on an output (input) stream, or a FILE pointer designates corrupt or otherwise unintelligible FILE data.

NAME

strcat, strncat, strcmp, strncmp, strcpy, strncpy, strlen, index, rindex — string operations

SYNOPSIS

```
char *strcat(s1, s2)
char *s1, *s2;

char *strncat(s1, s2, n)
char *s1, *s2;

strcmp(s1, s2)
char *s1, *s2;

strncmp(s1, s2, n)
char *s1, *s2;

char *strcpy(s1, s2)
char *s1, *s2;

char *strncpy(s1, s2, n)
char *s1, *s2;

strlen(s)
char *s;

char *index(s, c)
char *s, c;

char *rindex(s, c)
char *s;
```

DESCRIPTION

These functions operate on null-terminated strings. They do not check for overflow of any receiving string.

Strcat appends a copy of string *s2* to the end of string *s1*. *Strncat* copies at most *n* characters. Both return a pointer to the null-terminated result.

Strcmp compares its arguments and returns an integer greater than, equal to, or less than 0, according as *s1* is lexicographically greater than, equal to, or less than *s2*. *Strncmp* makes the same comparison but looks at at most *n* characters.

Strcpy copies string *s2* to *s1*, stopping after the null character has been moved. *Strncpy* copies exactly *n* characters, truncating or null-padding *s2;* the target may not be null-terminated if the length of *s2* is *n* or more. Both return *s1*.

Strlen returns the number of non-null characters in *s*.

Index (*rindex*) returns a pointer to the first (last) occurrence of character *c* in string *s*, or zero if *c* does not occur in the string.

BUGS

Strcmp uses native character comparison, which is signed on PDP11's, unsigned on other machines.

NAME

　　　swab − swap bytes

SYNOPSIS

　　　swab(from, to, nbytes)
　　　char *from, *to;

DESCRIPTION

　　　Swab copies *nbytes* bytes pointed to by *from* to the position pointed to by *to*, exchanging adjacent even and odd bytes. It is useful for carrying binary data between PDP11's and other machines. *Nbytes* should be even.

NAME

system — issue a shell command

SYNOPSIS

system(string)
char *string;

DESCRIPTION

System causes the *string* to be given to *sh*(1) as input as if the string had been typed as a command at a terminal. The current process waits until the shell has completed, then returns the exit status of the shell.

SEE ALSO

popen(3), exec(2), wait(2)

DIAGNOSTICS

Exit status 127 indicates the shell couldn't be executed.

NAME

ttyname, isatty, ttyslot — find name of a terminal

SYNOPSIS

char *ttyname(fildes)

isatty(fildes)

ttyslot( )

DESCRIPTION

Ttyname returns a pointer to the null-terminated path name of the terminal device associated with file descriptor *fildes*.

Isatty returns 1 if *fildes* is associated with a terminal device, 0 otherwise.

Ttyslot returns the number of the entry in the *ttys*(5) file for the control terminal of the current process.

FILES

/dev/*
/etc/ttys

SEE ALSO

ioctl(2), ttys(5)

DIAGNOSTICS

Ttyname returns a null pointer (0) if *fildes* does not describe a terminal device in directory '/dev'.

Ttyslot returns 0 if '/etc/ttys' is inaccessible or if it cannot determine the control terminal.

BUGS

The return value points to static data whose content is overwritten by each call.

NAME

    ungetc — push character back into input stream

SYNOPSIS

    #include <stdio.h>

    ungetc(c, stream)
    FILE *stream;

DESCRIPTION

    Ungetc pushes the character *c* back on an input stream. That character will be returned by the next *getc* call on that stream. *Ungetc* returns *c*.

    One character of pushback is guaranteed provided something has been read from the stream and the stream is actually buffered. Attempts to push EOF are rejected.

    Fseek(3) erases all memory of pushed back characters.

SEE ALSO

    getc(3), setbuf(3), fseek(3)

DIAGNOSTICS

    Ungetc returns **EOF** if it can't push a character back.

Section 4
SPECIAL FILES

NAME

      cat — phototypesetter interface

DESCRIPTION

      Cat provides the interface to a Graphic Systems C/A/T phototypesetter. Bytes written on the file specify font, size, and other control information as well as the characters to be flashed. The coding will not be described here.

      Only one process may have this file open at a time. It is write-only.

FILES

      /dev/cat

SEE ALSO

      troff(1)

      Phototypesetter interface specification

NAME

dn — DN-11 ACU interface

DESCRIPTION

The *dn?* files are write-only. The permissible codes are:

0-9   dial 0-9
:   dial *
;   dial #
—   4 second delay for second dial tone
<   end-of-number

The entire telephone number must be presented in a single *write* system call.

It is recommended that an end-of-number code be given even though not all ACU's actually require it.

FILES

/dev/dn0   connected to 801 with dp0
/dev/dn1   not currently connected
/dev/dn2   not currently connected

SEE ALSO

dp(4)

NAME

du, dp — DU-11 201 data-phone interface

DESCRIPTION

The *dp0* file is a 201 data-phone interface. *Read* and *write* calls to dp0 are limited to a maximum of 512 bytes. Each write call is sent as a single record. Seven bits from each byte are written along with an eighth odd parity bit. The sync must be user supplied. Each read call returns characters received from a single record. Seven bits are returned unaltered; the eighth bit is set if the byte was not received in odd parity. A 10 second time out is set and a zero-byte record is returned if nothing is received in that time.

FILES

/dev/dp0

SEE ALSO

dn(4)

BUGS

The name *dp0* is a historical dreg.

NAME

hp — RH-11/RP04, RP05, RP06 moving-head disk

DESCRIPTION

The octal representation of the minor device number is encoded *idp*, where *i* is an interleave flag, *d* is a physical drive number, and *p* is a pseudodrive (subsection) within a physical unit. If *i* is 0, the origins and sizes of the pseudodisks on each drive, counted in cylinders of 418 512-byte blocks, are:

disk	start	length
0	0	23
1	23	21
2	0	0
3	0	0
4	44	386
5	430	385
6	44	367
7	44	771

If *i* is 1, the minor device consists of the specified pseudodisk on drives numbered 0 through the designated drive number. Successively numbered blocks are distributed across the drives in rotation.

Systems distributed for these devices use disk 0 for the root, disk 1 for swapping, and disk 4 (RP04/5) or disk 7 (RP06) for a mounted user file system.

The block files access the disk via the system's normal buffering mechanism and may be read and written without regard to physical disk records.

A 'raw' interface provides for direct transmission between the disk and the user's read or write buffer. A single read or write call results in exactly one I/O operation and therefore raw I/O is considerably more efficient when many words are transmitted. The names of the raw files conventionally begin with an extra 'r.' In raw I/O the buffer must begin on a word boundary, and raw I/O to an interleaved device is likely to have disappointing results.

FILES

/dev/rp?, /dev/rrp?

SEE ALSO

rp(4)

BUGS

In raw I/O *read* and *write*(2) truncate file offsets to 512-byte block boundaries, and *write* scribbles on the tail of incomplete blocks. Thus, in programs that are likely to access raw devices, *read, write* and *lseek*(2) should always deal in 512-byte multiples.

Raw device drivers don't work on interleaved devices.

NAME

    hs — RH11/RS03-RS04 fixed-head disk file

DESCRIPTION

    The files *hs0* ... *hs7* refer to RJS03 disk drives 0 through 7. The files *hs8* ... *hs15* refer to RJS04 disk drives 0 through 7. The RJS03 drives are each 1024 blocks long and the RJS04 drives are 2048 blocks long.

    The *hs* files access the disk via the system's normal buffering mechanism and may be read and written without regard to physical disk records. There is also a 'raw' inteface which provides for direct transmission between the disk and the user's read or write buffer. A single read or write call results in exactly one I/O operation and therefore raw I/O is considerably more efficient when many words are transmitted. The names of the raw HS files begin with *rhs*. The same minor device considerations hold for the raw interface as for the normal interface.

    In raw I/O the buffer must begin on a word boundary, and counts should be a multiple of 512 bytes (a disk block). Likewise *lseek* calls should specify a multiple of 512 bytes.

FILES

    /dev/hs?, /dev/rhs?

NAME

ht − RH-11/TU-16 magtape interface

DESCRIPTION

The files *mt0, mt1,* ... refer to the DEC RH/TM/TU16 magtape. When opened for reading or writing, the tape is not rewound. When closed, it is rewound (unless the 0200 bit is on, see below). If the tape was open for writing, a double end-of-file is written. If the tape is not to be rewound the tape is backspaced to just between the two tapemarks.

A standard tape consists of a series of 512 byte records terminated by a double end-of-file. To the extent possible, the system makes it possible, if inefficient, to treat the tape like any other file. Seeks have their usual meaning and it is possible to read or write a byte at a time. Writing in very small units is inadvisable, however, because it tends to create monstrous record gaps.

The last octal digit of the minor device number selects the drive. The middle digit selects a controller. The initial digit is even to select 800 BPI, odd to select 1600 BPI. If the 0200 bit is on (initial digit 2 or 3), the tape is not rewound on close. Note that the minor device number has no necessary connection with the file name, and in fact *tp*(1) turns the short name *x* into '/dev/mt*x*'.

The *mt* files discussed above are useful when it is desired to access the tape in a way compatible with ordinary files. When foreign tapes are to be dealt with, and especially when long records are to be read or written, the 'raw' interface is appropriate. The associated files may be named *rmt0,* ..., *rmt7,* but the same minor-device considerations as for the regular files still apply.

Each *read* or *write* call reads or writes the next record on the tape. In the write case the record has the same length as the buffer given. During a read, the record size is passed back as the number of bytes read, provided it is no greater than the buffer size; if the record is long, an error is indicated. In raw tape I/O, the buffer must begin on a word boundary and the count must be even. Seeks are ignored. A zero count is returned when a tape mark is read; another read will fetch the first record of the next tape file.

FILES

/dev/mt?, /dev/rmt?

SEE ALSO

tp(1)

BUGS

The magtape system is supposed to be able to take 64 drives. Such addressing has never been tried.

Taking a drive off line, or running off the end of tape, while writing have been known to hang the system.

If any non-data error is encountered, it refuses to do anything more until closed. In raw I/O, there should be a way to perform forward and backward record and file spacing and to write an EOF mark explicitly.

NAME

mem, kmem — core memory

DESCRIPTION

Mem is a special file that is an image of the core memory of the computer. It may be used, for example, to examine, and even to patch the system. *Kmem* is the same as *mem* except that kernel virtual memory rather than physical memory is accessed.

Byte addresses are interpreted as memory addresses. References to non-existent locations return errors.

Examining and patching device registers is likely to lead to unexpected results when read-only or write-only bits are present.

On PDP11's, the I/O page begins at location 0160000 of *kmem* and per-process data for the current process begins at 0140000.

FILES

/dev/mem, /dev/kmem

BUGS

On PDP11's, memory files are accessed one byte at a time, an inapproriate method for some device registers.

NAME

    null — data sink

DESCRIPTION

    Data written on a null special file is discarded.

    Reads from a null special file always return 0 bytes.

FILES

    /dev/null

NAME
        pk — packet driver

DESCRIPTION
        The packet driver implements a full-duplex end-to-end flow control strategy for machine-to-machine communication. Packet driver protocol is established by calling *pkon*(2) with a character device file descriptor and a desired packet size in bytes. The packet size must be a power of 2, $32 \leq size \leq 4096$. The file descriptor must represent an 8-bit data path. This is normally obtained by setting the device in raw mode (see *ioctl*(2)).

        The actual packet size, which may be smaller than the desired packet size, is arrived at by negotiation with the packet driver at the remote end of the data link.

        The packet driver maintains two data areas for incoming and outgoing packets. The output area is needed to implement retransmission on errors, and arriving packets are queued in the input area. Data arriving for a file not open for reading is discarded. Initially the size of both areas is set to two packets.

        It is not necessary that reads and writes be multiples of the packet size although there is less system overhead if they are. Read operations return the maximum amount of data available from the input area up to the number of bytes specified in the system call. The buffer sizes in write operations are not normally transmitted across the link. However, writes of zero length are treated specially and are reflected at the remote end as a zero-length read. This facilitates marking the serial byte stream, usually for delimiting files.

        When one side of a packet driver link is shut down by *close*(2) *or pkoff* (see *pkon*(2)), *read*(2) on the other side will return 0, and *write* on the other side will raise a SIGPIPE signal.

SEE ALSO
        pkon(2), pkopen(3)

NAME

rf — RF11/RS11 fixed-head disk file

DESCRIPTION

This file refers to the concatenation of all RS-11 disks.

Each disk contains 1024 256-word blocks. The length of the combined RF file is 1024×(minor+1) blocks. That is minor device zero is taken to be 1024 blocks long; minor device one is 2048, etc.

The *rf0* file accesses the disk via the system's normal buffering mechanism and may be read and written without regard to physical disk records. There is also a 'raw' interface which provides for direct transmission between the disk and the user's read or write buffer. A single read or write call results in exactly one I/O operation and therefore raw I/O is considerably more efficient when many words are transmitted. The name of the raw RF file is *rrf0*. The same minor device considerations hold for the raw interface as for the normal interface.

In raw I/O the buffer must begin on a word boundary, and counts should be a multiple of 512 bytes (a disk block). Likewise *seek* calls should specify a multiple of 512 bytes.

FILES

/dev/rf0, /dev/rrf0

BUGS

The 512-byte restrictions on the raw device are not physically necessary, but are still imposed.

NAME

    rk — RK-11/RK03 or RK05 disk

DESCRIPTION

Rk? refers to an entire disk as a single sequentially-addressed file. Its 256-word blocks are numbered 0 to 4871. Minor device numbers are drive numbers on one controller.

The *rk* files discussed above access the disk via the system's normal buffering mechanism and may be read and written without regard to physical disk records. There is also a 'raw' interface which provides for direct transmission between the disk and the user's read or write buffer. A single read or write call results in exactly one I/O operation and therefore raw I/O is considerably more efficient when many words are transmitted. The names of the raw RK files begin with *rrk* and end with a number which selects the same disk as the corresponding *rk* file.

In raw I/O the buffer must begin on a word boundary, and counts should be a multiple of 512 bytes (a disk block). Likewise *seek* calls should specify a multiple of 512 bytes.

FILES

    /dev/rk?, /dev/rrk?

BUGS

In raw I/O *read* and *write*(2) truncate file offsets to 512-byte block boundaries, and *write* scribbles on the tail of incomplete blocks. Thus, in programs that are likely to access raw devices, *read, write* and *lseek*(2) should always deal in 512-byte multiples.

NAME

rp — RP-11/RP03 moving-head disk

DESCRIPTION

The files *rp0* ... *rp7* refer to sections of RP disk drive 0. The files *rp8* ... *rp15* refer to drive 1 etc. This allows a large disk to be broken up into more manageable pieces.

The origin and size of the pseudo-disks on each drive are as follows:

disk	start	length
0	0	81000
1	0	5000
2	5000	2000
3	7000	74000
4-7	unassigned	

Thus rp0 covers the whole drive, while rp1, rp2, rp3 can serve usefully as a root, swap, and mounted user file system respectively.

The *rp* files access the disk via the system's normal buffering mechanism and may be read and written without regard to physical disk records. There is also a 'raw' interface which provides for direct transmission between the disk and the user's read or write buffer. A single read or write call results in exactly one I/O operation and therefore raw I/O is considerably more efficient when many words are transmitted. The names of the raw RP files begin with *rrp* and end with a number which selects the same disk section as the corresponding *rp* file.

In raw I/O the buffer must begin on a word boundary.

FILES

/dev/rp?, /dev/rrp?

SEE ALSO

hp(4)

BUGS

In raw I/O *read* and *write*(2) truncate file offsets to 512-byte block boundaries, and *write* scribbles on the tail of incomplete blocks. Thus, in programs that are likely to access raw devices, *read, write* and *lseek*(2) should always deal in 512-byte multiples.

NAME

    tc — TC-11/TU56 DECtape

DESCRIPTION

    The files *tap0* ... *tap7* refer to the TC-11/TU56 DECtape drives 0 to 7.

    The 256-word blocks on a standard DECtape are numbered 0 to 577.

FILES

    /dev/tap?

SEE ALSO

    tp(1)

NAME
     tm — TM-11/TU-10 magtape interface

DESCRIPTION
     The files *mt0, ..., mt7* refer to the DEC TU10/TM11 magtape. When closed it can be rewound
     or not, see below. If it was open for writing, two end-of-files are written. If the tape is not to
     be rewound it is positioned with the head between the two tapemarks.

     If the 0200 bit is on in the minor device number the tape is not rewound when closed.

     A standard tape consists of a series of 512 byte records terminated by an end-of-file. To the
     extent possible, the system makes it possible, if inefficient, to treat the tape like any other file.
     Seeks have their usual meaning and it is possible to read or write a byte at a time. Writing in
     very small units is inadvisable, however, because it tends to create monstrous record gaps.

     The *mt* files discussed above are useful when it is desired to access the tape in a way compatible
     with ordinary files. When foreign tapes are to be dealt with, and especially when long records
     are to be read or written, the 'raw' interface is appropriate. The associated files are named
     rmt0, ..., rmt7. Each *read* or *write* call reads or writes the next record on the tape. In the write
     case the record has the same length as the buffer given. During a read, the record size is
     passed back as the number of bytes read, provided it is no greater than the buffer size; if the
     record is long, an error is indicated. In raw tape I/O, the buffer must begin on a word boun-
     dary and the count must be even. Seeks are ignored. A zero byte count is returned when a
     tape mark is read, but another read will fetch the first record of the new tape file.

FILES
     /dev/mt?, /dev/rmt?

SEE ALSO
     tp(1)

BUGS
     If any non-data error is encountered, it refuses to do anything more until closed. In raw I/O,
     there should be a way to perform forward and backward record and file spacing and to write an
     EOF mark.

NAME

tty — general terminal interface

DESCRIPTION

This section describes both a particular special file, and the general nature of the terminal interface.

The file */dev/tty* is, in each process, a synonym for the control terminal associated with that process. It is useful for programs that wish to be sure of writing messages on the terminal no matter how output has been redirected. It can also be used for programs that demand a file name for output, when typed output is desired and it is tiresome to find out which terminal is currently in use.

As for terminals in general: all of the low-speed asynchronous communications ports use the same general interface, no matter what hardware is involved. The remainder of this section discusses the common features of the interface.

When a terminal file is opened, it causes the process to wait until a connection is established. In practice user's programs seldom open these files; they are opened by *init* and become a user's input and output file. The very first terminal file open in a process becomes the *control terminal* for that process. The control terminal plays a special role in handling quit or interrupt signals, as discussed below. The control terminal is inherited by a child process during a *fork*, even if the control terminal is closed. The set of processes that thus share a control terminal is called a *process group*; all members of a process group receive certain signals together, see DEL below and *kill*(2).

A terminal associated with one of these files ordinarily operates in full-duplex mode. Characters may be typed at any time, even while output is occurring, and are only lost when the system's character input buffers become completely choked, which is rare, or when the user has accumulated the maximum allowed number of input characters that have not yet been read by some program. Currently this limit is 256 characters. When the input limit is reached all the saved characters are thrown away without notice.

Normally, terminal input is processed in units of lines. This means that a program attempting to read will be suspended until an entire line has been typed. Also, no matter how many characters are requested in the read call, at most one line will be returned. It is not however necessary to read a whole line at once; any number of characters may be requested in a read, even one, without losing information. There are special modes, discussed below, that permit the program to read each character as typed without waiting for a full line.

During input, erase and kill processing is normally done. By default, the character '#' erases the last character typed, except that it will not erase beyond the beginning of a line or an EOT. By default, the character '@' kills the entire line up to the point where it was typed, but not beyond an EOT. Both these characters operate on a keystroke basis independently of any backspacing or tabbing that may have been done. Either '@' or '#' may be entered literally by preceding it by '\'; the erase or kill character remains, but the '\' disappears. These two characters may be changed to others.

When desired, all upper-case letters are mapped into the corresponding lower-case letter. The upper-case letter may be generated by preceding it by '\'. In addition, the following escape sequences can be generated on output and accepted on input:

```
for    use
`      \`
|      \!
~      \^
{      \(
}      \)
```

Certain ASCII control characters have special meaning. These characters are not passed to a reading program except in raw mode where they lose their special character. Also, it is possible to change these characters from the default; see below.

EOT   (Control-D) may be used to generate an end of file from a terminal. When an EOT is received, all the characters waiting to be read are immediately passed to the program, without waiting for a new-line, and the EOT is discarded. Thus if there are no characters waiting, which is to say the EOT occurred at the beginning of a line, zero characters will be passed back, and this is the standard end-of-file indication.

DEL   (Rubout) is not passed to a program but generates an *interrupt* signal which is sent to all processes with the associated control terminal. Normally each such process is forced to terminate, but arrangements may be made either to ignore the signal or to receive a trap to an agreed-upon location. See *signal*(2).

FS   (Control-\ or control-shift-L) generates the *quit* signal. Its treatment is identical to the interrupt signal except that unless a receiving process has made other arrangements it will not only be terminated but a core image file will be generated.

DC3   (Control-S) delays all printing on the terminal until something is typed in.

DC1   (Control-Q) restarts printing after DC3 without generating any input to a program.

When the carrier signal from the dataset drops (usually because the user has hung up his terminal) a *hangup* signal is sent to all processes with the terminal as control terminal. Unless other arrangements have been made, this signal causes the processes to terminate. If the hangup signal is ignored, any read returns with an end-of-file indication. Thus programs that read a terminal and test for end-of-file on their input can terminate appropriately when hung up on.

When one or more characters are written, they are actually transmitted to the terminal as soon as previously-written characters have finished typing. Input characters are echoed by putting them in the output queue as they arrive. When a process produces characters more rapidly than they can be typed, it will be suspended when its output queue exceeds some limit. When the queue has drained down to some threshold the program is resumed. Even parity is always generated on output. The EOT character is not transmitted (except in raw mode) to prevent terminals that respond to it from hanging up.

Several *ioctl*(2) calls apply to terminals. Most of them use the following structure, defined in <*sgtty.h*>:

```
struct sgttyb {
        char    sg_ispeed;
        char    sg_ospeed;
        char    sg_erase;
        char    sg_kill;
        int     sg_flags;
};
```

The *sg_ispeed* and *sg_ospeed* fields describe the input and output speeds of the device according to the following table, which corresponds to the DEC DH-11 interface. If other hardware is used, impossible speed changes are ignored. Symbolic values in the table are as defined in <*sgtty.h*>.

B0	0	(hang up dataphone)
B50	1	50 baud
B75	2	75 baud
B110	3	110 baud
B134	4	134.5 baud
B150	5	150 baud

B200	6	200 baud
B300	7	300 baud
B600	8	600 baud
B1200	9	1200 baud
B1800	10	1800 baud
B2400	11	2400 baud
B4800	12	4800 baud
B9600	13	9600 baud
EXTA	14	External A
EXTB	15	External B

In the current configuration, only 110, 150, 300 and 1200 baud are really supported on dial-up lines. Code conversion and line control required for IBM 2741's (134.5 baud) must be implemented by the user's program. The half-duplex line discipline required for the 202 dataset (1200 baud) is not supplied; full-duplex 212 datasets work fine.

The *sg_erase* and *sg_kill* fields of the argument structure specify the erase and kill characters respectively. (Defaults are # and @.)

The *sg_flags* field of the argument structure contains several bits that determine the system's treatment of the terminal:

ALLDELAY	0177400	Delay algorithm selection
BSDELAY	0100000	Select backspace delays (not implemented):
BS0	0	
BS1	0100000	
VTDELAY	0040000	Select form-feed and vertical-tab delays:
FF0	0	
FF1	0100000	
CRDELAY	0030000	Select carriage-return delays:
CR0	0	
CR1	0010000	
CR2	0020000	
CR3	0030000	
TBDELAY	0006000	Select tab delays:
TAB0	0	
TAB1	0001000	
TAB2	0004000	
XTABS	0006000	
NLDELAY	0001400	Select new-line delays:
NL0	0	
NL1	0000400	
NL2	0001000	
NL3	0001400	
EVENP	0000200	Even parity allowed on input (most terminals)
ODDP	0000100	Odd parity allowed on input
RAW	0000040	Raw mode: wake up on all characters, 8-bit interface
CRMOD	0000020	Map CR into LF; echo LF or CR as CR-LF
ECHO	0000010	Echo (full duplex)
LCASE	0000004	Map upper case to lower on input
CBREAK	0000002	Return each character as soon as typed
TANDEM	0000001	Automatic flow control

The delay bits specify how long transmission stops to allow for mechanical or other movement when certain characters are sent to the terminal. In all cases a value of 0 indicates no delay.

Backspace delays are currently ignored but might be used for Terminet 300's.

If a form-feed/vertical tab delay is specified, it lasts for about 2 seconds.

Carriage-return delay type 1 lasts about .08 seconds and is suitable for the Terminet 300. Delay type 2 lasts about .16 seconds and is suitable for the VT05 and the TI 700. Delay type 3 is unimplemented and is 0.

New-line delay type 1 is dependent on the current column and is tuned for Teletype model 37's. Type 2 is useful for the VT05 and is about .10 seconds. Type 3 is unimplemented and is 0.

Tab delay type 1 is dependent on the amount of movement and is tuned to the Teletype model 37. Type 3, called XTABS, is not a delay at all but causes tabs to be replaced by the appropriate number of spaces on output.

Characters with the wrong parity, as determined by bits 200 and 100, are ignored.

In raw mode, every character is passed immediately to the program without waiting until a full line has been typed. No erase or kill processing is done; the end-of-file indicator (EOT), the interrupt character (DEL) and the quit character (FS) are not treated specially. There are no delays and no echoing, and no replacement of one character for another; characters are a full 8 bits for both input and output (parity is up to the program).

Mode 020 causes input carriage returns to be turned into new-lines; input of either CR or LF causes LF-CR both to be echoed (for terminals with a new-line function).

CBREAK is a sort of half-cooked (rare?) mode. Programs can read each character as soon as typed, instead of waiting for a full line, but quit and interrupt work, and output delays, case-translation, CRMOD, XTABS, ECHO, and parity work normally. On the other hand there is no erase or kill, and no special treatment of \ or EOT.

TANDEM mode causes the system to produce a stop character (default DC3) whenever the input queue is in danger of overflowing, and a start character (default DC1) when the input queue has drained sufficiently. It is useful for flow control when the 'terminal' is actually another machine that obeys the conventions.

Several *ioctl* calls have the form:

#include <sgtty.h>

ioctl(fildes, code, arg)
struct sgttyb *arg;

The applicable codes are:

TIOCGETP
   Fetch the parameters associated with the terminal, and store in the pointed-to structure.

TIOCSETP
   Set the parameters according to the pointed-to structure. The interface delays until output is quiescent, then throws away any unread characters, before changing the modes.

TIOCSETN
   Set the parameters but do not delay or flush input. Switching out of RAW or CBREAK mode may cause some garbage input.

With the following codes the *arg* is ignored.

TIOCEXCL
   Set "exclusive-use" mode: no further opens are permitted until the file has been closed.

TIOCNXCL
>	Turn off "exclusive-use" mode.

TIOCHPCL
>	When the file is closed for the last time, hang up the terminal. This is useful when the line is associated with an ACU used to place outgoing calls.

TIOCFLUSH
>	All characters waiting in input or output queues are flushed.

The following codes affect characters that are special to the terminal interface. The argument is a pointer to the following structure, defined in *<sgtty.h>*:

```
struct tchars {
        char    t_intrc;            /* interrupt */
        char    t_quitc;            /* quit */
        char    t_startc;           /* start output */
        char    t_stopc;            /* stop output */
        char    t_eofc;             /* end-of-file */
        char    t_brkc;             /* input delimiter (like nl) */
};
```

The default values for these characters are DEL, FS, DC1, DC3, EOT, and -1. A character value of -1 eliminates the effect of that character. The *t_brkc* character, by default -1, acts like a new-line in that it terminates a 'line,' is echoed, and is passed to the program. The 'stop' and 'start' characters may be the same, to produce a toggle effect. It is probably counterproductive to make other special characters (including erase an kill) identical.

The calls are:

TIOCSETC
>	Change the various special characters to those given in the structure.

TIOCSETP
>	Set the special characters to those given in the structure.

FILES
>	/dev/tty
>	/dev/tty*
>	/dev/console

SEE ALSO
>	getty(8), stty (1), signal(2), ioctl(2)

BUGS
>	Half-duplex terminals are not supported.
>
>	The terminal handler has clearly entered the race for ever-greater complexity and generality. It's still not complex and general enough for TENEX fans.

NAME

vp — Versatec printer-plotter

DESCRIPTION

Vp0 is the interface to a Versatec D1200A printer-plotter with a Versatec C-PDP11(DMA) controller. Ordinarily bytes written on it are interpreted as ASCII characters and printed. As a printer, it writes 64 lines of 132 characters each on 11 by 8.5 inch paper. Only some of the ASCII control characters are interpreted.

NL   performs the usual new-line function, i.e. spaces up the paper and resets to the left margin. It is ignored however following a CR which ends a non-empty line.

CR   is ignored if the current line is empty but is otherwise like NL.

FF   resets to the left margin and then to the top of the next page.

EOT   resets to the left margin, advances 8 inches, and then performs a FF.

The *ioctl*(2) system call may be used to change the mode of the device. Only the first word of the 3-word argument structure is used. The bits mean:

0400   Enter simultaneous print/plot mode.
0200   Enter plot mode.
0100   Enter print mode (default on open).
040   Send remote terminate.
020   Send remote form-feed.
010   Send remote EOT.
04   Send remote clear.
02   Send remote reset.

On open a reset, clear, and form-feed are performed automatically. Notice that the mode bits are not encoded, so that it is required that exactly one be set.

In plot mode each byte is interpreted as 8 bits of which the high-order is plotted to the left; a '1' leaves a visible dot. A full line of dots is produced by 264 bytes; lines are terminated only by count or by a remote terminate function. There are 200 dots per inch both vertically and horizontally.

When simultaneous print-plot mode is entered exactly one line of characters, terminated by NL, CR, or the remote terminate function, should be written. Then the device enters plot mode and at least 20 lines of plotting bytes should be sent. As the line of characters (which is 20 dots high) is printed, the plotting bytes overlay the characters. Notice that it is impossible to print characters on baselines that differ by fewer than 20 dot-lines.

In print mode lines may be terminated either with an appropriate ASCII character or by using the remote terminate function.

FILES

/dev/vp0

SEE ALSO

opr(1)

Section 5
FILE FORMATS AND CONVENTIONS

NAME

acct — execution accounting file

SYNOPSIS

#include <sys/acct.h>

DESCRIPTION

Acct(2) causes entries to be made into an accounting file for each process that terminates. The accounting file is a sequence of entries whose layout, as defined by the include file is:

```
/*
 * Accounting structures
 */

typedef ushort comp_t;          /* "floating point" */
                /* 13-bit fraction, 3-bit exponent  */

struct   acct
{
        char    ac_flag;        /* Accounting flag */
        char    ac_stat;        /* Exit status */
        ushort  ac_uid;         /* Accounting user ID */
        ushort  ac_gid;         /* Accounting group ID */
        dev_t   ac_tty;         /* control typewriter */
        time_t  ac_btime;       /* Beginning time */
        comp_t  ac_utime;       /* acctng user time in clock ticks */
        comp_t  ac_stime;       /* acctng system time in clock ticks */
        comp_t  ac_etime;       /* acctng elapsed time in clock ticks */
        comp_t  ac_mem;         /* memory usage */
        comp_t  ac_io;          /* chars transferred */
        comp_t  ac_rw;          /* blocks read or written */
        char    ac_comm[8];     /* command name */
};

extern   struct   acct          acctbuf;
extern   struct   inode         *acctp;/* inode of accounting file */

#define AFORK 01                /* has executed fork, but no exec */
#define ASU    02               /* used super-user privileges */
#define ACCTF 0300              /* record type: 00 = acct */
```

If the process does an *exec*(2), the first 10 characters of the filename appear in *ac_comm*. The accounting flag contains bits indicating whether *exec*(2) was ever accomplished, and whether the process ever had super-user privileges.

SEE ALSO

acct(2), sa(1)

NAME

a.out − assembler and link editor output

SYNOPSIS

#include <a.out.h>

DESCRIPTION

A.out is the output file of the assembler *as*(1) and the link editor *ld*(1). Both programs make *a.out* executable if there were no errors and no unresolved external references. Layout information as given in the include file for the PDP11 is:

```
struct    exec {       /* a.out header */
          int       a_magic;    /* magic number */
          unsigned  a_text;     /* size of text segment */
          unsigned  a_data;     /* size of initialized data */
          unsigned  a_bss;      /* size of unitialized data */
          unsigned  a_syms;     /* size of symbol table */
          unsigned  a_entry;    /* entry point */
          unsigned  a_unused;   /* not used */
          unsigned  a_flag;     /* relocation info stripped */
};

#define A_MAGIC1        0407    /* normal */
#define A_MAGIC2        0410    /* read-only text */
#define A_MAGIC3        0411    /* separated I&D */
#define A_MAGIC4        0405    /* overlay */
```

```
struct    nlist {        /* symbol table entry */
          char      n_name[8];  /* symbol name */
          int       n_type;     /* type flag */
          unsigned  n_value;    /* value */
};

                        /* values for type flag */
#define N_UNDF 0              /* undefined */
#define N_ABS  01             /* absolute */
#define N_TEXT 02             /* text symbol */
#define N_DATA 03             /* data symbol */
#define N_BSS  04             /* bss symbol */
#define N_TYPE 037
#define N_REG  024            /* register name */
#define N_FN   037            /* file name symbol */
#define N_EXT  040            /* external bit, or'ed in */
#define FORMAT"%.6o"          /* to print a value */
```

The file has four sections: a header, the program and data text, relocation information, and a symbol table (in that order). The last two may be empty if the program was loaded with the '−s' option of *ld* or if the symbols and relocation have been removed by *strip*(1).

In the header the sizes of each section are given in bytes, but are even. The size of the header is not included in any of the other sizes.

When an *a.out* file is loaded into core for execution, three logical segments are set up: the text segment, the data segment (with uninitialized data, which starts off as all 0, following initialized), and a stack. The text segment begins at 0 in the core image; the header is not loaded. If the magic number in the header is 0407(8), it indicates that the text segment is not to be write-protected and shared, so the data segment is immediately contiguous with the text segment. If the magic number is 0410, the data segment begins at the first 0 mod 8K byte boundary following the text segment, and the text segment is not writable by the program; if other processes are executing the same file, they will share the text segment. If the magic number is 411, the text segment is again pure, write-protected, and shared, and moreover instruction and data space are separated; the text and data segment both begin at location 0. If the magic number is 0405, the text segment is overlaid on an existing (0411 or 0405) text segment and the existing data segment is preserved.

The stack will occupy the highest possible locations in the core image: from 0177776(8) and growing downwards. The stack is automatically extended as required. The data segment is only extended as requested by *brk*(2).

The start of the text segment in the file is 020(8); the start of the data segment is $020 + S_t$ (the size of the text) the start of the relocation information is $020 + S_t + S_d$; the start of the symbol table is $020 + 2(S_t + S_d)$ if the relocation information is present, $020 + S_t + S_d$ if not.

The layout of a symbol table entry and the principal flag values that distinguish symbol types are given in the include file. Other flag values may occur if an assembly language program defines machine instructions.

If a symbol's type is undefined external, and the value field is non-zero, the symbol is interpreted by the loader *ld* as the name of a common region whose size is indicated by the value of the symbol.

The value of a word in the text or data portions which is not a reference to an undefined external symbol is exactly that value which will appear in core when the file is executed. If a word in the text or data portion involves a reference to an undefined external symbol, as indicated by the relocation information for that word, then the value of the word as stored in the file is an offset from the associated external symbol. When the file is processed by the link editor and the external symbol becomes defined, the value of the symbol will be added into the word in the file.

If relocation information is present, it amounts to one word per word of program text or initialized data. There is no relocation information if the 'relocation info stripped' flag in the header is on.

Bits 3-1 of a relocation word indicate the segment referred to by the text or data word associated with the relocation word:

000	absolute number
002	reference to text segment
004	reference to initialized data
006	reference to uninitialized data (bss)
010	reference to undefined external symbol

Bit 0 of the relocation word indicates, if 1, that the reference is relative to the pc (e.g. 'clr x'); if 0, that the reference is to the actual symbol (e.g., 'clr *$x').

The remainder of the relocation word (bits 15-4) contains a symbol number in the case of external references, and is unused otherwise. The first symbol is numbered 0, the second 1, etc.

SEE ALSO

      as(1), ld(1), nm(1)

NAME

ar — archive (library) file format

SYNOPSIS

#include <ar.h>

DESCRIPTION

The archive command *ar* is used to combine several files into one. Archives are used mainly as libraries to be searched by the link-editor *ld*.

A file produced by *ar* has a magic number at the start, followed by the constituent files, each preceded by a file header. The magic number and header layout as described in the include file are:

```
#define ARMAG 0177545
struct   ar_hdr {
         char     ar_name[14];
         long     ar_date;
         char     ar_uid;
         char     ar_gid;
         int      ar_mode;
         long     ar_size;
};
```

The name is a null-terminated string; the date is in the form of *time*(2); the user ID and group ID are numbers; the mode is a bit pattern per *chmod*(2); the size is counted in bytes.

Each file begins on a word boundary; a null byte is inserted between files if necessary. Nevertheless the size given reflects the actual size of the file exclusive of padding.

Notice there is no provision for empty areas in an archive file.

SEE ALSO

ar(1), ld(1), nm(1)

BUGS

Coding user and group IDs as characters is a botch.

NAME

    core — format of core image file

DESCRIPTION

    UNIX writes out a core image of a terminated process when any of various errors occur. See *signal*(2) for the list of reasons; the most common are memory violations, illegal instructions, bus errors, and user-generated quit signals. The core image is called 'core' and is written in the process's working directory (provided it can be; normal access controls apply).

    The first 1024 bytes of the core image are a copy of the system's per-user data for the process, including the registers as they were at the time of the fault; see the system listings for the format of this area. The remainder represents the actual contents of the user's core area when the core image was written. If the text segment is write-protected and shared, it is not dumped; otherwise the entire address space is dumped.

    In general the debugger *adb*(1) is sufficient to deal with core images.

SEE ALSO

    adb(1), signal(2)

NAME

dir — format of directories

SYNOPSIS

#include <sys/dir.h>

DESCRIPTION

A directory behaves exactly like an ordinary file, save that no user may write into a directory. The fact that a file is a directory is indicated by a bit in the flag word of its i-node entry see, *filsys*(5). The structure of a directory entry as given in the include file is:

```
#ifndef DIRSIZ
#define DIRSIZ14
#endif
struct    direct
{
        ino_t  d_ino;
        char   d_name[DIRSIZ];
};
```

By convention, the first two entries in each directory are for '.' and '..'. The first is an entry for the directory itself. The second is for the parent directory. The meaning of '..' is modified for the root directory of the master file system and for the root directories of removable file systems. In the first case, there is no parent, and in the second, the system does not permit off-device references. Therefore in both cases '..' has the same meaning as '.'.

SEE ALSO

filsys(5)

NAME

dump, ddate — incremental dump format

SYNOPSIS

#include <sys/types.h>
#include <sys/ino.h>
include <dumprestor.h>

DESCRIPTION

Tapes used by *dump* and *restor*(1) contain:

      a header record
      two groups of bit map records
      a group of records describing directories
      a group of records describing files

The format of the header record and of the first record of each description as given in the include file <*dumprestor.h*> is:

```
#define NTREC    20
#define MLEN     16
#define MSIZ     4096

#define TS_TAPE  1
#define TS_INODE 2
#define TS_BITS  3
#define TS_ADDR  4
#define TS_END   5
#define TS_CLRI  6
#define MAGIC    (int)60011
#define CHECKSUM(int)84446
struct  spcl
{
        int        c_type;
        time_t     c_date;
        time_t     c_ddate;
        int        c_volume;
        daddr_t    c_tapea;
        ino_t      c_inumber;
        int        c_magic;
        int        c_checksum;
        struct     dinodec_dinode;
        int        c_count;
        char       c_addr[BSIZE];
} spcl;

struct  idates
{
        char       id_name[16];
        char       id_incno;
        time_t     id_ddate;
};
```

NTREC is the number of 512 byte records in a physical tape block. *MLEN* is the number of bits in a bit map word. *MSIZ* is the number of bit map words.

The *TS_* entries are used in the *c_type* field to indicate what sort of header this is. The types and their meanings are as follows:

TS_TAPE   Tape volume label
TS_INODE   A file or directory follows. The *c_dinode* field is a copy of the disk inode and con-
            tains bits telling what sort of file this is.
TS_BITS   A bit map follows. This bit map has a one bit for each inode that was dumped.
TS_ADDR   A subrecord of a file description. See *c_addr* below.
TS_END   End of tape record.
TS_CLRI   A bit map follows. This bit map contains a zero bit for all inodes that were empty
            on the file system when dumped.
MAGIC   All header records have this number in *c_magic*.
CHECKSUM
            Header records checksum to this value.

The fields of the header structure are as follows:

c_type   The type of the header.
c_date   The date the dump was taken.
c_ddate   The date the file system was dumped from.
c_volume   The current volume number of the dump.
c_tapea   The current number of this (512-byte) record.
c_inumber   The number of the inode being dumped if this is of type *TS_INODE*.
c_magic   This contains the value *MAGIC* above, truncated as needed.
c_checksum
            This contains whatever value is needed to make the record sum to *CHECKSUM*.
c_dinode   This is a copy of the inode as it appears on the file system; see *filsys*(5).
c_count   The count of characters in *c_addr*.
c_addr   An array of characters describing the blocks of the dumped file. A character is zero
            if the block associated with that character was not present on the file system, other-
            wise the character is non-zero. If the block was not present on the file system, no
            block was dumped; the block will be restored as a hole in the file. If there is not
            sufficient space in this record to describe all of the blocks in a file, *TS_ADDR*
            records will be scattered through the file, each one picking up where the last left
            off.

Each volume except the last ends with a tapemark (read as an end of file). The last volume
ends with a *TS_END* record and then the tapemark.

The structure *idates* describes an entry of the file */etc/ddate* where dump history is kept. The
fields of the structure are:

id_name   The dumped filesystem is '/dev/*id_nam*'.
id_incno   The level number of the dump tape; see *dump*(1).
id_ddate   The date of the incremental dump in system format see *types*(5).

FILES

/etc/ddate

SEE ALSO

dump(1), dumpdir(1), restor(1), filsys(5), types(5)

NAME

environ — user environment

SYNOPSIS

extern char **environ;

DESCRIPTION

An array of strings called the 'environment' is made available by *exec*(2) when a process begins. By convention these strings have the form 'name=value'. The following names are used by various commands:

PATH   The sequence of directory prefixes that *sh, time, nice*(1), etc., apply in searching for a file known by an incomplete path name. The prefixes are separated by ':'. *Login*(1) sets PATH=:/bin:/usr/bin.

HOME A user's login directory, set by *login*(1) from the password file *passwd*(5).

TERM   The kind of terminal for which output is to be prepared. This information is used by commands, such as *nroff* or *plot*(1), which may exploit special terminal capabilities. See *term*(7) for a list of terminal types.

Further names may be placed in the environment by the *export* command and 'name=value' arguments in *sh*(1), or by *exec*(2). It is unwise to conflict with certain Shell variables that are frequently exported by '.profile' files: MAIL, PS1, PS2, IFS.

SEE ALSO

exec(2), sh(1), term(7), login(1)

NAME

filsys, fblk, ino — format of file system volume

SYNOPSIS

#include <sys/types.h>
#include <sys/fblk.h>
#include <sys/filsys.h>
#include <sys/ino.h>

DESCRIPTION

Every file system storage volume (e.g. RF disk, RK disk, RP disk, DECtape reel) has a common format for certain vital information. Every such volume is divided into a certain number of 512-byte blocks. Block 0 is unused and is available to contain a bootstrap program, pack label, or other information.

Block 1 is the *super block*. The layout of the super block as defined by the include file *<sys/filsys.h>* is:

```
/*
 * Structure of the super-block
 */
struct filsys
{
        ushort  s_isize;                /* size in blocks of i-list */
        daddr_t s_fsize;                /* size in blocks of entire volume */
        short   s_nfree;                /* number of addresses in s_free */
        daddr_t s_free[NICFREE];        /* free block list */
        short   s_ninode;               /* number of i-nodes in s_inode */
        ino_t   s_inode[NICINOD];       /* free i-node list */
        char    s_flock;                /* lock during free list manipulation */
        char    s_ilock;                /* lock during i-list manipulation */
        char    s_fmod;                 /* super block modified flag */
        char    s_ronly;                /* mounted read-only flag */
        time_t  s_time;                 /* last super block update */
        short   s_dinfo[4];             /* device information */
        daddr_t s_tfree;                /* total free blocks*/
        ino_t   s_tinode;               /* total free inodes */
        char    s_fname[6];             /* file system name */
        char    s_fpack[6];             /* file system pack name */
};
```

S_isize is the address of the first block after the i-list, which starts just after the super-block, in block 2. Thus is i-list is *s_isize* − 2 blocks long. *S_fsize* is the address of the first block not potentially available for allocation to a file. These numbers are used by the system to check for bad block addresses; if an 'impossible' block address is allocated from the free list or is freed, a diagnostic is written on the on-line console. Moreover, the free array is cleared, so as to prevent further allocation from a presumably corrupted free list.

The free list for each volume is maintained as follows. The *s_free* array contains, in *s_free[1]*, ... , *s_free[s_nfree* − *1]*, up to NICFREE free block numbers. NICFREE is a configuration constant. *S_free[0]* is the block address of the head of a chain of blocks constituting the free list. The layout of each block of the free chain as defined in the include file *<sys/fblk.h>* is:

```
struct fblk
{
        int     df_nfree;
        daddr_t df_free[NICFREE];
```

};

The fields *df_nfree* and *df_free* in a free block are used exactly like *s_nfree* and *s_free* in the super block. To allocate a block: decrement *s_nfree,* and the new block number is *s_free[s_nfree].* If the new block address is 0, there are no blocks left, so give an error. If *s_nfree* became 0, read the new block into *s_nfree* and *s_free.* To free a block, check if *s_nfree* is NICFREE; if so, copy *s_nfree* and the *s_free* array into it, write it out, and set *s_nfree* to 0. In any event set *s_free[s_nfree]* to the freed block's address and increment *s_nfree.*

S_ninode is the number of free i-numbers in the *s_inode* array. To allocate an i-node: if *s_ninode* is greater than 0, decrement it and return *s_inode[s_ninode].* If it was 0, read the i-list and place the numbers of all free inodes (up to NICINOD) into the *s_inode* array, then try again. To free an i-node, provided *s_ninode* is less than NICINODE, place its number into *s_inode[s_ninode]* and increment *s_ninode.* If *s_ninode* is already NICINODE, don't bother to enter the freed i-node into any table. This list of i-nodes is only to speed up the allocation process; the information as to whether the inode is really free or not is maintained in the inode itself.

S_flock and *s_ilock* are flags maintained in the core copy of the file system while it is mounted and their values on disk are immaterial. The value of *s_fmod* on disk is likewise immaterial; it is used as a flag to indicate that the super-block has changed and should be copied to the disk during the next periodic update of file system information. *S_ronly* is a write-protection indicator; its disk value is also immaterial.

S_time is the last time the super-block of the file system was changed. During a reboot, *s_time* of the super-block for the root file system is used to set the system's idea of the time.

The fields *s_tfree, s_tinode, s_fname* and *s_fpack* are not currently maintained.

I-numbers begin at 1, and the storage for i-nodes begins in block 2. I-nodes are 64 bytes long, so 8 of them fit into a block. I-node 2 is reserved for the root directory of the file system, but no other i-number has a built-in meaning. Each i-node represents one file. The format of an i-node as given in the include file *<sys/ino.h>* is:

```
        /* Inode structure as it appears on a disk block. */
struct dinode
{
        ushort di_mode;     /* mode and type of file */
        short  di_nlink;    /* number of links to file */
        ushort di_uid;      /* owner's user id */
        ushort di_gid;      /* owner's group id */
        off_t  di_size;     /* number of bytes in file */
        char   di_addr[40]; /* disk block addresses */
        time_t di_atime;    /* time last accessed */
        time_t di_mtime;    /* time last modified */
        time_t di_ctime;    /* time created */
};
/*
 * the 40 address bytes:
 *      39 used; 13 addresses
 *      of 3 bytes each.
 */
```

Di_mode tells the kind of file; it is encoded identically to the *st_mode field of stat* (2). *Di_nlink* is the number of directory entries (links) that refer to this i-node. *Di_uid* and *di_gid* are the owner's user and group IDs. *Size* is the number of bytes in the file. *Di_atime* and *di_mtime* are the times of last access and modification of the file contents (read, write or create) (see *times* (2)); *Di_ctime* records the time of last modification to the inode or to the file, and is used to determine whether it should be dumped.

Special files are recognized by their modes and not by i-number. A block-type special file is one which can potentially be mounted as a file system; a character-type special file cannot, though it is not necessarily character-oriented. For special files, the *di_addr* field is occupied by the device code (see *types*(5)). The device codes of block and character special files overlap.

Disk addresses of plain files and directories are kept in the array *di_addr* packed into 3 bytes each. The first 10 addresses specify device blocks directly. The last 3 addresses are singly, doubly, and triply indirect and point to blocks of 128 block pointers. Pointers in indirect blocks have the type *daddr_t* (see *types*(5)).

For block *b* in a file to exist, it is not necessary that all blocks less than *b* exist. A zero block number either in the address words of the i-node or in an indirect block indicates that the corresponding block has never been allocated. Such a missing block reads as if it contained all zero words.

SEE ALSO

icheck(1), dcheck(1), dir(5), mount(1), stat(2), types(5)

NAME

      group — group file

DESCRIPTION

      Group contains for each group the following information:

      group name
      encrypted password
      numerical group ID
      a comma separated list of all users allowed in the group

      This is an ASCII file. The fields are separated by colons; Each group is separated from the next by a new-line. If the password field is null, no password is demanded.

      This file resides in directory /etc. Because of the encrypted passwords, it can and does have general read permission and can be used, for example, to map numerical group ID's to names.

FILES

      /etc/group

SEE ALSO

      newgrp(1), crypt(3), passwd(1), passwd(5)

NAME

mpxio — multiplexed i/o

SYNOPSIS

#include <sys/mx.h>

#include <sgtty.h>

DESCRIPTION

Data transfers on mpx files (see *mpx*(2)) are multiplexed by imposing a record structure on the io stream. Each record represents data from/to a particular channel or a control or status message associated with a particular channel.

The prototypical data record read from an mpx file is as follows

```
struct input_record {
        short   index;
        short   count;
        short   ccount;
        char    data[];
};
```

where *index* identifies the channel, and *count* specifies the number of characters in *data*. If *count* is zero, *ccount* gives the size of *data*, and the record is a control or status message. Although *count* or *ccount* might be odd, the operating system aligns records on short (i.e. 16—bit) boundaries by skipping bytes when necessary.

Data written to an mpx file must be formatted as an array of record structures defined as follows

```
struct output_record {
        short   index;
        short   count;
        short   ccount;
        char    *data;
};
```

where the data portion of the record is referred to indirectly and the other cells have the same interpretation as in *input_record*.

The control messages listed below may be read from a multiplexed file descriptor. They are presented as two 16-bit integers: the first number is the message code (defined in <*sys/mx.h*>), the second is an optional parameter meaningful only with M_WATCH and M_BLK.

    M_WATCH — a process 'wants to attach' on this channel. The second parameter is the 16-bit user-id of the process that executed the open.

    M_CLOSE — the channel is closed. This message is generated when the last file descriptor referencing a channel is closed. The *detach* command (see *mpx*(2) should be used in response to this message.

    M_EOT — indicates logical end of file on a channel. If the channel is joined to a typewriter, EOT (control-d) will cause the M_EOT message under the conditions specified in *tty*(4) for end of file. If the channel is attached to a process, M_EOT will be generated whenever the process writes zero bytes on the channel.

    M_BLK — if non-blocking mode has been enabled on an mpx file descriptor *xd* by executing *ioctl(xd, MXNBLK, 0)*, write operations on the file are truncated in the kernel when internal queues become full. This is done on a per-channel basis: the parameter is a count of the number of characters not transferred to the channel on which M_BLK is received.

M_UBLK — is generated for a channel after M_BLK when the internal queues have drained below a threshold.

Two other messages may be generated by the kernel. As with other messages, the first 16-bit quantity is the message code.

M_OPEN — is generated in conjunction with 'listener' mode (see *mpx*(2)). The uid of the calling process follows the message code as with M_WATCH. This is followed by a null-terminated string which is the name of the file being opened.

M_IOCTL — is generated for a channel connected to a process when that process executes the *ioctl(fd, cmd, &vec)* call on the channel file descriptor. The M_IOCTL code is followed by the *cmd* argument given to *ioctl* followed by the contents of the structure *vec*. It is assumed, not needing a better compromise at this time, that the length of *vec* is determined by *sizeof (struct sgttyb)* as declared in *<sgtty.h>*.

Two control messages are understood by the operating system. M_EOT may be sent through an mpx file to a channel. It is equivalent to propagating a zero-length record through the channel; i.e. the channel is allowed to drain and the process or device at the other end receives a zero-length transfer before data starts flowing through the channel again. M_IOCTL can also be sent through a channel. The format is identical to that described above.

NAME

    mtab − mounted file system table

DESCRIPTION

    Mtab resides in directory */etc* and contains a table of devices mounted by the *mount* command. *Umount* removes entries.

    Each entry is 64 bytes long; the first 32 are the null-padded name of the place where the special file is mounted; the second 32 are the null-padded name of the special file. The special file has all its directories stripped away; that is, everything through the last '/' is thrown away.

    This table is present only so people can look at it. It does not matter to *mount* if there are duplicated entries nor to *umount* if a name cannot be found.

FILES

    /etc/mtab

SEE ALSO

    mount(1)

NAME

    passwd — password file

DESCRIPTION

    Passwd contains for each user the following information:

    name (login name, contains no upper case)
    encrypted password
    numerical user ID
    numerical group ID
    GCOS job number, box number, optional GCOS user-id
    initial working directory
    program to use as Shell

    This is an ASCII file. Each field within each user's entry is separated from the next by a colon. The GCOS field is used only when communicating with that system, and in other installations can contain any desired information. Each user is separated from the next by a new-line. If the password field is null, no password is demanded; if the Shell field is null, the Shell itself is used.

    This file resides in directory /etc. Because of the encrypted passwords, it can and does have general read permission and can be used, for example, to map numerical user ID's to names.

FILES

    /etc/passwd

SEE ALSO

    getpwent(3), login(1), crypt(3), passwd(1), group(5)

NAME

plot — graphics interface

DESCRIPTION

Files of this format are produced by routines described in *plot*(3), and are interpreted for various devices by commands described in *plot*(1). A graphics file is a stream of plotting instructions. Each instruction consists of an ASCII letter usually followed by bytes of binary information. The instructions are executed in order. A point is designated by four bytes representing the x and y values; each value is a signed integer. The last designated point in an **l, m, n,** or **p** instruction becomes the 'current point' for the next instruction.

Each of the following descriptions begins with the name of the corresponding routine in *plot*(3).

m move: The next four bytes give a new current point.

n cont: Draw a line from the current point to the point given by the next four bytes. See *plot*(1).

p point: Plot the point given by the next four bytes.

l line: Draw a line from the point given by the next four bytes to the point given by the following four bytes.

t label: Place the following ASCII string so that its first character falls on the current point. The string is terminated by a newline.

a arc: The first four bytes give the center, the next four give the starting point, and the last four give the end point of a circular arc. The least significant coordinate of the end point is used only to determine the quadrant. The arc is drawn counter-clockwise.

c circle: The first four bytes give the center of the circle, the next two the radius.

e erase: Start another frame of output.

f linemod: Take the following string, up to a newline, as the style for drawing further lines. The styles are 'dotted,' 'solid,' 'longdashed,' 'shortdashed,' and 'dotdashed.' Effective only in *plot 4014* and *plot ver*.

s space: The next four bytes give the lower left corner of the plotting area; the following four give the upper right corner. The plot will be magnified or reduced to fit the device as closely as possible.

Space settings that exactly fill the plotting area with unity scaling appear below for devices supported by the filters of *plot*(1). The upper limit is just outside the plotting area. In every case the plotting area is taken to be square; points outside may be displayable on devices whose face isn't square.

4014	space(0, 0, 3120, 3120);
ver	space(0, 0, 2048, 2048);
300, 300s	space(0, 0, 4096, 4096);
450	space(0, 0, 4096, 4096);

SEE ALSO

plot(1), plot(3), graph(1)

NAME

     tp − DEC/mag tape formats

DESCRIPTION

     The command *tp* dumps files to and extracts files from DECtape and magtape. The formats of these tapes are the same except that magtapes have larger directories.

     Block zero contains a copy of a stand-alone bootstrap program. See *bproc*(8).

     Blocks 1 through 24 for DECtape (1 through 62 for magtape) contain a directory of the tape. There are 192 (resp. 496) entries in the directory; 8 entries per block; 64 bytes per entry. Each entry has the following format:

```
struct {
        char    pathname[32];
        int     mode;
        char    uid;
        char    gid;
        char    unused1;
        char    size[3];
        long    modtime;
        int     tapeaddr;
        char    unused2[16];
        int     checksum;
};
```

     The path name entry is the path name of the file when put on the tape. If the pathname starts with a zero word, the entry is empty. It is at most 32 bytes long and ends in a null byte. Mode, uid, gid, size and time modified are the same as described under i-nodes (see file system *filsys*(5)). The tape address is the tape block number of the start of the contents of the file. Every file starts on a block boundary. The file occupies (size+511)/512 blocks of continuous tape. The checksum entry has a value such that the sum of the 32 words of the directory entry is zero.

     Blocks above 25 (resp. 63) are available for file storage.

     A fake entry has a size of zero.

SEE ALSO

     filsys(5), tp(1)

BUGS

     The *pathname, uid, gid,* and *size* fields are too small.

NAME

ttys — terminal initialization data

DESCRIPTION

The *ttys* file is read by the *init* program and specifies which terminal special files are to have a process created for them which will allow people to log in. It contains one line per special file.

The first character of a line is either '0' or '1'; the former causes the line to be ignored, the latter causes it to be effective. The second character is used as an argument to *getty*(8), which performs such tasks as baud-rate recognition, reading the login name, and calling *login*. For normal lines, the character is '0'; other characters can be used, for example, with hard-wired terminals where speed recognition is unnecessary or which have special characteristics. (*Getty* will have to be fixed in such cases.) The remainder of the line is the terminal's entry in the device directory, /dev.

FILES

/etc/ttys

SEE ALSO

init(8), getty(8), login(1)

NAME

  types − primitive system data types

SYNOPSIS

  #include <sys/types.h>

DESCRIPTION

  The data types defined in the include file are used in UNIX system code; some data of these
  types are accessible to user code:

  typedef struct { int r[1]; } * physadr;
  typedef long   daddr_t;
  typedef char *   caddr_t;
  typedef unsigned short ushort;
  typedef ushort   ino_t;
  #ifdef vax
  typedef short   cnt_t;
  #else
  typedef char   cnt_t;
  #endif
  typedef long   time_t;
  #ifdef vax
  typedef int   label_t[10];
  #else
  typedef int   label_t[6];
  #endif
  typedef short   dev_t;
  typedef long   off_t;
  typedef long   paddr_t;

  The form *daddr_t* is used for disk addresses except in an i-node on disk, see *filsys*(5). Times
  are encoded in seconds since 00:00:00 GMT, January 1, 1970. The major and minor parts of a
  device code specify kind and unit number of a device and are installation-dependent. Offsets
  are measured in bytes from the beginning of a file. The *label_t* variables are used to save the
  processor state while another process is running.

SEE ALSO

  filsys(5), time(2), lseek(2), adb(1)

NAME

utmp, wtmp — login records

SYNOPSIS

#include <utmp.h>

DESCRIPTION

The *utmp* file allows one to discover information about who is currently using UNIX. The file is a sequence of entries with the following structure declared in the include file:

```
/*
 * Format of /etc/utmp and /usr/adm/wtmp
 */

struct utmp {
        char    ut_line[8];             /* tty name */
        char    ut_name[8];             /* user id */
        long    ut_time;                /* time on */
};
```

This structure gives the name of the special file associated with the user's terminal, the user's login name, and the time of the login in the form of *time*(2).

The *wtmp* file records all logins and logouts. Its format is exactly like *utmp* except that a null user name indicates a logout on the associated terminal. Furthermore, the terminal name '~' indicates that the system was rebooted at the indicated time; the adjacent pair of entries with terminal names '|' and '}' indicate the system-maintained time just before and just after a *date* command has changed the system's idea of the time.

Wtmp is maintained by *login*(1) and *init*(8). Neither of these programs creates the file, so if it is removed record-keeping is turned off. It is summarized by *ac*(1).

FILES

/etc/utmp
/usr/adm/wtmp

SEE ALSO

login(1), init(8), who(1), ac(1)

Section 6
GAMES

NAME

arithmetic − provide drill in number facts

SYNOPSIS

/usr/games/arithmetic [+−x/] [range]

DESCRIPTION

Arithmetic types out simple arithmetic problems, and waits for an answer to be typed in. If the answer is correct, it types back "Right!", and a new problem. If the answer is wrong, it replies "What?", and waits for another answer. Every twenty problems, it publishes statistics on correctness and the time required to answer.

To quit the program, type an interrupt (delete).

The first optional argument determines the kind of problem to be generated; +−x/ respectively cause addition, subtraction, multiplication, and division problems to be generated. One or more characters can be given; if more than one is given, the different types of problems will be mixed in random order; default is +−

Range is a decimal number; all addends, subtrahends, differences, multiplicands, divisors, and quotients will be less than or equal to the value of *range*. Default *range* is 10.

At the start, all numbers less than or equal to *range* are equally likely to appear. If the respondent makes a mistake, the numbers in the problem which was missed become more likely to reappear.

As a matter of educational philosophy, the program will not give correct answers, since the learner should, in principle, be able to calculate them. Thus the program is intended to provide drill for someone just past the first learning stage, not to teach number facts *de novo*. For almost all users, the relevant statistic should be time per problem, not percent correct.

NAME
      backgammon — the game

SYNOPSIS
      /usr/games/backgammon

DESCRIPTION
      This program does what you expect. It will ask whether you need instructions.

NAME

> banner − make long posters

SYNOPSIS

> **/usr/games/banner**

DESCRIPTION

> *Banner* reads the standard input and prints it sideways in huge built-up letters on the standard output.

NAME

      bcd, ppt − convert to antique media

SYNOPSIS

      /usr/games/bcd text

      /usr/games/ppt

DESCRIPTION

      Bcd converts the literal *text* into a form familiar to old-timers.

      Ppt converts the standard input into yet another form.

SEE ALSO

      dd(1)

NAME

bj — the game of black jack

SYNOPSIS

/usr/games/bj

DESCRIPTION

Bj is a serious attempt at simulating the dealer in the game of black jack (or twenty-one) as might be found in Reno. The following rules apply:

The bet is $2 every hand.

  A player 'natural' (black jack) pays $3. A dealer natural loses $2. Both dealer and player naturals is a 'push' (no money exchange).

  If the dealer has an ace up, the player is allowed to make an 'insurance' bet against the chance of a dealer natural. If this bet is not taken, play resumes as normal. If the bet is taken, it is a side bet where the player wins $2 if the dealer has a natural and loses $1 if the dealer does not.

  If the player is dealt two cards of the same value, he is allowed to 'double'. He is allowed to play two hands, each with one of these cards. (The bet is doubled also; $2 on each hand.)

  If a dealt hand has a total of ten or eleven, the player may 'double down'. He may double the bet ($2 to $4) and receive exactly one more card on that hand.

  Under normal play, the player may 'hit' (draw a card) as long as his total is not over twenty-one. If the player 'busts' (goes over twenty-one), the dealer wins the bet.

  When the player 'stands' (decides not to hit), the dealer hits until he attains a total of seventeen or more. If the dealer busts, the player wins the bet.

  If both player and dealer stand, the one with the largest total wins. A tie is a push.

The machine deals and keeps score. The following questions will be asked at appropriate times. Each question is answered by y followed by a new line for 'yes', or just new line for 'no'.

?   (means, 'do you want a hit?')
Insurance?
Double down?

Every time the deck is shuffled, the dealer so states and the 'action' (total bet) and 'standing' (total won or lost) is printed. To exit, hit the interrupt key (DEL) and the action and standing will be printed.

NAME

checkers — game

SYNOPSIS

/usr/games/checkers

DESCRIPTION

Checkers uses standard notation for the board:

BLACK

//// ////	1	//// ////	2	//// ////	3	//// ////	4
5	//// ////	6	//// ////	7	//// ////	8	//// ////
//// ////	9	//// ////	10	//// ////	11	//// ////	12
13	//// ////	14	//// ////	15	//// ////	16	//// ////
//// ////	17	//// ////	18	//// ////	19	//// ////	20
21	//// ////	22	//// ////	23	//// ////	24	//// ////
//// ////	25	//// ////	26	//// ////	27	//// ////	28
29	//// ////	30	//// ////	31	//// ////	32	//// ////

WHITE

Black plays first. The program normally plays white. To specify a move, name the square moved from and the square moved to. For multiple jumps name all the squares touched.

Certain commands may be given instead of moves:

reverse Reverse roles; the program takes over your pieces.

backup Undo the last move for each player.

list Print the record of the game.

move Let the program select a move for you.

print Print a map of the present position.

NAME

chess — the game of chess

SYNOPSIS

/usr/games/chess

DESCRIPTION

Chess is a computer program that plays class D chess. Moves may be given either in standard (descriptive) notation or in algebraic notation. The symbol '+' is used to specify check; 'o-o' and 'o-o-o' specify castling. To play black, type 'first'; to print the board, type an empty line.

Each move is echoed in the appropriate notation followed by the program's reply.

FILES

/usr/lib/book   opening 'book'

DIAGNOSTICS

The most cryptic diagnostic is 'eh?' which means that the input was syntactically incorrect.

WARNING

Over-use of this program will cause it to go away.

BUGS

Pawns may be promoted only to queens.

NAME
ching, fortune − the book of changes and other cookies

SYNOPSIS
/usr/games/ching [hexagram]

. **/usr/games/fortune**

DESCRIPTION
The *I Ching* or *Book of Changes* is an ancient Chinese oracle that has been in use for centuries as a source of wisdom and advice.

The text of the *oracle* (as it is sometimes known) consists of sixty-four *hexagrams,* each symbolized by a particular arrangement of six straight (−−−) and broken (− −) lines. These lines have values ranging from six through nine, with the even values indicating the broken lines.

Each hexagram consists of two major sections. The **Judgement** relates specifically to the matter at hand (E.g., "It furthers one to have somewhere to go.") while the **Image** describes the general attributes of the hexagram and how they apply to one's own life ("Thus the superior man makes himself strong and untiring.").

When any of the lines have the values six or nine, they are moving lines; for each there is an appended judgement which becomes significant. Furthermore, the moving lines are inherently unstable and change into their opposites; a second hexagram (and thus an additional judgement) is formed.

Normally, one consults the oracle by fixing the desired question firmly in mind and then casting a set of changes (lines) using yarrow−stalks or tossed coins. The resulting hexagram will be the answer to the question.

Using an algorithm suggested by S. C. Johnson, the Unix *oracle* simply reads a question from the standard input (up to an EOF) and hashes the individual characters in combination with the time of day, process id and any other magic numbers which happen to be lying around the system. The resulting value is used as the seed of a random number generator which drives a simulated coin−toss divination. The answer is then piped through **nroff** for formatting and will appear on the standard output.

For those who wish to remain steadfast in the old traditions, the oracle will also accept the results of a personal divination using, for example, coins. To do this, cast the change and then type the resulting line values as an argument.

The impatient modern may prefer to settle for Chinese cookies; try *fortune.*

SEE ALSO
It furthers one to see the great man.

DIAGNOSTICS
The great prince issues commands,
Founds states, vests families with fiefs.
Inferior people should not be employed.

BUGS
Waiting in the mud
Brings about the arrival of the enemy.

If one is not extremely careful,
Somebody may come up from behind and strike him.
Misfortune.

NAME

    maze — generate a maze problem

SYNOPSIS

    /usr/games/maze/

DESCRIPTION

    Maze asks a few questions and then prints a maze.

BUGS

    Some mazes (especially small ones) have no solutions.

NAME

moo — guessing game

SYNOPSIS

/usr/games/moo

DESCRIPTION

Moo is a guessing game imported from England. The computer picks a number consisting of four distinct decimal digits. The player guesses four distinct digits being scored on each guess. A 'cow' is a correct digit in an incorrect position. A 'bull' is a correct digit in a correct position. The game continues until the player guesses the number (a score of four bulls).

NAME

quiz — test your knowledge

SYNOPSIS

/usr/games/quiz [−i file] [−t] [category1 category2]

DESCRIPTION

Quiz gives associative knowledge tests on various subjects. It asks items chosen from *category1* and expects answers from *category2*. If no categories are specified, *quiz* gives instructions and lists the available categories.

Quiz tells a correct answer whenever you type a bare newline. At the end of input, upon interrupt, or when questions run out, *quiz* reports a score and terminates.

The −t flag specifies 'tutorial' mode, where missed questions are repeated later, and material is gradually introduced as you learn.

The −i flag causes the named file to be substituted for the default index file. The lines of these files have the syntax:

```
line      = category newline | category ':' line
category  = alternate | category '|' alternate
alternate = empty | alternate primary
primary   = character | '[' category ']' | option
option    = '{' category '}'
```

The first category on each line of an index file names an information file. The remaining categories specify the order and contents of the data in each line of the information file. Information files have the same syntax. Backslash '\' is used as with *sh*(1) to quote syntactically significant characters or to insert transparent newlines into a line. When either a question or its answer is empty, *quiz* will refrain from asking it.

FILES

/usr/games/quiz.k/*

BUGS

The construct 'a|b' doesn't work in an information file. Use 'a{b}'.

NAME

　　　　reversi — a game of dramatic reversals

SYNOPSIS

　　　　/usr/games/reversi [[−r] *file*]

DESCRIPTION

　　　　Reversi (also known as 'friends', 'Chinese friends' and 'Othello') is played on an 8×8 board using two-sided tokens. Each player takes his turn by placing a token with his side up in an empty square. During the first four turns, players may only place tokens in the four central squares of the board. Subsequently, with each turn, a player *must* capture one or more of his opponent's tokens. He does this by placing one of his tokens such that it and another of his tokens embrace a solid line of his opponent's horizontally, vertically or diagonally. Captured tokens are flipped over and thus can be re-captured. If a player cannot outflank his opponent he forfeits his turn. The play continues until the board is filled or until no more outflanking is possible.

　　　　In this game, your tokens are asterisks and the machine's are at-signs. You move by typing in the row and column at which you want to place your token as two digits (1-8), optionally separated by blanks or tabs. You can also type

　　c　　　　to continue the game after hitting break (this is only necessary if you interrupt the machine while it is deliberating).

　　g *n*　　　to start *reversi* playing against itself for the next *n* moves (or until the break key is hit).

　　n　　　　to stop printing the board after each move.

　　o　　　　to start it up again.

　　p　　　　to print the board regardless.

　　q　　　　to quit (without dishonor).

　　s　　　　to print the score.

　　　　Reversi also recognizes several commands which are valid only at the start of the game, before any moves have been made. They are

　　f　　　　to let the machine go first.

　　h *n*　　　to ask for a handicap of from one to four corner squares. If you're good, you can give the machine a handicap by typing a negative number.

　　l *n*　　　to set the amount of lookahead used by the machine in searching for moves. Zero means none at all. Four is the default. Greater than six means you may fall asleep waiting for the machine to move.

　　t *n*　　　to tell *reversi* that you will only need *n* seconds to consider each move. If you fail to respond in the alloted time, you forfeit your turn.

　　　　If *reversi* is given a file name as an argument, it will checkpoint the game, move by move, by dumping the board onto *file*. The −r option will cause *reversi* to restart the game from *file* and continue logging.

NAME

    ttt, cubic — tic-tac-toe

SYNOPSIS

    /usr/games/ttt

    /usr/games/cubic

DESCRIPTION

    Ttt is the X and O game popular in the first grade. This is a learning program that never makes the same mistake twice.

    Although it learns, it learns slowly. It must lose nearly 80 games to completely know the game.

    Cubic plays three-dimensional tic-tac-toe on a 4×4×4 board. Moves are specified as a sequence of three coordinate numbers in the range 1-4.

FILES

    /usr/games/ttt.k   learning file

NAME

hangman, words — word games

SYNOPSIS

/usr/games/hangman [dict]

/usr/games/words

DESCRIPTION

Hangman chooses a word at least seven letters long from a word list. The user is to guess letters one at a time.

The optional argument names an alternate word list. The special name '−a' gets a particular very large word list.

Words prints all the uncapitalized words in the word list that can be made from letters in *string*.

FILES

/usr/dict/words	the regular word list
/crp/dict/web2	the the −a word list

DIAGNOSTICS

After each round, *hangman* reports the average number of guesses per round and the number of rounds.

BUGS

Hyphenated compounds are run together.

UNIX software is distributed without the −a word list.

NAME

wump — the game of hunt-the-wumpus

SYNOPSIS

/usr/games/wump

DESCRIPTION

Wump plays the game of 'Hunt the Wumpus.' A Wumpus is a creature that lives in a cave with several rooms connected by tunnels. You wander among the rooms, trying to shoot the Wumpus with an arrow, meanwhile avoiding being eaten by the Wumpus and falling into Bottomless Pits. There are also Super Bats which are likely to pick you up and drop you in some random room.

The program asks various questions which you answer one per line; it will give a more detailed description if you want.

This program is based on one described in *People's Computer Company, 2,* 2 (November 1973).

BUGS

It will never replace Space War.

Section 7
MACRO PACKAGES AND LANGUAGE CONVENTIONS

NAME

ascii − map of ASCII character set

SYNOPSIS

cat /usr/pub/ascii

DESCRIPTION

Ascii is a map of the ASCII character set, to be printed as needed. It contains:

```
|000 nul|001 soh|002 stx|003 etx|004 eot|005 enq|006 ack|007 bel|
|010 bs |011 ht |012 nl |013 vt |014 np |015 cr |016 so |017 si |
|020 dle|021 dc1|022 dc2|023 dc3|024 dc4|025 nak|026 syn|027 etb|
|030 can|031 em |032 sub|033 esc|034 fs |035 gs |036 rs |037 us |
|040 sp |041  ! |042  " |043  # |044  $ |045  % |046  & |047  ´ |
|050  ( |051  ) |052  * |053  + |054  , |055  − |056  . |057  / |
|060  0 |061  1 |062  2 |063  3 |064  4 |065  5 |066  6 |067  7 |
|070  8 |071  9 |072  : |073  ; |074  < |075  = |076  > |077  ? |
|100  @ |101  A |102  B |103  C |104  D |105  E |106  F |107  G |
|110  H |111  I |112  J |113  K |114  L |115  M |116  N |117  O |
|120  P |121  Q |122  R |123  S |124  T |125  U |126  V |127  W |
|130  X |131  Y |132  Z |133  [ |134  \ |135  ] |136  ^ |137  _ |
|140  ` |141  a |142  b |143  c |144  d |145  e |146  f |147  g |
|150  h |151  i |152  j |153  k |154  l |155  m |156  n |157  o |
|160  p |161  q |162  r |163  s |164  t |165  u |166  v |167  w |
|170  x |171  y |172  z |173  { |174  | |175  } |176  ~ |177 del|
```

FILES

/usr/pub/ascii

NAME

eqnchar — special character definitions for eqn

SYNOPSIS

eqn **/usr/pub/eqnchar** [files] | **troff** [options]

neqn **/usr/pub/eqnchar** [files] | **nroff** [options]

DESCRIPTION

Eqnchar contains *troff* and *nroff* character definitions for constructing characters that are not available on the Graphic Systems typesetter. These definitions are primarily intended for use with *eqn* and *neqn*. It contains definitions for the following characters

ciplus	⊕	‖	‖	*square*	□
citimes	⊗	*langle*	⟨	*circle*	○
wig	∼	*rangle*	⟩	*blot*	■
-wig	≃	*hbar*	ℏ	*bullet*	●
>wig	≳	*ppd*	⊥	*prop*	∝
<wig	≲	*<->*	⟷	*empty*	∅
=wig	≅	*<=>*	⟺	*member*	∈
star	∗		≮	*nomem*	∉
bigstar	✳	*|>*	≯	*cup*	∪
=dot	≐	*ang*	∠	*cap*	∩
orsign	∨	*rang*	∟	*incl*	⊑
andsign	∧	*3dot*	⋮	*subset*	⊂
=del	≜	*thf*	∴	*supset*	⊃
oppA	∀	*quarter*	¼	*!subset*	⊆
oppE	∃	*3quarter*	¾	*!supset*	⊇
angstrom	Å	*degree*	°		

FILES

/usr/pub/eqnchar

SEE ALSO

troff(1), eqn(1)

NAME

hier — file system hierarchy

DESCRIPTION

The following outline gives a quick tour through a representative directory hierarchy.

/	root	
/dev/	devices (4)	
	console	
		main console, *tty*(4)
	tty*	terminals, *tty*(4)
	cat	phototypesetter *cat*(4)
	rp*	disks, *rp, hp*(4)
	rrp*	raw disks, *rp, hp*(4)
	...	
/bin/	utility programs, cf /usr/bin/ (1)	
	as	assembler first pass, cf /usr/lib/as2
	cc	C compiler executive, cf /usr/lib/c[012]
	...	
/lib/	object libraries and other stuff, cf /usr/lib/	
	libc.a	system calls, standard I/O, etc. (2,3,3S)
	libm.a	math routines (3M)
	libplot.a	
		plotting routines, *plot*(3)
	libF77.a	
		Fortran runtime support
	libI77.a	
		Fortran I/O
	...	
	as2	second pass of *as*(1)
	c[012]	passes of *cc*(1)
	...	
/etc/	essential data and dangerous maintenance utilities	
	passwd	password file, *passwd*(5)
	group	group file, *group*(5)
	motd	message of the day, *login*(1)
	mtab	mounted file table, *mtab*(5)
	ddate	dump history, *dump*(1)
	ttys	properties of terminals, *ttys*(5)
	getty	part of *login*, *getty*(8)
	init	the father of all processes, *init*(8)
	rc	shell program to bring the system up
	cron	the clock daemon, *cron*(8)
	mount	*mount*(1)
	wall	*wall*(1)
	...	
/tmp/	temporary files, usually on a fast device, cf /usr/tmp/	
	e*	used by *ed*(1)
	ctm*	used by *cc*(1)
	...	
/usr/	general-pupose directory, usually a mounted file system	
	adm/	administrative information
		wtmp login history, *utmp*(5)

```
                messages
                        hardware error messages
                tracct  phototypesetter accounting, troff(1)
                vpacct  line printer accounting lpr(1)
/usr    /bin
        utility programs, to keep /bin/ small
        tmp/    temporaries, to keep /tmp/ small
                stm*    used by sort(1)
                raster  used by plot(1)
        dict/   word lists, etc.
                words   principal word list, used by look(1)
                spellhist
                        history file for spell(1)
        games/
                bj      blackjack
                hangman
                quiz.k/ what quiz(6) knows
                        index   category index
                        africa  countries and capitals
                        ...
        ...
        include/
                standard #include files
                a.out.h object file layout, a.out(5)
                stdio.h standard I/O, stdio(3)
                math.h  (3M)
                ...
                sys/    system-defined layouts, cf /usr/sys/h
                        acct.h  process accounts, acct(5)
                        buf.h   internal system buffers
                        ...
        lib/    object libraries and stuff, to keep /lib/ small
                lint[12]
                        subprocesses for lint(1)
                llib-lc dummy declarations for /lib/libc.a, used by lint(1)
                llib-lm dummy declarations for /lib/libc.m
                atrun   scheduler for at(1)
                struct/ passes of struct(1)
                ...
                tmac/   macros for troff(1)
                        tmac.an
                                macros for man(7)
                        tmac.s  macros for ms(7)
                        ...
                font/   fonts for troff(1)
                        R       Times Roman
                        B       Times Bold
                        ...
                uucp/   programs and data for uucp(1)
                        L.sys   remote system names and numbers
                        uucico  the real copy program
```

		...	
	suftab	table of suffixes for hyphenation, used by *troff*(1)	
	units	conversion tables for *units*(1)	
	eign	list of English words to be ignored by *ptx*(1)	

/usr/ man/
    volume 1 of this manual, *man*(1)

        man0/ general
            intro   introduction to volume 1, *ms*(7) format
            xx   template for manual page

        man1/ chapter 1
            as.1
            mount.1m
            ...

        cat1/   preprinted pages for man1/
            as.1
            mount.1m
    ...

    spool/ delayed execution files
        at/   used by *at*(1)
        lpd/   used by *lpr*(1)
            lock   present when line printer is active
            cf*   copy of file to be printed, if necessary
            df*   daemon control file, *lpd*(8)
            tf*   transient control file, while *lpr* is working
        uucp/ work files and staging area for *uucp*(1)
            LOGFILE
                summary log
            LOG.* log file for one transaction

    mail/ mailboxes for *mail*(1)
        uid   mail file for user *uid*
        uid.lock
            lock file while *uid* is receiving mail

    wd   initial working directory of a user, typically *wd* is the user's login name
        .profile set environment for *sh*(1), *environ*(5)
        calendar
            user's datebook for *calendar*(1)

    doc/   papers, mostly in volume 2 of this manual, typically in *ms*(7) format
        as/   assembler manual
        c   C manual
        ...

    sys/   system source
        dev/   device drivers
            bio.c   common code
            cat.c   *cat*(4)
            dh.c   DH11, *tty*(4)
            tty   *tty*(4)
            ...

        conf/ hardware-dependent code
            mch.s assembly language portion
            conf   configuration generator
            ...

```
            h/      header (include) files
                    acct.h   acct(5)
                    stat.h   stat(2)
                    ...
            sys/    source for system proper
                    main.c
                    pipe.c
                    sysent.c
                            system entry points
                    ...
/usr/   src/
        source programs for utilities, etc.
            cmd/    source of commands
                    as/     assembler
                            makefile
                                    recipe for rebuilding the assembler
                            as1?.s   source of pass1
                    ar.c    source for ar(1)
                    ...
                    troff/  source for nroff and troff(1)
                            nmake  makefile for nroff
                            tmake  makefile for troff
                            font/   source for font tables, /usr/lib/font/
                                    ftR.c    Roman
                                    ...
                            term/   terminal characteristics tables, /usr/lib/term/
                                    tab300.c
                                        DASI 300
                                    ...
                    ...
            libc/   source for functions in /lib/libc.a
                    crt/    C runtime support
                            ldiv.s   division into a long
                            lmul.s   multiplication to produce long
                            ...
                    csu/    startup and wrapup routines needed with every C program
                            crt0.s   regular startup
                            mcrt0.s modified startup for cc −p
                    sys/    system calls (2)
                            access.s
                            alarm.s
                            ...
                    stdio/  standard I/O functions (3S)
                            fgets.c
                            fopen.c
                            ...
                    gen/    other functions in (3)
                            abs.c
                            atof.c
                            ...
                    compall
                            shell procedure to compile libc
```

          mklib shell procedure to make /lib/libc.a
     libI77/ source for /lib/libI77
     libF77/
     ...
     games/ source for /usr/games

SEE ALSO

   ls(1), ncheck(1), find(1), grep(1)

BUGS

   The position of files is subject to change without notice.

NAME

man – macros to typeset manual

SYNOPSIS

nroff   **–man**   file ...

troff   **–man**   file ...

DESCRIPTION

These macros are used to lay out pages of this manual. A skeleton page may be found in the file /usr/man/man0/xx.

Any text argument *t* may be zero to six words. Quotes may be used to include blanks in a 'word'. If *text* is empty, the special treatment is applied to the next input line with text to be printed. In this way .I may be used to italicize a whole line, or .SM followed by .B to make small bold letters.

A prevailing indent distance is remembered between successive indented paragraphs, and is reset to default value upon reaching a non-indented paragraph. Default units for indents *i* are ens.

Type font and size are reset to default values before each paragraph, and after processing font and size setting macros.

These strings are predefined by **–man**:

*R   '®', '(Reg)' in *nroff*.

*S   Change to default type size.

FILES

/usr/lib/tmac/tmac.an
/usr/man/man0/xx

SEE ALSO

troff(1), man(1)

REQUESTS

Request	Cause Break	If no Argument	Explanation
.B *t*	no	*t*=n.t.l.*	Text *t* is bold.
.BI *t*	no	*t*=n.t.l.	Join words of *t* alternating bold and italic.
.BR *t*	no	*t*=n.t.l.	Join words of *t* alternating bold and Roman.
.DT	no	.5i 1i...	Restore default tabs.
.HP *i*	yes	*i*=p.i.*	Set prevailing indent to *i*. Begin paragraph with hanging indent.
.I *t*	no	*t*=n.t.l.	Text *t* is italic.
.IB *t*	no	*t*=n.t.l.	Join words of *t* alternating italic and bold.
.IP *x i*	yes	*x*=""	Same as .TP with tag *x*.
.IR *t*	no	*t*=n.t.l.	Join words of *t* alternating italic and Roman.
.LP	yes	-	Same as .PP.
.PD *d*	no	*d*=.4v	Interparagraph distance is *d*.
.PP	yes	-	Begin paragraph. Set prevailing indent to .5i.
.RE	yes	-	End of relative indent. Set prevailing indent to amount of starting .RS.
.RB *t*	no	*t*=n.t.l.	Join words of *t* alternating Roman and bold.
.RI *t*	no	*t*=n.t.l.	Join words of *t* alternating Roman and italic.
.RS *i*	yes	*i*=p.i.	Start relative indent, move left margin in distance *i*. Set prevailing indent to .5i for nested indents.
.SH *t*	yes	*t*=n.t.l.	Subhead.
.SM *t*	no	*t*=n.t.l.	Text *t* is small.
.TH *n c x*	yes	-	Begin page named *n* of chapter *c*; *x* is extra commentary, e.g. 'local', for page foot. Set prevailing indent and tabs to .5i.
.TP *i*	yes	*i*=p.i.	Set prevailing indent to *i*. Begin indented paragraph with hanging tag given by

next text line. If tag doesn't fit, place it on separate line.

* n.t.l. = next text line; p.i. = prevailing indent

NAME
ms – macros for formatting manuscripts

SYNOPSIS
nroff **−ms** [options] file ...
troff **−ms** [options] file ...

DESCRIPTION
This package of *nroff* and *troff* macro definitions provides a canned formatting facility for technical papers in various formats. When producing 2-column output on a terminal, filter the output through *col*(1).

The macro requests are defined below. Many *nroff* and *troff* requests are unsafe in conjunction with this package, but these requests may be used with impunity after the first .PP:

>   .bp   begin new page
>   .br   break output line here
>   .sp n insert n spacing lines
>   .ls n (line spacing) n=1 single, n=2 double space
>   .na   no alignment of right margin

Output of the *eqn, neqn, tbl,* and *refer*(1) preprocessors for equations, tables and references is acceptable as input.

Diacritical marks may be applied to letters, as in these examples:

*`e	*`a	*´e	*^e	*^o	*:u	*~n	*,c	*vc
è	à	é	ê	ô	ü	ñ	ç	č

FILES
/usr/lib/tmac/tmac.s

SEE ALSO
eqn(1), troff(1), refer(1), tbl(1)

REQUESTS

Request	Initial Value	Cause Break	Explanation
.1C	yes	yes	One column format on a new page.
.2C	no	yes	Two column format.
.AB	no	yes	Begin abstract.
.AE	-	yes	End abstract.
.AI	no	yes	Author's institution follows. Suppressed in TM.
.AT	no	yes	Print 'Attached' and turn off line filling.
.AU *x y*	no	yes	Author's name follows. *x* is location and *y* is extension, ignored except in TM.
.B *x*	no	no	Print *x* in boldface and append *y*; if no argument switch to boldface.
.B1	no	yes	Begin text to be enclosed in a box.
.B2	no	yes	End boxed text.
.BT	date	no	Bottom title, automatically invoked at foot of page. May be redefined.
.BX *x*	no	no	Print *x* in a box.
.CS *x...*	-	yes	Cover sheet info if TM format, suppressed otherwise. Arguments are number of text pages, other pages, total pages, figures, tables, references.
.CT	no	yes	Print 'Copies to' and turn off line filling.
.DA *x*	nroff	no	'Date line' at bottom of page is *x*. Default is today.
.DE	-	yes	End displayed text. Implies .KE.
.DS *x*	no	yes	Start of displayed text, to appear verbatim line-by-line. *x*=I for indented display (default), *x*=L for left-justified on the page, *x*=C for centered, *x*=B (block) for centered with straight left margin. Implies .KS.
.EG	no	-	Print document in BTL format for 'Engineer's Notes.' Must be first.

.EN	-	yes	Space after equation produced by *eqn* or *neqn*.
.EQ *x y*	-	yes	Display equation. Equation number is *y*. Optional argument *x*=I, L, C as in .DS.
.FE	-	yes	End footnote.
.FS	no	no	Start footnote. The note will be moved to the bottom of the page.
.HO	-	no	'Bell Laboratories, Holmdel, New Jersey 07733'.
.I *x y*	no	no	Italicize *x* and append *y*; if no argument switch to Italic.
.IH	no	no	'Bell Laboratories, Naperville, Illinois 60540'
.IM	no	no	Print document in BTL format for an internal memorandum. Must be first.
.IP *x y*	no	yes	Start indented paragraph, with hanging tag *x*. Indentation is *y* ens (default 5).
.KE	-	yes	End keep. Put kept text on next page if not enough room.
.KF	no	yes	Start floating keep. If the kept text must be moved to the next page, float later text back to this page.
.KS	no	yes	Start keeping following text.
.LG	no	no	Make letters larger.
.LP	yes	yes	Start left-blocked paragraph.
.LT	no	yes	Start a letter with today's date; address follows.
.MF	-	-	Print document in BTL format for 'Memorandum for File.' Must be first.
.MH	-	no	'Bell Laboratories, Murray Hill, New Jersey 07974'.
.MR	-	-	Print document in BTL format for 'Memorandum for Record.' Must be first.
.ND *date*	troff	no	Use date supplied (if any) only in special BTL format positions; omit from page footer.
.NH *n*	-	yes	Same as .SH, with section number supplied automatically. Numbers are multilevel, like 1.2.3, where *n* tells what level is wanted (default is 1).
.NL	yes	no	Make letters normal size.
.OK	-	yes	'Other keywords' for TM cover sheet follow.
.PP	no	yes	Begin paragraph. First line indented.
.PT	pg #	-	Page title, automatically invoked at top of page. May be redefined.
.PY	-	no	'Bell Laboratories, Piscataway, New Jersey 08854'
.QE	-	yes	End quoted (indented and shorter) material.
.QP	-	yes	Begin single paragraph which is indented and shorter.
.QS	-	yes	Begin quoted (indented and shorter) material.
.R	yes	no	Roman text follows.
.RE	-	yes	End relative indent level.
.RP	no	-	Cover sheet and first page for released paper. Must precede other requests.
.RS	-	yes	Start level of relative indentation. Following .IP's are measured from current indentation.
.SG *x*	no	yes	Insert signature(s) of author(s), ignored except in TM. *x* is the reference line (initials of author and typist).
.SH	-	yes	Section head follows, font automatically bold.
.SM	no	no	Make letters smaller.
.TA *x*...	5...	no	Set tabs in ens. Default is 5 10 15 ...
.TE	-	yes	End table.
.TH	-	yes	End heading section of table.
.TL	no	yes	Title follows.
.TM *x*...	no	-	Print document in BTL technical memorandum format. Arguments are TM number, (quoted list of) case number(s), and file number. Must precede other requests.
.TR *x*	-	-	Print in BTL technical report format; report number is *x*. Must be first.
.TS *x*	-	yes	Begin table; if *x* is *H* table heading is repeated on new pages.
.UL *x*	-	no	Underline argument (even in troff).
.UX	-	no	'UNIX'; first time used, add footnote 'UNIX is a trademark of Bell Laboratories.'
.WH	-	no	'Bell Laboratories, Whippany, New Jersey 07981'.

NAME

terminals— conventional names

DESCRIPTION

These names are used by certain commands and are maintained as part of the shell environment (see *sh*(1), *environ*(5)).

1620	DIABLO 1620 (and others using HyType II)
1620−12	same, in 12-pitch mode
300	DASI/DTC/GSI 300 (and others using HyType I)
300−12	same, in 12-pitch mode
300s	DASI/DTC 300/S
300s−12	same, in 12-pitch mode
33	TELETYPE® Model 33
37	TELETYPE Model 37
40−2	TELETYPE Model 40/2
43	TELETYPE Model 43
450	DASI 450 (same as Diablo 1620)
450−12	same, in 12-pitch mode
450−12−8	same, in 12-pitch, 8 lines/inch mode
735	Texas Instruments TI735 (and TI725)
745	Texas Instruments TI745
dumb	terminals with no special features
hp	Hewlett-Packard HP264? series terminals
4014	Tektronix 4014
tn1200	General Electric TermiNet 1200
tn300	General Electric TermiNet 300
vt05	Digital Equipment Corp. VT05

Commands whose behavior may depend on the terminal accept arguments of the form −**T**term, where *term* is one of the names given above. If no such argument is present, a command may consult the shell environment for the terminal type.

SEE ALSO

stty(1), tabs(1), plot(1), sh(1), environ(5)
troff(1) for *nroff*

BUGS

The programs that ought to adhere to this nomenclature do so only fitfully.

Section 8
MAINTENANCE

NAME

boot — startup procedures

DESCRIPTION

A PDP11/45 and PDP11/70 UNIX system is started by a two-stage process. The first is a primary bootstrap which is able to read in relatively small stand-alone programs; the second (called *boot*) is used to read in the system itself.

The primary bootstrap must reside in the otherwise unused block zero of the boot device. It can be read in and started by the standard ROM programs, or if necessary by keying in a small startup routine. This program is capable of loading type 407 executable files (not shared, not separate I&D). The user types on the system console the name of the program wished, in this case *boot*, followed by a carriage return; the named program is retrieved from the file system that starts at block 0 of drive 0 of the boot device. No prompt is given, no diagnostic results if the file cannot be found, and no provision is made for correcting typographical errors.

The second step, called *boot,* actually brings in the system. When read into location 0 and executed, *boot* sets up memory management, relocates itself into high memory, and types a ':' on the console. Then it reads from the console a device specification (see below) followed immediately by a pathname. *Boot* finds the corresponding file on the given device, loads that file into memory location zero, sets up memory management as required, and calls the program by executing a 'trap' instruction. Normal line editing characters can be used.

Conventionally, the name of the secondary boot program is '/boot' and the name of the current version of the system is '/unix'. Then, the recipe is:

1)   Load block 0 of the boot device by fiddling with the console keys as appropriate for your hardware. If you have no appropriate ROM, some programs suitable for manual use are given below.

2)   Type *boot*.

3)   When the prompt is given, type

        hp(0,0)unix

    or

        rp(0,0)unix

depending on whether you are loading from an RP04/5/6 or an RP03 respectively. The first 0 indicates the physical unit number; the second indicates the block number of the beginning of the logical file system to be searched. (See below).

When the system is running, it types a '#' prompt. After doing any file system checks and setting the date (*date*(8)) a multi-user system is brought up by typing an EOT (control-d) in response to the '#' prompt.

Device specifications. A device specification has the following form:

    device(unit,offset)

where *device* is the type of the device to be searched, *unit* is the unit number of the device, and *offset* is the block offset of the file system on the device. *Device* is one of the following

    rp   RP03
    hp   RP04/5/6
    rk   RK05

For example, the specification

    hp(1,7000)

indicates an RP03 disk, unit 1, and the file system found starting at block 7000 (cylinder 35).

ROM programs. The following programs to call the primary bootstrap may be installed in read-only memories or manually keyed into main memory. Each program is position-independent but should be placed well above location 0 so it will not be overwritten. Each reads a block from the beginning of a device into core location zero. The octal words constituting the program are listed on the left.

RK (drive 0):

```
012700          mov     $rkda,r0
177412
005040          clr     −(r0)                    / rkda cleared by start
010040          mov     r0,−(r0)
012740          mov     $5,−(r0)
000005
105710     1:   tstb    (r0)
002376          bge     1b
005007          clr     pc
```

RP (drive 0)

```
012700          mov     $rpmr,r0
176726
005040          clr     −(r0)
005040          clr     −(r0)
005040          clr     −(r0)
010040          mov     r0,−(r0)
012740          mov     $5,−(r0)
000005
105710     1:   tstb    (r0)
002376          bge     1b
005007          clr     pc
```

FILES

/unix − system code
/usr/mdec/rpuboot, /usr/mdec/hpuboot − copies of primary bootstrap
/boot − second stage bootstrap

SEE ALSO

init(8)

NAME

cron — clock daemon

SYNOPSIS

/etc/cron

DESCRIPTION

Cron executes commands at specified dates and times according to the instructions in the file /usr/lib/crontab. Since *cron* never exits, it should only be executed once. This is best done by running *cron* from the initialization process through the file /etc/rc; see *init*(8).

Crontab consists of lines of six fields each. The fields are separated by spaces or tabs. The first five are integer patterns to specify the minute (0-59), hour (0-23), day of the month (1-31), month of the year (1-12), and day of the week (1-7 with 1=monday). Each of these patterns may contain a number in the range above; two numbers separated by a minus meaning a range inclusive; a list of numbers separated by commas meaning any of the numbers; or an asterisk meaning all legal values. The sixth field is a string that is executed by the Shell at the specified times. A percent character in this field is translated to a new-line character. Only the first line (up to a % or end of line) of the command field is executed by the Shell. The other lines are made available to the command as standard input.

Crontab is examined by *cron* every minute.

FILES

/usr/lib/crontab

NAME

crash — what to do when the system crashes

DESCRIPTION

This section gives at least a few clues about how to proceed if the system crashes. It can't pretend to be complete.

Bringing it back up. If the reason for the crash is not evident (see below for guidance on 'evident') you may want to try to dump the system if you feel up to debugging. At the moment a dump can be taken only on magtape. With a tape mounted and ready, stop the machine, load address 44, and start. This should write a copy of all of core on the tape with an EOF mark. Caution: Any error is taken to mean the end of core has been reached. This means that you must be sure the ring is in, the tape is ready, and the tape is clean and new. If the dump fails, you can try again, but some of the registers will be lost. See below for what to do with the tape.

In restarting after a crash, always bring up the system single-user. This is accomplished by following the directions in *boot*(8) as modified for your particular installation; a single-user system is indicated by having a particular value in the switches (173030 unless you've changed *init*) as the system starts executing. When it is running, perform a *dcheck* and *icheck*(1) on all file systems which could have been in use at the time of the crash. If any serious file system problems are found, they should be repaired. When you are satisfied with the health of your disks, check and set the date if necessary, then come up multi-user. This is most easily accomplished by changing the single-user value in the switches to something else, then logging out by typing an EOT.

To even boot UNIX at all, three files (and the directories leading to them) must be intact. First, the initialization program */etc/init* must be present and executable. If it is not, the CPU will loop in user mode at location 6. For *init* to work correctly, */dev/tty8* and */bin/sh* must be present. If either does not exist, the symptom is best described as thrashing. *Init* will go into a *fork/exec* loop trying to create a Shell with proper standard input and output.

If you cannot get the system to boot, a runnable system must be obtained from a backup medium. The root file system may then be doctored as a mounted file system as described below. If there are any problems with the root file system, it is probably prudent to go to a backup system to avoid working on a mounted file system.

Repairing disks. The first rule to keep in mind is that an addled disk should be treated gently; it shouldn't be mounted unless necessary, and if it is very valuable yet in quite bad shape, perhaps it should be dumped before trying surgery on it. This is an area where experience and informed courage count for much.

The problems reported by *icheck* typically fall into two kinds. There can be problems with the free list: duplicates in the free list, or free blocks also in files. These can be cured easily with an *icheck* −*s*. If the same block appears in more than one file or if a file contains bad blocks, the files should be deleted, and the free list reconstructed. The best way to delete such a file is to use *clri*(1), then remove its directory entries. If any of the affected files is really precious, you can try to copy it to another device first.

Dcheck may report files which have more directory entries than links. Such situations are potentially dangerous; *clri* discusses a special case of the problem. All the directory entries for the file should be removed. If on the other hand there are more links than directory entries, there is no danger of spreading infection, but merely some disk space that is lost for use. It is sufficient to copy the file (if it has any entries and is useful) then use *clri* on its inode and remove any directory entries that do exist.

Finally, there may be inodes reported by *dcheck* that have 0 links and 0 entries. These occur on the root device when the system is stopped with pipes open, and on other file systems when the system stops with files that have been deleted while still open. A *clri* will free the inode, and an *icheck -s* will recover any missing blocks.

Why did it crash? UNIX types a message on the console typewriter when it voluntarily crashes. Here is the current list of such messages, with enough information to provide a hope at least of the remedy. The message has the form 'panic: ...', possibly accompanied by other information. Left unstated in all cases is the possibility that hardware or software error produced the message in some unexpected way.

blkdev
>   The *getblk* routine was called with a nonexistent major device as argument. Definitely hardware or software error.

devtab
>   Null device table entry for the major device used as argument to *getblk*. Definitely hardware or software error.

iinit
>   An I/O error reading the super-block for the root file system during initialization.

out of inodes
>   A mounted file system has no more i-nodes when creating a file. Sorry, the device isn't available; the *icheck* should tell you.

no fs
>   A device has disappeared from the mounted-device table. Definitely hardware or software error.

no imt
>   Like 'no fs', but produced elsewhere.

no inodes
>   The in-core inode table is full. Try increasing NINODE in param.h. Shouldn't be a panic, just a user error.

no clock
>   During initialization, neither the line nor programmable clock was found to exist.

swap error
>   An unrecoverable I/O error during a swap. Really shouldn't be a panic, but it is hard to fix.

unlink − iget
>   The directory containing a file being deleted can't be found. Hardware or software.

out of swap space
>   A program needs to be swapped out, and there is no more swap space. It has to be increased. This really shouldn't be a panic, but there is no easy fix.

out of text
>   A pure procedure program is being executed, and the table for such things is full. This shouldn't be a panic.

trap
>   An unexpected trap has occurred within the system. This is accompanied by three numbers: a 'ka6', which is the contents of the segmentation register for the area in which the system's stack is kept; 'aps', which is the location where the hardware stored the program status word during the trap; and a 'trap type' which encodes which trap occurred. The trap types are:

0   bus error

1	illegal instruction
2	BPT/trace
3	IOT
4	power fail
5	EMT
6	recursive system call (TRAP instruction)
7	11/70 cache parity, or programmed interrupt
10	floating point trap
11	segmentation violation

In some of these cases it is possible for octal 20 to be added into the trap type; this indicates that the processor was in user mode when the trap occurred. If you wish to examine the stack after such a trap, either dump the system, or use the console switches to examine core; the required address mapping is described below.

Interpreting dumps. All file system problems should be taken care of before attempting to look at dumps. The dump should be read into the file */usr/sys/core; cp*(1) will do. At this point, you should execute *ps —alxk* and *who* to print the process table and the users who were on at the time of the crash. You should dump (*od*(1)) the first 30 bytes of */usr/sys/core*. Starting at location 4, the registers R0, R1, R2, R3, R4, R5, SP and KDSA6 (KISA6 for 11/40s) are stored. If the dump had to be restarted, R0 will not be correct. Next, take the value of KA6 (location 022(8) in the dump) multiplied by 0100(8) and dump 01000(8) bytes starting from there. This is the per-process data associated with the process running at the time of the crash. Relabel the addresses 140000 to 141776. R5 is C's frame or display pointer. Stored at (R5) is the old R5 pointing to the previous stack frame. At (R5)+2 is the saved PC of the calling procedure. Trace this calling chain until you obtain an R5 value of 141756, which is where the user's R5 is stored. If the chain is broken, you have to look for a plausible R5, PC pair and continue from there. Each PC should be looked up in the system's name list using *adb*(1) and its ':' command, to get a reverse calling order. In most cases this procedure will give an idea of what is wrong. A more complete discussion of system debugging is impossible here.

SEE ALSO

clri(1), icheck(1), dcheck(1), boot(8)

NAME

getty − set typewriter mode

SYNOPSIS

/etc/getty [char]

DESCRIPTION

Getty is invoked by *init*(8) immediately after a typewriter is opened following a dial-up. It reads the user's login name and calls *login*(1) with the name as argument. While reading the name *getty* attempts to adapt the system to the speed and type of terminal being used.

Init calls *getty* with a single character argument taken from the *ttys*(5) file entry for the terminal line. This argument determines a sequence of line speeds through which *getty* cycles, and also the 'login:' greeting message, which can contain character sequences to put various kinds of terminals in useful states.

The user's name is terminated by a new-line or carriage-return character. In the second case CRMOD mode is set (see *ioctl*(2)).

The name is scanned to see if it contains any lower-case alphabetic characters; if not, and if the name is nonempty, the system is told to map any future upper-case characters into the corresponding lower-case characters.

If the terminal's 'break' key is depressed, *getty* cycles to the next speed appropriate to the type of line and prints the greeting message again.

Finally, login is called with the user's name as argument.

The following arguments from the *ttys* file are understood.

0   Cycles through 300-1200-150-110 baud. Useful as a default for dialup lines accessed by a variety of terminals.

−   Intended for an on-line Teletype model 33, for example an operator's console.

1   Optimized for a 150-baud Teletype model 37.

2   Intended for an on-line 9600-baud terminal, for example the Textronix 4014.

3   Starts at 1200 baud, cycles to 300 and back. Useful with 212 datasets where most terminals run at 1200 speed.

5   Same as '3' but starts at 300.

4   Useful for on-line console DECwriter (LA36).

SEE ALSO

init(8), login(1), ioctl(2), ttys(5)

NAME

init, rc — process control initialization

SYNOPSIS

/etc/init

/etc/rc

DESCRIPTION

Init is invoked as the last step of the boot procedure (see *boot*(8)). Generally its role is to create a process for each typewriter on which a user may log in.

When *init* first is executed the console typewriter */dev/console.* is opened for reading and writing and the shell is invoked immediately. This feature is used to bring up a single-user system. If the shell terminates, *init* comes up multi-user and the process described below is started.

When *init* comes up multiuser, it invokes a shell, with input taken from the file */etc/rc.* This command file performs housekeeping like removing temporary files, mounting file systems, and starting daemons.

Then *init* reads the file */etc/ttys* and forks several times to create a process for each typewriter specified in the file. Each of these processes opens the appropriate typewriter for reading and writing. These channels thus receive file descriptors 0, 1 and 2, the standard input, output and error files. Opening the typewriter will usually involve a delay, since the *open* is not completed until someone is dialed up and carrier established on the channel. Then */etc/getty* is called with argument as specified by the last character of the *ttys* file line. *Getty* reads the user's name and invokes *login*(1) to log in the user and execute the shell.

Ultimately the shell will terminate because of an end-of-file either typed explicitly or generated as a result of hanging up. The main path of *init*, which has been waiting for such an event, wakes up and removes the appropriate entry from the file *utmp*, which records current users, and makes an entry in */usr/adm/wtmp*, which maintains a history of logins and logouts. Then the appropriate typewriter is reopened and *getty* is reinvoked.

Init catches the hangup signal SIGHUP and interprets it to mean that the system should be brought from multi user to single user. Use 'kill -1 1' to send the hangup signal.

FILES

/dev/tty?, /etc/utmp, /usr/adm/wtmp, /etc/ttys, /etc/rc

SEE ALSO

login(1), kill(1), sh(1), ttys(5), getty(8)

NAME

    makekey — generate encryption key

SYNOPSIS

    /usr/lib/makekey

DESCRIPTION

    Makekey improves the usefulness of encryption schemes depending on a key by increasing the amount of time required to search the key space. It reads 10 bytes from its standard input, and writes 13 bytes on its standard output. The output depends on the input in a way intended to be difficult to compute (i.e. to require a substantial fraction of a second).

    The first eight input bytes (the *input key*) can be arbitrary ASCII characters. The last two (the *salt*) are best chosen from the set of digits, upper- and lower-case letters, and '.' and '/'. The salt characters are repeated as the first two characters of the output. The remaining 11 output characters are chosen from the same set as the salt and constitute the *output key*.

    The transformation performed is essentially the following: the salt is used to select one of 4096 cryptographic machines all based on the National Bureau of Standards DES algorithm, but modified in 4096 different ways. Using the input key as key, a constant string is fed into the machine and recirculated a number of times. The 64 bits that come out are distributed into the 66 useful key bits in the result.

    Makekey is intended for programs that perform encryption (e.g. *ed* and *crypt*(1)). Usually its input and output will be pipes.

SEE ALSO

    crypt(1), ed(1)

NAME
update — periodically update the super block

SYNOPSIS
/etc/update

DESCRIPTION
Update is a program that executes the *sync*(2) primitive every 30 seconds. This insures that the file system is fairly up to date in case of a crash. This command should not be executed directly, but should be executed out of the initialization shell command file.

SEE ALSO
sync(2), sync(1), init(8)

BUGS

With *update* running, if the CPU is halted just as the *sync* is executed, a file system can be damaged. This is partially due to DEC hardware that writes zeros when NPR requests fail. A fix would be to have *sync*(1) temporarily increment the system time by at least 30 seconds to trigger the execution of *update*. This would give 30 seconds grace to halt the CPU.

Section 9
QUICK UNIX
REFERENCE

†UNIX is a Trademark of Bell Laboratories.

adb [−w] [*objfil* [*corfil*]]   { −w = open *objfil* and *corfil*
for both reading and writing; defaults: **a.out core**

ar $\begin{Bmatrix} d \\ m \\ p \\ q \\ r \\ t \\ x \end{Bmatrix}$ [**abciluv**][*posname*] afile file ...

d = delete	**a** = after *posname*
m = move to end or *posname*	**b** or **i** = before *posname*
p = print	**c** = suppress create message
q = quickly (no checking)	**l** = local temp files
r = replace	**u** = update
t = list	**v** = verbose
x = extract	

as [−] [−**o** *objfil*] *file* ...
   − = make undefined symbols global
   −**o** = use next argument as output; default: **a.out**

at *time* [*day*] [*file*]
   time = *hours* [*minutes*] [**apnm**] (AM, PM, noon, midnight)
   day = *month day-no* or *day-of-week* [**week**]
   week = 7 days more

awk [−F*c*] [−**f** *progfile*] [*prog*] [*file*] ...
   −F*c* = use *c* as field separator
   −**f** = use next argument as *prog*

bas [*file*]

basename *string* [*suffix*]

bc [−**l**] [−**c**] [*file* ...]
   −**l** = load the function library
   −**c** = compile only

calendar [−]   { − sends all users their calendar entries

cat [−**u**] *file* ...   { −**u** causes output to be unbuffered

cc [−**c**] [−**p**] [−**f**] [−**O**] [−**S**] [−**P**] [−**o** *output*]
   [−**D***name*=*def*] [−**U***name*] [−**I***dir*] *file.c*... [−*l*] *ofile*...
   −**c** = suppress loading
   −**p** = profile
   −**f** = floating-point interpreter
   −**O** = optimize
   −**S** = keep assembler code; output to *file*.**s**
   −**P** = just preprocess; output to *file*.**i**
   −**o** *output* = output to *output* ; default: **a.out**
   −**D***name*=*def* = define preprocessor variable
   −**D***name* = *name* is set to 1
   −**U***name* = undefine *name*
   −**I***dir* = after home, look in *dir* for include files
   −*l* = loader options

cd *directory*

chgrp *group file* ...

chmod *mode file* ...   {*mode* may be symbolic [**ugoa**]{+ − =}{**rwxst**}
   where **a** = **ugo**, **s** = set id and **t** = sticky
   or *mode* may be the octal OR of the following:
   4000   set user id on execution
   2000   set group id on execution
   1000   sticky bit
   0700   read, write, execute by owner
   0070   read, write, execute by group
   0007   read, write, execute by others

chown *owner file* ...

cmp [−**l**] [−**s**] *file1 file2*
   −**l** = print byte number and differing bytes
   −**s** = print nothing; return codes: 0=same
   1=different, 2=problem

col [−**bfx**]
   −**b** = do not output backspace
   −**f** = output half line motions
   −**x** = do not convert spaces to tabs

comm [−**123**] *file1 file2*
   −**1** = suppress lines only in *file1*
   −**2** = suppress lines only in *file2*
   −**3** = suppress lines in both files

cp *oldfile newfile*

cp *file* ... *directory*

crypt [*password*]

date [*yymmddhhmm* [*.ss*]]   {date set to *year-month-day-hour-minute*
   .ss = seconds
   no arguments - print date

dc [*file*]

dd [*option*=*value*] ...   {options are:
   if= input file
   of= output file
   ibs= input block size; default: 512
   obs= output block size; default: 512
   bs= block size
   cbs= conversion block size
   files= copy *n* files
   skip= skip *n* input records
   seek= skip *n* output records
   count= copy only *n* input records
   conv=ascii,ebcdic,ibm,lcase,ucase,swab,sync,noerror

deroff [−**w**] *file* ...   { −**w** = output word list

diff [−**befh**] *file1 file2*
   −**b** = ignore trailing blanks
   −**e** = output **ed** script to make *file2* from *file1*
   −**f** = opposite script from −**e** but useless to **ed**
   −**h** = fast but half-hearted; no size limits

diff3 [−**ex3**] *file1 file2 file3*
   −**e** = output **ed** script to add changes between *file2* and
   file3 to *file1*
   −**x** = output script for changes in all 3 files
   −**3** = output script only for changes in *file3*

du [−**s**] [−**a**] [*file* ...]
   −**s** = only give grand total
   −**a** = give entry for each file

echo [−**n**] [*args*]   { −**n** adds no newline to output

ed [−] [−**x**] [*name*]
   − = no character count on **e**, **r**, **w** commands
   −**x** = file is encrypted

eqn [−**d***xy*] [−**f***n*] [−**p***n*] [−**s***n*] [*file*] ...
   −**d***xy* = use *x* and *y* as delimiters
   −**f***n* = use *n* as font
   −**p***n* = use ±*n* for subscript point size changes; default: 3
   −**s***n* = use *n* as point size

expr *arg* ...

f77 [−**c**] [−**p**] [−**O**] [−**S**] [−**f**] [−**o** *output*] [−**onetrip**] [−**u**] [−**C**]
   [−**w**] [−**F**] [−**m**] [−**E***x*] [−**R***x*] *file.f* ... [−*l*] *ofile* ...
   −**c** = suppress loading; output in *file*.**o**
   −**p** = profile
   −**O** = optimize
   −**S** = compile only; output to *file*.**s**
   −**f** = floating point interpreter
   −**o** *output* = output to *output* ; default: **a.out**
   −**onetrip** = compile onetime loops
   −**u** = default variable type undefined
   −**C** = subscript checking
   −**w** = no warning messages
   −**w66** = no Fortran 66 warning messages
   −**F** = run only EFL and Ratfor preprocessors
   −**m** = run M4 preprocessor before EFL or Ratfor
   −**E***x* = use *x* as EFL option
   −**R***x* = use *x* as Ratfor option
   −*l* = loader options

factor [*number*]

file *file* ...

find *pathname expression*
   expression is made of the following primitives,
   n is integer , +*n* means more than *n*,
   −*n* means less than *n*
   −**name** *filename*   true if *filename* matches current file
   −**perm** *onum*   true if permission flags = *onum* (octal)
   −**type** *c*   true if file type is **b**,**c**,**d**,**f**
   −**links** *n*   true if file has *n* links
   −**user** *uname*   true if file belongs to *uname*
   −**group** *gname*   true if file belongs to *gname*
   −**size** *n*   true if file is *n* blocks long
   −**inum** *n*   true if file has inode *n*
   −**atime** *n*   true if file has been accessed in *n* days
   −**mtime** *n*   true if file has been modified in *n* days
   −**exec** *command*   true if exit status of *command* is 0
   −**ok** *command*   like −**exec** but asks
   −**print**   true; prints current pathname
   −**newer** *file*   true if file was modified before *file*

   combined with the following operators:
   !   prefix *not*
   −**a**   infix *and*
   −**o**   infix *or*
   ( )   parentheses for grouping; must be escaped with \

399

graph [−a] [−b] [−c c] [−g n] [−l lab] [−m n]
  [−h f] [−w f] [−r f] [−u f] [−s] [−t]
    [−x[l] low [upper [sp]]]   [−y[l] low [upper [sp]]]
        −a = automatic abscissas
        −b = disconnect after each label
        −c c = use c as label for each point
        −g n = n is grid type; 0 (no grid), 1(frame+ticks), 2(full)
        −l lab = label graph with lab
        −m n = mode; 0(disconnected), 1(connected); default: 1
        −s = save screen; don't erase before plotting
        −h f = f is fraction of space for height
        −w f = f is fraction of space for width
        −r f = f is fraction of space to move right before plotting
        −u f = f is fraction of space to move up before plotting
        −t = transpose horizontal and vertical axes
        −x[l] = next 3 arguments are lower, upper, & spacing limits
                for x; l for logarithmic x axis
        −y[l] = next 3 arguments are lower, upper, & spacing limits
                for y; l for logarithmic y axis

grep [−v] [−b] [−c] [−n] [−l] [−s] [−h] [−y] [−e expr] expr [file] ...
  egrep [grep-option] [−f file] [expr] [file] ...
  fgrep [grep-option] [−x] [−f file] [strings] [file]
        −v = print all but those that match
        −b = print block numbers
        −c = print count of matching lines
        −n = print line number
        −l = list files with matching lines
        −s = just return status
        −h = no filename headers on output lines
        −y = fold lower and upper case (**grep**)
        −x = output only lines matching totally (**fgrep**)
        −e expr = use expr for matching
        −f file = use file for matching (**egrep,fgrep**)

join [−an] [−e s] [−jn m] [−j m] [−o m.n ...] [−tc] file1 file2
        −an = output unpaired lines in file n also
        −e s = use string s for white space
        −jn m = join on m th field of file n
        −j m = join on m th field
        −o n.m ... = output m th field of n th file ...
        −tc = use c as input separator

kill [−signo] processid ...   {signo is sent with the following meanings:
  (name following description is in **#include** <**signal.h**>)
        1 = hangup (SIGHUP)
        2 = interrupt (SIGINT)
        3 = quit (SIGQUIT)
        4 = illegal instruction (SIGILL)
        5 = trace trap (SIGTRAP)
        6 = IOT (SIGIOT)
        7 = EMT (SIGEMT)
        8 = floating exception (SIGFPE)
        9 = kill (SIGKILL)
        10 = bus error (SIGBUS)
        11 = segment violation (SIGSEGV)
        12 = bad system call (SIGSYS)
        13 = write on pipe with no one to read (SIGPIPE)
        14 = alarm clock (SIGALRM)
        15 = software terminate (SIGTERM) (default)
        16 = unassigned

ld [−sulxXrdnioeOD] name ...
        s = strip
        u = make following argument undefined
        lx = load library **/lib/libx.a**; x is a string
        x = do not save local symbols
        X = used by **cc**
        r = generate relocation bits
        d = define common storage
        n = share text
        i = separate instruction and data space
        o = use next argument as output not **a.out**
        e = use next argument as entry point; default: 0
        O = overlay file
        D = use next argument as data segment size

learn [−directory] [subject [lesson [speed]]]

lex [−fntv] [file]
        −f = fast; no packing; only for small programs
        −n = no summary statistics; default
        −t = output to **stdout** not **lex.yy.c**
        −v = generate summary statistics

lint [−abchnpuvx] file ...
        a = report longs assigned to int variables
        b = report **break** statements not reached
        c = report unportable casts
        h = use heuristic tests
        n = don't check for standard library
        p = check portability to IBM and GCOS C
        u = don't report on defined and unused variables
        v = don't report on unused arguments in functions
        x = report externally declared variables not used

ln oldname [newname]   {newname is the name of the link

login [username]

look [−df] string [file]
        d = dictionary order
        f = fold upper case letters to lower case
        default input: **/usr/dict/words** folded

lorder file ...

ls [−ltasdrucifg] name ...
        l = long format
        t = sort by time modified
        a = list all entries
        s = give size in blocks
        d = list only directory names
        r = list in reverse order
        u = sort on last access time
        c = sort on last inode change
        i = print i-number
        f = interpret all entries as directories
        g = give group ID instead of owner ID

m4 [file]

mail person ...

mail [−p] [−r] [−f file]
        −r = first-in, first-out order
        −p = don't ask questions
        −f file = use file as mail file

make [−f makefile] [−iknrts] file ...
        i = ignore returning status
        k = on bad status, continue unrelated entries
        n = trace and print, don't execute
        t = touch
        r = no suffix list
        s = work silently

man [−tnkew] [chapter] title ...
        t = phototypeset
        n = output to **stdout** (default)
        k = output to Tektronix 4014
        e = run **eqn**; append or prefix **e** with above
        w = print only path names

mesg [ny]
        n = forbid messages
        y = allow messages
        no argument; report current permission

mkdir dirname ...

mv oldname newname

mv file ... directory

newgrp group

nice [−number] command [arguments]
        {number is a priority from 1 to 20, lowest 20; default: 10.

nm [−gnopru] [file]
        g = print only global symbols
        n = sort by value instead of by name
        o = output file name on each line
        p = do not sort
        r = sort in reverse order
        u = print only undefined symbols

nohup command [arguments]

nroff [−ol] [−nn] [−ran] [−mname] [−sn] [−h] [−i] [−q]
  [−T name] [−e] file ...
        −ol = list of pages to output, separated by , or −(range)
        −nn = number first generated page n
        −ran = set number register a to the value n
        −mname = prepend macro file **/usr/lib/tmac/tmac.**name
        −sn = stop after n pages; default: 1
        −h = replace spaces with tabs
        −i = read **stdin** after files
        −q = for insertions, send bell not name, do not echo
        −Tname = output for terminal name
                37 tn300 300s 300 450
        −e = equally-spaced words in adjusted lines

od [−bcdox] [file] [[+] offset [.] [b]]
        b = bytes in octal
        c = bytes in ascii
        d = words in decimal
        o = words in octal
        x = words in hex
        offset = where to begin (octal; . for decimal; **b** for blocks)

passwd [*name*]

plot [−T*term* [*raster*]]
    term = **4014 450 300 300S ver**

pr [−*n*] [+*n*] [−**h** *hdr*] [−**w***n*] [−**l***n*] [−**t**] [−**s***c*] [−**m**] *name* ...
    −*n* = *n*-column output
    +*n* = begin with page *n*
    −**h** = use next argument as header
    −**w***n* = use page width *n* ; default: 72
    −**l***n* = use page length *n* ; default: 66
    −**t** = do not print header or trailer
    −**s***c* = separate columns by the character *c*
    −**m** = print each file in a separate column

prof [−**v**] [−**a**] [−**l**] [−*low* [−*high*]] [*file*]
    −**v** = output only graphic profile
    −**a** = report all symbols, not just externals
    −**l** = order output by symbol value
    low, high = percentages for plotting; default: 0,100

ps [**aklx**] [*namelist*]
    a = give all processes with typewriters
    k = system debugging
    l = output long listing
    x = give all processes

ptx [−**f**] [−**w** *n*] [−**g** *n*] [−**o** *only*] [−**i** *ignore*] [−**b** *break*] [−**r**]
    [−**t**] [*input* [*output*]]
    −**f** = fold upper and lower case
    −**w** *n* = set line width to *n* ; default: 72
    −**g** *n* = set column gap to *n* ; default: 3
    −**o** *only* = use only keywords from *only*
    −**i** *ignore* = don't use keywords from *ignore*
    −**b** *break* = use characters in *break* to separate words
    −**r** = use 1st word as reference; use as 5th field
    −**t** = phototypeset

ratfor [−**C**] [−**h**] [−**6***x*] [*file*] ...
    −**C** = copy comments
    −**h** = convert quoted strings to **H** convention
    −**6***x* = use *x* as continuation character

refer [−**a***r*] [−**b**] [−**c***s*] [−**e**] [−**k***x*] [−**l***m,n*] [−**p** *f*] [−**n**] [−**s***keys*] ...
  lookbib [*file*] ...
    −**a***r* = reverse the first *r* author names
    −**a** = reverse all author names
    −**b** = omit all flags
    −**c***s* = capitalize fields in *s*
    −**e** = accumulate references
    −**k***x* = labels specified with *x*
    −**l***m,n* = label with *m* name letters and *n* year digits
    −**p** *f* = use file *f* as references
    −**n** = don't search default file
    −**s***keys* = sort on *keys*

rev [*file* ...]

rm [−**fir**] *file* ...
    −**f** = do not ask about mode
    −**i** = interactive
    −**r** = remove directory contents recursively

rmdir *dir* ...

roff [+*n*] [−*n*] [−**s**] [−**h**] *file* ...
    +*n* = start with page *n*
    −*n* = stop after page *n*
    −**s** = pause before each page
    −**h** = use tabs for spaces

sed [−**n**] [−**f** *commandfile*] [−**e** *script*] [*file*] ...
    −**n** = only output lines operated on by **p** command
    −**f** = next argument is command file
    −**e** = next argument is editor command

sh [−**ceiknrstuvx**] [*arg*] ...
    c = use next argument as command
    e = if non interactive, exit on bad status
    i = interactive
    k = keywords
    n = don't execute, just read commands
    r = restricted environment
    s = read from **stdin**
    t = exit after 1 command
    u = treat unset variables as error
    v = print input as it's read
    x = print on execution

size [*object* ...]

sleep *seconds*

sort [−**cmubdfinrt***x*] [+*m.n* [−*m.n*]] ... [−**o** *name*] [−**T** *dir*] [*file*] ...
    c = just check order, don't sort
    m = merge only, files should be sorted
    u = output only 1 copy of equal lines
    b = ignore leading blanks
    d = dictionary order
    f = fold upper case to lower case
    i = ignore characters outside 040-0176
    n = sort initial string by arithmetic value
    r = reverse sort
    t*x* = tab character is *x*
    +*m.n* = skip *m* fields and *n* characters
    −*m.n* = end of key (used with +*m.n*)
    −**o** *name* = output to *file*
    −**T** *dir* = use *dir* for temporaries

spell [−**b**] [−**v**] [−**x**] [*file* ...]
    b = British
    v = output derived words from list
    x = print stems

spline [−**a**] [−**k**] [−**n**] [−**p**] [−**x**]
    −**a** = automatic abscissas; next argument is spacing
    −**k** = next argument is used to compute boundary value
    −**n** = next argument is number of intervals between limits
    −**p** = make output periodic
    −**x** = next 1 or 2 arguments are lower and upper x limits

split [−*n*] [*file* [*name*]]   {*n* lines per file; default: 1000

strip *name* ...

struct [−**s**] [−**i**] [−**a**] [−**b**] [−**n**] [−**e***n*] [*file*]
    −**s** = input in standard format
    −**i** = don't make computed goto's switches
    −**a** = turn else if sequences into switch
    −**b** = generate goto's, not breaks
    −**n** = generate goto's, not nexts
    −**e***n* = loop control parameter

stty *option* ...   {options, preceded by − to indicate negation are:

even	allow even parity
odd	allow odd parity
raw	raw mode input
cbreak	pass characters on as received
nl	accept only new-line to end lines
echo	echo back every character typed
lcase	map upper case to lower case
tabs	preserve tabs
ek	reset erase and kill to # and @
erase *c*	set erase character to *c*
kill *c*	set kill character to *c*
hup	hang up on last close
0	hang up immediately
cr*n*	set delay for carriage return *n*=(0,1,2,3)
nl*n*	set delay for linefeed *n*=(0,1,2,3)
tab*n*	set delay for tab *n*=(0,1,2,3)
ff*n*	set delay for formfeed *n*=(0,1)
tty33	modes for Teletype model 33
tty37	modes for Teletype model 37
vt05	modes for DEC VT05
tn300	modes for GE TermiNet 300
ti700	modes for Texas Instruments 700
tek	modes for Tektronix 4014
50 75 110 134 150 200 300 600 1200 1800 2400	
4800 9600 exta extb set baud rate	

su [*userid*]

sum *file* ...

tabs [−**n**] [*terminal*]
    −**n** = don't indent left margin
    terminal =
            1620[−12]
            300[**s**][−12]
            33, 37, 40−**2, 43**
            450[−12][−8]
            735, 745
            dumb
            hp
            4014
            tn1200, tn300
            vt05

tail [±*number* [**lbc**]] [*file*]   { *number* = lines, blocks, characters
    from beginning (+) or end (−)

tar [*key*] [*name* ...]   {*key* is a string containing at most
one function and optionally several modifiers.
functions are:
    r = write files on end of tape
    x = extract from tape
    t = list
    u = update
    c = create new tape (implies **r**)
modifiers are:
    0,...,7 = tape drive
    v = verbose
    w = wait for user response
    f = use next argument as tape
    b = use next argument as blocking factor
    l = complain on unresolved links

tbl [*file* ...]

tc [−**t**] [−**s***n*] [−**p***l*] [*file*]
    −**t** = don't wait between pages
    −**s***n* = skip the first *n* pages
    −**p***l* = set page length to *l* [**picP**]
        (points, inches, centimeters, Picas); default: **P**

tee [−**i**] [−**a**] [*file*] ...
    −**i** = ignore interrupts
    −**a** = append don't overwrite

test *expr*   {*expr* is made of the following primitives:
    −**r** *file* = true if *file* is readable
    −**w** *file* = true if *file* is writable
    −**f** *file* = true if *file* is not a directory
    −**d** *file* = true if *file* is a directory
    −**s** *file* = true if *file* longer than 0
    −**t** [*fildes*] = true if *fildes* is a terminal; default: 1
    −**z** *s1* = true if length of *s1* = 0
    −**n** *s1* = true if length of *s1* not 0
    s1 = *s2* = true if *s1* = *s2*
    s1 != *s2* = true if *s1* != *s2*
    s1 = true if *s1* not null
    n1 op n2 = algebraic comparison of integers
        op = −**eq**, −**ne**, −**gt**, −**ge**, −**lt**, −**le**
combined with the following operators:
    ! = unary negation
    −**a** = binary *and*
    −**o** = binary *or*
    (*expr*) = parentheses for grouping

time *command* [*arguments*]

tk [−**t**] [−*n*] [−**p***l*] [*file*]
    −**t** = don't wait between pages
    −*n* = *n* column output
    −**p***l* = set page length to *l*

touch [−**c**] *file* ...   { −**c** = create *file*

tp [*key*] [*name* ...]   {*key* is a character string containing at most
one function and possibly several modifiers.
    functions are:
        r = replace
        u = update
        d = delete
        x = extract
        t = list
    and modifiers are:
        m = magtape
        0,...,7 = tape drive
        v = verbose
        c = create new tape
        f = use first file in place of tape
        i = ignore errors
        w = wait for user response

tr [−**cds**] [*string1* [*string2*]]
    c = complement characters in *string1*
    d = delete all characters in *string1*
    s = make repeated characters in *string2* one character

troff [−**o***l*] [−**s***n*] [−**n***n*] [−**r***an*] [−**m***x*] [−**t**] [−**f**] [−**w**] [−**a**]
[−**i**] [−**q**] [−**b**] [−**p***n*] [−**g**] *file* ...
    −**o***l* = list of pages to output, separated by , or −(range)
    −**s***n* = stop after every *n* pages
    −**n***n* = number first generated page *n*
    −**r***an* = set number register *a* to the value *n*
    −**m***x* = prepend file **/usr/lib/tmac/tmac**.*x*
    −**t** = output to standard output
    −**f** = do not feed paper or stop phototypesetter at end
    −**w** = wait until phototypesetter available
    −**a** = send printable approximation to standard output
    −**i** = read **stdin** after files
    −**q** = do **rd** in simultaneous input-output mode
    −**b** = just report if phototypesetter busy
    −**p***n* = print all characters in size *n*
    −**g** = output for GCOS

tsort [**file**]

uniq [−**udc**] [+*n*] [−*n*] [*input* [*output*]]
    u = output lines not repeated
    d = output one copy of repeated lines
    c = output count with each line
    +*n* = skip first *n* fields in each line
    −*n* = skip first *n* characters in each line

wc [−**lwc**] [*name* ...]   { −**lwc** = just count lines, words or chars

who [*who-file*] [**am i**]
    no arguments tells who is on
    1 argument is file to be examined
    2 arguments tells who you are

write *user* [*ttyname*]

xsend *person*

yacc [−**vd**] [*grammar*]
    v = make file **y.output**
    d = make file **y.tab.h** for *define* statements

COMMUNICATIONS COMMANDS

cu *telno* [−**t**] [−**s** *speed*] [−**a** *acu*] [−**l** *line*]
    in *telno* use − for delays
    −**t** = to dial a terminal
    −**s** = *speed* = **110 134 150 300 1200**; default 300
    −**a** = *acu* = acu pathname; default /dev/cua0
    −**l** = *line* = line name; default /dev/cul0

The following are interpreted by the *send* process:
    `~.`   terminate connection
    `~EOT`   terminate connection
    `~<file`   send contents of *file* as though typed
    `~!`   run shell on local system
    `~!cmd ...`   run *cmd* on local system
    `~$cmd ...`   run *cmd* on local system and send output
    `~%take` *from* [*to*]   copy file from remote to local
    `~%put` *from* [*to*]   copy file from local to remote
    `~~ ...`   send line ~ ...

The *receive* process recognizes output diversions:
    `~>[>][:]file`
        lines
    `~>`
where *file* is created or appended to (>>)
on the local system; : for silent

uucp [−**d**] [−**c**] [−**m**] *source-file* ... *destination-file*
    −**d** = make necessary directories
    −**c** = don't spool; copy from source
    −**m** = send mail when done
file names may be *pathname* or *system-name!pathname*
pathname is either a full pathname,
    ~*user pathname*, or anything else (current
    directory is prefixed automatically)

uulog [−**s***sys*] [−**u***user*]
    −**s***sys* = report only about *sys*
    −**u***user* = report only about *user*

uux [−] *command*   { − makes **stdin** for *command* same as
    stdin for **uux**

SYSTEM MAINTENANCE COMMANDS

ac [−**w** *wtemp*] [−**p**] [−**d**] [*people*] ...
    −**w** *wtemp* = use alternate **wtemp** file
    −**p** = print individual totals
    −**d** = print by day (midnight to midnight)
    people = only those login names specified

/etc/accton [*file*]

arcv *file* ...

clri *filesys i-number* ...

dcheck [−**i** *numbers*] [*filesys*]   {−**i** report on specified i-numbers

df [**filesys**] ...   {no argument, report on all normally mounted systems

dump [**key** [*arg*] ... filesys]   *key* is chosen from:
        f = place dump on next argument
        u = if successful, write date on **/etc/ddate**; default
        0−9 = dump level; default 9
        s = size of dump tape; default 2300ft
        d = tape density; default 1600

dumpdir [**f** *filename*]   { **f** causes dump to go to *filename*

icheck [−**s**] [−**b** *numbers*] [*filesys*]
        −**s** = reconstruct new free list
        −**b** = report on specified block numbers

iostat [−**tisb**] [*interval* [*count*]]
        −**t** = report characters/second
        −**i** = report percentages
        −**s** = report raw timing info
        −**b** = report i/o buffer usage

/etc/mkfs *special-file proto*

/etc/mknod *name* [**bc**] *major minor*
        b = block-type device (disk, tape)
        c = character-type device

/etc/mount [*device directory* [−**r**]]   { −**r** = read-only

/etc/umount *device*

ncheck [−**i** *numbers*] [−**a**] [−**s**] [*filesys*]
        −**i** = report only on specified i-numbers
        −**a** = also report names beginning with . and ..
        −**s** = only report special files

pstat [−**aixptuf**] [*suboptions*] [*file*]
        −**a** = report on all process slots
        −**i** = report inode table
        −**x** = report text table
        −**p** = report active processes
        −**t** = report on terminals
        −**u** *addr* = report on user process at *addr*
        −**f** = report on open files

quot [−**n**] [−**c**] [−**f**] [*filesys*]
        −**n** = list all files and their owners
        −**c** = list files by size
        −**f** = list space and number of files for each user

restor *key* [*argument*] ...
   { *key* is one of following with optional **f**:
        f = use first argument as tape
        r = tape is loaded into file system *argument*
        R = asks which tape to start on - allows restart
        x = extract named files
        t = print date of dump

sa [−**abcjlnrstuv**] [*file*]
        a = report commands used once as **other**
        b = sort by (user time + system time)/number of calls
        c = print percentages
        j = print seconds/call
        l = separate system and user time
        m = print processes and CPU minutes for each user
        n = sort by number of calls
        r = sort in reverse order
        s = merge results into **/usr/adm/savacct**
        t = report (realtime)/(usertime+systime) for each command
        u = print user ID and command name
        v*n* = print commands used *n* times or less

Special Characters

|	pipeline
!	pipeline
;	sequential command separator
&	return without waiting for command to finish
&&	only execute command following if previous command returned 0 value
||	only execute command following if previous command returned non-zero value
`' ... '`	take enclosed characters literally
`" ... "`	literal except for parameter substitution
\	negates special meaning of following character

Input-Output

[d]<	use next argument as standard input with file descriptor d ; default 0
[d]>	use next argument as standard output with file descriptor d ; default 1
[d]>>	same as > but append to file if it exists
[d]<<	use as standard input shell input up to a line that matches the next argument
[d]<&digit	duplicate standard input from digit
[d]<&−	close standard input
[d]<>	open next argument for reading & writing

File Name Generation

?	match single character
*	match string of characters (including null)
[...]	match a class of characters
	a pair of characters separated by a − matches all characters lexically between the pair

Parameter Substitution

$n	replace $n with argument n
$*	"$1 $2 ..."
$@	"$1" "$2" ...
$#	number of positional parameters
$−	options supplied on invocation or by set
$?	value returned by last command
$$	process number of this shell
$!	process number of last background command
name=value	set variable
${parm−word }	use parm if set; otherwise word
${parm=word }	if parm not set, set it to word and use it
${parm?word }	use parm if set; otherwise print word and exit
${parm+word }	use word if parm is set; otherwise nothing
$HOME	default argument for cd
$PATH	search path for commands
$MAIL	mail file
$PS1	primary prompt string; default $
$PS2	secondary prompt string; default >
$IFS	field separators; default blank, tab, newline
$TERM	terminal type (see command tabs)

Command Language

for name [**in** word ...] **do** list **done**
case word **in** [patl [\| pat2] ...) list ;;] ... **esac**
if list **then** list [**elif** list **then** list] ... [**else** list] **fi**
while list [**do** list] **done**

until list [**do** list] **done**
(list)
{ list }

break [n]	exit from **for** or **while** n levels
continue [n]	do next iteration of n th **for** or **while**
exit [n]	exit with return value n
:	no-op command but may contain text

Special Commands

. file	read and execute commands from file
eval [arg ...]	arg ... is read and executed
exec [arg ...]	execute arg ...
export [name ...]	export name to environment of commands
read name ...	read **stdin** and assign to name ...
readonly [name ...]	mark name read-only
set [−eknptuvx [arg ...]]	see **sh** command for flags
shift	rename positional parameters; $1=$2 ...
times	print accumulated process times
trap [arg] [n]	execute arg if signal n is received
umask [nnn]	file creation mask is complement of octal nnn
wait [pid]	wait for process pid

Regular Expressions

c	the character c
\c	the character c
.	any character except <nl>
[str]	only those characters in str; a−b all characters from ascii a to b
[^str]	any character except those in str and <nl>
re*	all adjacent occurrences of re
\(re \)	re
\n	n th re enclosed in \(\)
^	beginning of line
$	end of line
string of re's	
null-re	last re encountered

Addresses

.	current line
$	last line
n	n-th line
´x	line marked with name x
/re /	first line searching forward containing re
?re ?	first line searching backward containing re
addr ± n	addr + (or −) n
± [n]	. + (or −) n ; default 1
addr ±	addr + (or −) 1

Commands

(.)a	append
(. , .)c	change
(. , .)d	delete
e [filename]	edit
E [filename]	edit; no diagnostics
f [filename]	remembered name
(1 , $)g/re /commands	global
(.)i	insert
(. , .+1)j	join
(.)kx	mark (addressed by ´x)
(. , .)l	list
(. , .)ma	move (after a)
(. , .)p	print
q	quit
Q	quit; no diagnostics
($)r[filename]	read
(. , .)s/re /repl /	substitute; & in repl is re
(. , .)s/re /repl /g	substitute globally
(. , .)ta	move copy (after a)
(. , .)u	undo previous substitution
(1 , $)v/re /commands	like global but lines that don't match
(1,$)w [filename]	write
(1,$)W [filename]	append to file
x	encrypt
($)=	line number
!UNIX command	execute
(.+1) newline	print one line

ADB

General Command Format

[addr] [, count] [command] [;]

Commands

?[format]	print from objfil
/[format]	print from corfil
=[format]	print address
newline	repeat last command
[?\]l value mask	mask words until value is found (L used for 4 bytes)
[?\]w value ...	write 2 byte value at addr (W writes 4 bytes)
[?\]m bl el fl [?\]	modify map
>name	assign dot to **adb** name
!	escape to system
$<file	read commands from file
$>file	output to file
$r	print general registers
$f	print floating registers
$b	print all breakpoints
$a	print ALGOL 68 stack backtrace

$c	print C stack backtrace
$C	print C stack backtrace and automatic variables
$e	print external variables
$w	set page width; default 80
$s	set symbol match limit to *addr*; default 255
$o	input base is octal
$d	reset input base
$q	exit
$v	print **adb** variables in octal
$m	print address map
:b[*c*]	set breakpoint; execute breakpoint *c* − 1 times
:d	delete breakpoint
:r [*args*]	run *objfil* with *args*
:c[*s*]	continue subprocess with signal *s* ; default previous
:s[*s*]	single step subprocess with signal *s* ; default previous
:k	kill subprocess

Printing Formats

[*n*]*c* ...   where n is a repeat count for format
   c chosen from the following:
   (* indicates capital c used for field twice as long)
   ((*n*) is temporary increment of *dot*)

o	print in octal * (2)
q	print in signed octal * (2)
d	print in decimal * (2)
x	print in hexadecimal * (2)
u	print unsigned decimal * (2)
f	print floating point * (4)
c	print character (1)
C	print character using @ as escape char (1)
s	print characters until 0 encountered (*n*)
S	print characters using @ as escape (*n*)
b	print byte in octal (1)
Y	print date format (4)
i	print PDP11 instruction (*n*)
a	print *dot* in symbolic form (0)
	/ = data, ? = text, = = absolute
p	print in symbolic form (2)
t	print tab (0)

r	print a space (0)
n	print a newline (0)
"..."	print enclosed string (0)
^	decrement *dot* by current *incr* ; print nothing
+	increment *dot* by 1; print nothing
−	decrement *dot* by 1; print nothing

Expressions

used for *addr* and *count*

.	value of *dot*
+	. + *incr*
^	. − *incr*
"	last *addr* typed
[0#]*integer*	number; **0**=octal, **#** = hexadecimal
integer .fraction	32 bit floating point number
'cccc'	up to 4 ascii characters
**< ***name*	value of *name* ; *name* as follows:

0	last value printed
1	last offset part of instr. source
2	previous value of **1**
r0 ... r5 sp pc ps	registers
b	data segment base addr
d	data segment size
e	entry point
m	magic number
s	stack segment size
t	text segment size

symbol	value from symbol table in *objfil*
	initial _ or ˉ will be added if needed
routine.name	variable *name* in C *routine*
(*exp* **)**	value of *exp*
***exp*	contents of *corfil* at *exp*
@*exp*	contents of *objfil* at *exp*
−*exp*	integer negation
ˉ*exp*	bitwise complement
e1 op e2	*op* one of [+ − * %] (%=division)
e1 **&** *e2*	bitwise conjunction
e1 **|** *e2*	bitwise disjunction
e1 **#** *e2*	*e1* rounded up to multiple of *e2*

* − command causes a break (suppressed by ´, see **.c2**)
() − initial value (*troff,nroff*); [] − value if no argument
F = R, I, B, S, G, C, P, etc.
point size = 6, 7, 8, 9, 10, 11, 12, 14, 16, 18, 20, 22, 24, 28, 36
±*N* may be *N*, +*N* (increment) or −*N* (decrement)
−*N* may be *N* or −*N*
N is distance to place *N* from current place

Scale Indicators - troff; nroff

*N*i	inches	*N**432; *N**240
*N*c	cm.	*N**170; *N**94
*N*p	points	*N**6; *N**3
*N*u	units	*N*; *N*
*N*m	Ems	*N**6*(point size); *N**nominal character width
*N*n	Ens	*N**3*(point size); same as **m**
*N*P	Picas	*N**72; *N**40
*N*v	spaces	*N**current line spacing (see **.vs**)

Font and Character Size Control - troff only

.ps ±*N*	point size (10) [previous]
.ss *N*	space character size *N*/36m (12/36m) [ignored]
.cs *F N M*	constant character spacing; *N*/36m *M*/36m *N* is width; *M* is size of Em; no *N* turns **cs** off; no *M* implies size dependent (off)
.bd *F N*	embolden font by *N*-1 (off)
.bd S *F N*	embolden special font when in font *F* (off)
.ft *F*	font change (Roman) [previous]
.fp *N F*	font position, 1 to 4 (R,I,B,S) [ignored]
.fz *F* ±*N*	font *F* always in size *N*
.fz S *F* ±*N*	special font in size *N* when in *F*

Page Control

.pl ±*N*	page length (11 **i**) [11 **i**]
.bp ±*N*	begin page; *N* is page number * (1)
.pn ±*N*	page number (1) [ignored]
.po ±*N*	page offset (26/27 **i**,0) [previous]
.ne *N*	need *N* vertical space [1**v**]
.mk *a*	mark vertical place in register *a* (none) [internal]
.rt −*N*	return (upward) to vertical place; *N* from top; −*N* relative to current place; [last marked place]

Text Filling, Adjusting, Centering, and Underlining

.br	break *
.fi	fill * (on)
.nf	no filling & adjusting * (off)
.ad *c*	adjust mode; **n** or **b**(both adjusted),**r**(right adjusted), **l**(left adjusted), **c**(centered) (**n**) [unchanged]
.na	no adjusting (off)
.mc *c N*	specify margin character (off) [off]
.ce *N*	center *N* input lines * (off) [1]
.ul *N*	**nroff** underline alphanumerics; **troff** italicize [1 line]
.cu *N*	**nroff** continuous underline; **troff** italicize [1 line]
.uf *F*	underline font set to *F* (I) [I]

Vertical Spacing

.vs *N*	vertical spacing; **v** (12**p**, 1/6**i**) [previous]
.ls *N*	line spacing (1) [previous]
.sp −*N*	space vertically −*N* * [1**v**]
.sv *N*	save vertical distance [1**v**]
.os	output saved vertical distance
.ns	no space mode (off)
.rs	restore spacing
`q	disconnest from TSS
¯ *file*	receive *file* from HIS routine **csr/daccopy**
¯ *file*	send *file* to HIS routine **csr/daccopy**

to send files to TSS run: **csr/daccopy (s)** *aftname* with ´s above
to receive files from TSS run: **csr/daccopy (r)** *aftname* with ¯r above

Line Length and Indenting

.ll ±*N*	line length (6.5**i**) [previous]
.in ±*N*	indent * (0) [previous]
.ti ±*N*	temporary indent * [ignored]

Macros, Diversion, and Line Traps

.de *xx yy*	define macro; end at call of *yy* (*yy*=.) [ignored] called by .*xx*
.am *xx yy*	append to macro [ignored]
.ds *xx str*	define string; invoked by *x or *(*xx* [ignored]
.as *xx str*	append to string [ignored]

.rn *xx yy*	rename *xx* to *yy*
.rm *xx*	remove string or macro [ignored]
.di *xx*	divert output to macro [end]
.da *xx*	divert and append to *xx* [end]
.wh −*N xx*	invoke *xx* when at or beyond place *N*; −*N* means with respect to bottom of page
.ch *xx N*	change line trap for *xx* to place *N*
.em *xx*	end-macro name specification (none) [none]
.dt *N xx*	set diversion trap [off]
.it *N xx*	set input text line count trap [off]

Number Registers

.nr *a* ±*N M*	number & increment register; called by \\n*a*, \\n+*a* or \\n−*a*
.nr *ab* ±*N −M*	number register; called by \\n(*ab*, \\n(+*ab* or \\n−(*ab*
.af *xx c*	assign format to *xx*; 1(1,2,), **001**(001,002,), i(i,ii,), I(I,II,), **a**(a,b,), **A**(A,B,)
.rr *xx*	remove register

Tabs, Leaders, and Fields

.ta *N* [RC] ...	tab settings & types; +*N* = increment ((.5i ...),(.8i ...) left justified) [none]
.tc *c*	tab repetition character (none) [none]
.lc *c*	leader repetition character (.) [none]
.fc *a b*	set field delimiter & pad character (off) [off]

Input and Output Conversions & Character Translations

.ec *c*	set escape character (\\) [\\]
.eo	turn off escape processing (off) [off]
.lg *N*	**troff** ligature mode; 0=off (on) [on]
.cc *c*	basic control character (.) [.]
.c2 *c*	nobreak control character (´) [´]
.li *N*	accept input lines literally [1 line]
.tr *abcd*...	translate on output; *a* to *b*,... (none)

Hyphenation

.nh	no hyphenation (off)
.hy *N*	hyphenation; *N*=**0**(off), ≠**0**(on), =**2**(don't hyphenate last lines), =**4**(don't split off last 2 characters), =**8**(don't split off first 2 characters) (1)
.hc *c*	hyphenation indicator character (\\%) [\\%]
.hw *word1* ...	hyphenation exception list

Three Part Titles

.tl ´*l*´*c*´*r*´	title
.lt *N*	length of title (6.5i) [previous]
.pc *c*	page number character (%) [off]

Output Line Numbering

.nm ±*N M S I*	number mode on or off, set parameters [off]
.nn *n*	don't number next *n* lines [1]

Conditional Input Line Acceptance

.if *c anything*	if *c* true accept *anything*, *c*=**e**(even page number),
.if !*c anything*	**o**(odd page number),**t**(**troff**), **n**(**nroff**) !=not
.if *N anything*	if *N* > 0 accept *anything*, *N* is a number register
.if !*N anything*	!=not
.if ´*s1*´*s2*´ *anything*	if *s1* = *s2*
.if !´*s1*´*s2*´ *anything*	if *s1* != *s2*
.ie *c anything*	same as **.if** but has else with it
.el *anything*	else

Input Switching

.so *filename*	switch source file-push down
.nx *filename*	next file [EOF on current file]
.pi *prog*	**nroff** pipe output to *prog*
.rd *prompt*	read insert from **stdin** [bell]
.ex	exit

Miscellaneous

.ev *N*	environment pushed down (0) [previous]
.mc *c N*	right margin character (1**m**, .2**i**) [off]
.tm *string*	typewriter message
.ig *yy*	ignore until *yy* is called (*yy*=.)
.fl	flush output buffer *
.pm *t*	print macros; *t*=print only sum of sizes
.ab *str*	print string & abort

Escape Sequences - Characters, Indicators, & Functions

\\	prevent interpretation of \
\e	print current escape character
\'	´ (acute accent); same as \(aa
\`	` (grave accent); same as \(ga
\-	− (minus)
_	_ ; same as \(ul
\\|	1/6 **m** space character; 0 width in **nroff**
\^	1/12 **m** space character; 0 width in **nroff**
\(space)	unpaddable space
\&	zero width character
\0	digit width space
\!	transparent line indicator
\"	beginning of comment
\%	default optional hyphenation character
\{	beginning of conditional input
\}	end of conditional input
\$	argument indicator; args 1-9
\(xx	character named xx
*	string indicator; *x, *(xx
\a	leader character
\b´abc´	bracket building function
\c	interrupt text processing
\d	forward (down) 1/2 **m** (**troff**) or line (**nroff**)
\f	font change function
\h	local horizontal motion function
\k	mark horizontal place
\l	draw horizontal line
\L	draw vertical line
\n	number register indicator; \nx, \n(xx
\o´abc´	overstrike function
\p	break and spread output line
\r	reverse 1m or line vertical motion
\s	point size change function
\t	non-interpreted horizontal tab
\u	reverse (up) 1/2 **m** or line
\v	local vertical motion function
\w	width function
\x	extra line-space function
\z	zero width character function
\(newline)	concealed newline

Reserved Registers

(r) = read only

%	current page number
.$	number of arguments available at macro level (r)
.A	1 if **troff** −**a** or **nroff**, 0 otherwise (r)
.H	available horizontal resolution (r)
.L	current line-spacing parameter (r)
.P	1 if current page being printed; 0 otherwise (r)
.T	1 if **nroff** −**T**, 0 otherwise (r)
.V	available vertical resolution (r)
.a	most recent post-line application of \x (r)
.c	input line number in current file (r)
c.	input line number in current file
.d	current vertical place in diversion (r)
.f	physical quadrant of current font (r)
.h	high-water mark of **nl** for text on current page (r)
.i	current indent (r)
.j	current adjustment mode and type (r)
.k	horizontal size of current output line (r)
.l	current line length (r)
.n	length of text on last output line (r)
.o	current page offset (r)
.p	current page length (r)
.s	current point size (r)
.t	distance to next trap (r)
.u	1 in fill mode; 0 in nofill mode (r)
.v	current vertical line spacing (r)
.w	width of previous character (r)
.x	reserved version-dependent register (r)
.y	reserved version-dependent register (r)
.z	name of current diversion (r)
ct	character type
dl	width of last completed diversion
dn	height of last diversion
dw	current day of the week number
dy	current day of the month
hp	current horizontal place on input line
ln	output line number
mo	current month number
nl	current vertical place on the page
sb	depth of string below base line
st	height of string above base line
yr	last 2 digits of current year

TROFF SPECIAL CHARACTERS

´	\' close			fi	\(fi
`	\` open			fl	\(fl
−	\- minus			ff	\(ff
—	\(em			ffi	\(Fi
-	\(hy or −			ffl	\(Fl
●	\(bu			°	\(de
□	\(sq			†	\(dg
_	\(ru			'	\(fm
¼	\(14			¢	\(ct
½	\(12			®	\(rg
¾	\(34			©	\(co

+	\(pl	B	\(*B	×	\(mu
−	\(mi	Γ	\(*G	÷	\(di
=	\(eq	Δ	\(*D	±	\(+−
*	\(**	E	\(*E	∪	\(cu
§	\(sc	Z	\(*Z	∩	\(ca
´	\(aa	H	\(*Y	⊂	\(sb
`	\(ga	Θ	\(*H	⊃	\(sp
_	\(ul	I	\(*I	⊆	\(ib
/	\(sl	K	\(*K	⊇	\(ip
α	\(*a	Λ	\(*L	∞	\(if
β	\(*b	M	\(*M	∂	\(pd
γ	\(*g	N	\(*N	∇	\(gr
δ	\(*d	Ξ	\(*C	¬	\(no
ε	\(*e	O	\(*O	∫	\(is
ζ	\(*z	Π	\(*P	∝	\(pt
η	\(*y	P	\(*R	∅	\(es
θ	\(*h	Σ	\(*S	∈	\(mo
ι	\(*i	T	\(*T	|	\(br
κ	\(*k	Y	\(*U	‡	\(dd
λ	\(*l	Φ	\(*F	☞	\(rh
μ	\(*m	X	\(*X	☜	\(lh
ν	\(*n	Ψ	\(*Q	Ⓐ	\(bs
ξ	\(*c	Ω	\(*W	|	\(or
ο	\(*o	√	\(sr	○	\(ci
π	\(*p		\(rn	⌈	\(lt
ρ	\(*r	≥	\(>=	⌊	\(lb
σ	\(*s	≤	\(<=	⌉	\(rt
ς	\(ts	≡	\(==	⌋	\(rb
τ	\(*t	≃	\(~=	{	\(lk
υ	\(*u	~	\(ap	}	\(rk
φ	\(*f	≠	\(!=	|	\(bv
χ	\(*x	→	\(->	|	\(lf
ψ	\(*q	←	\(<-	⌡	\(rf
ω	\(*w	↑	\(ua	⌠	\(lc
A	\(*A	↓	\(da	⌡	\(rc

− ms Option for TROFF & NROFF

* − command causes a break; ( ) − initial value
general calling order:

   paper-type, **TL**, *author & other 1st page info*, *abstract*,
      heading-type, *body*, *trailing info*

Format & Abstract

.TM *x y z*	BTL TM format; tm# case# file#
.EG	BTL Engineer´s Notes format
.IM	BTL internal memorandum format
.MF	BTL Memorandum-for-File format
.MR	BTL Memorandum-for-Record format
.RP	released paper cover sheet
.TR *x*	BTL technical report format; report #
.TL	title follows *
.AU *ad ex*	authors names follow; address extension *
.AI	authors institute follows (.MH, .HO, .WH, .IH, .PY) *
.AB	begin abstract *
.AE	end of abstract *
.CS *data*	cover sheet data *
	#text #other total #fig #tab #ref
.OK	other keywords follow *
.SG *x*	signature line follows - for TM´s ; reference line *
.AT	attachments
.CT	copies to
.BT	bottom title
.PT	top title

Headings & Paragraphs

.PP	paragraph *
.IP *x y*	indented paragraph; hanging tag *x*, *y* ens indentation *
.RS	increment level of indent *
.RE	decrement level of indent *

.NH *n*	numbered headings in bold, *n*=level *	
.LP	block paragraph (on) *	
.SH	bold headings, no numbers *	

Fonts, Sizes, & Emphasis

.f *x*	change fonts or print *x* in font; Bold, Italic
.R	restore font
.sz	size change; LG=larger, SM=smaller, NL=normal
.UL *x*	underline *x*
.TA *x* ...	set tabs in ens; default: 5 10 ...
.BX *x*	print *x* in a box

Footnotes

.FS	start footnote
.FE	end footnote
.UX	UNIX trademark footnote
.US	"the .UX operating system"

Displays, Tables, & Equations

.DS [CLIB]	begin display; C=center, L=left adjust, I=indent, B=left-justified centered * [I]
.DE	end display *
.CD	long centered display *
.LD	long left adjusted display *
.ID	long indented display *
.KS	begin keep *
.KE	release keep *
.KF	keep floating *
.B1	begin boxed text
.B2	end boxed text
.QS	begin quoted text (indented, shorter)
.QE	end quoted text
.QP	begin single quoted paragraph
.EQ [CLI] *n*	begin equation; for **CLI** see **DS**, *n*=equation number *
.EN	end equation *
.TS *x*	begin table; repeated heading if *x*=**H**
.TE	end table
.TH	end table heading section

Miscellaneous

.2C	2 column *
.1C	1 column (on) *
.DA [*x*]	current date - on for **nroff**
.ND [*date*]	change or cancel date - on for **troff**

Registers & Strings

CF	center footer; string
CH	center heading; string
CW	column width for **2C**; register; (7/15 **LL**)
FL	footnote length; register; (11/12 **LL**)
FM	bottom margin; register; (1 in)
GW	intercolumn gap for **2C**; register; (1/15 **LL**)
HM	top margin; register; (1 in)
LF	left footer; string
LH	left heading; string
LL	line length; register; (6 in)
LT	title length; register; (6 in)
PD	paragraph spacing; register; (.3 **VS**)
PI	paragraph indent; register; (5 ens)
PN	page number; string
PO	page offset; register; (26/27 in)
PS	point size; register; (10)
RF	right footer; string
RH	right heading; string
VS	line spacing; register; (12 pts)

EQN & NEQN KEYWORDS

sub, sup
over
sqrt
...from...to...
left *c*, right *c*
pile { ...above... }, lpile, cpile, rpile
dot, dotdot, hat, bar, tilde, under, vec, dyad
size *n*, gsize *n*
roman, italic, bold, font *f*, gfont *f*
delim
define, tdefine, ndefine
mark, lineup
up, down, fwd, back
matrix, lcol, ccol, rcol

sum, int, integral, prod, union, inter
>=, <=, !=, ==, +-, ->, <-, approx
sin, cos, tan, tanh, coth, sinh, cosh
for, if
arc, times, lim, max, min, log, ln, exp
prime, cdot, del, half
,..., ...
uppercase and lowercase greek
infinity, inf, partial, grad

TBL

Options

center	center table
expand	expand to line length
box	enclose in a box
allbox	box all entries
doublebox	enclose in two boxes
tab(*c*)	change tab character to *c*
linesize(*n*)	line thickness is *n*
delim(*xx*)	forces **eqn** equations to be kept together

Formats

l	left-adjusted column
r	right-adjusted column
c	centered column
n	alligned number column
a	left-adjusted subcolumn
d	push vertical span to bottom
t	push vertical span to top
v	vertical spacing
s	spanned heading
^	vertically spanned heading
_	horizontal line
=	double horizontal line
|	vertical line
b	bold column
i	italic column
p*n*	point size for column
w(*n*)	column width
n	space between columns
e	equal width columns
.	end of format

Data

T{ ... **T}**	text block
_	short horizontal line
\`	above item spans downward to this row

−mm Option for TROFF & NROFF

[] − in macro definition, optional arg; otherwise, value if no arg
() − initial value; {} − select one
general order:
    TL, *author info*, *other cover-info*, *abstract*, **MT**,
        body, *trailing info*

Format & Abstract

.MT ["012345]	document type; 0="=no type, 1=mm for file, 2=programmer's notes, 3=engineer's notes, 4=released paper, 5=letter; **must** occur **after** all cover sheet info [1]
.ND *date*	new date
.TL [*chg#*] [*file#*]	title follows
.AF [*co-name*]	alternate 1st page format
.AU *name* [*initl*] [*loc*] [*dept*] [*ext*] [*room*] [*arg*] ...	author info
.TM [*number*]	technical memorandum numbers
.AS [01] [*indent*]	abstract start; 0=abstract on cover-sheet & 1st pg, 1=abstract only on cover-sheet
.AE	abstract end
.OK [*keyword* ...]	other keywords
.SG [*initls*] [1]	signature line
.NS ["0123456789]	notation start; "=0=copy-to, 1=copy-with-att, 2=copy-without-att, 3=att, 4=atts, 5=enc, 6=encs, 7=sep-cov, 8=letter-to, 9=mm-to
.NE	notation end
.CS [*pgs*] [*other*] [*tot*] [*figs*] [*tbls*] [*ref*]	cover sheet
.TC [*s*[*lev*]] [*spac*] lev [*tab*] [*head*] ...	table-of-contents
.TX	user exit for table-of-contents

Headings & Paragraphs

.P [01]	paragraph; 0=left-justified, 1=indented [\n(Pt]
.H {1234567} [*h-text*]	numbered headings
.HU *h-text*	unnumbered headings
.HM {1 0001 AaIi} ...	heading mark style; 1=arabic, 0001=arabic with leading 0's, A=upper case, a=lower case, I=upper roman, i=lower roman
.HX *dlev rlev h-text*	user exit before headings
.HZ *dlev rlev h-text*	user exit after headings

Lists

presence of last argument on start macros = no blank line between items

.AL [1AaIi] [*t-indent*] [1]	auto-incremented start [1 \n(Li]
.BL [*t-indent*] [1]	bullet start [\n(Pi]
.DL [*t-indent*] [1]	dash start; [\n(Pi]
.ML *mark* [t-indent] [1]	marked start; [mark-width + 1]
.RL [*t-indent*] [1]	reference start; [6]

408

.VL *t-indent* [*m-indent*] [**1**]   variable-item start [**0**]
.LI [*mark*] [**1**]   list item follows; **1**=*mark* is prefix [current mark]
.LE [**1**] list end; arg=blank line output [no blank]
.LB *t-indent m-indent pad type* [*mark*] [**01**] [**0**] list begin
    type: **1**=. **2**=) **3**=( ) **4**=[ ] **5**=< > **6**={ }
    6th arg=blank before each item; *7th arg*=blank before list
.LC [*lev*]   clear list-status

Displays, Tables, Equations, & Footnotes

.DS [**LIC CB**] [**01**]   start static display; **L**=no indent, **I**=indent,
    C=center each line, **CB**=center as a block; **0**=no-fill, **1**=fill
    [**L 0**]
.DF [**LIC CB**] [**01**]   start floating display; args same as .**DS**
.DE   end display
.FG [*titl*] [*o-ride*] [**012**]   figure caption
    0=prefix with o-ride, **1**=suffix, **2**=replace
.TS   start table
.TE   end table
.TB [*titl*] [*o-ride*] [**012**]   table caption
.EQ [*label*]   start equation display
.EN   end equation
.EC [*titl*] [*o-ride*] [**012**]   equation caption
.FS [*lab*]   start footnote
.FE   end footnote
.FD [*arg*] [**1**]   default footnote format
    arg is a decimal number < 12 created from bit definitions
    with the following meanings (each defines 1 bit):
    right-justified label ; *indented text* ; *ragged right margin* ;
    hyphenation on
    2nd arg=reset footnote counter on 1st level heading

Page Headers & Footers

.PH ´*left* ´*center* ´*right* ´ page header (´´page-number´´)
.OH ´*left* ´*center* ´*right* ´   odd-page header
.EH ´*left* ´*center* ´*right* ´ even-page header
.PF ´*left* ´*center* ´*right* ´ page footer
.OF   odd-page footer
.EF   even-page footer
.BS   bottom-block start
.BE   bottom-block end
.PX   user exit for page-header
.TP   top of page macro

Miscellaneous

.B [*arg*] [*prev-font-arg*]   bold
.I [*arg*] [*prev-font-arg*] italic
.R   return to regular font
.SP [*lines*] skip vertically
.SK [*pages*]   skip pages (next page)
.OP   odd-numbered page start
.2C   two-column
.1C   one-column
.SA [*a*]   set right-margin justification
.HS *c*   set hyphenation character
.S $\pm N$ set point size; vertical spacing=point size+2 (10) [previous]

Registers & Strings

Au   inhibit author info on 1st page (1)
BU   bullet string
Cl   contents level (2)
Ds   static display pre & post space; (on)
DT   current date string
Ec   equation counter
Ej   if 1, begin 1st level headings at top of page (0)
F   footnote numberer string
Fg   figure counter
Fs   footnote separation (1)
H1 ... H7   heading counters
Hb   heading level above which there's a break (2)
Hc   heading level below which heading is centered (0)
Hi   for stand alone headings; **0**=left-justify, **1**=indent by **Pt**,
    2=line-up with heading (1)
Hs   heading level below which blank line added (2)
Ht   heading type; **0**=concatenated nums, **1**=single nums; (0)
Hu   heading level for unnumbered heading
Hy   hyphenation control (1)
HF   heading level font string; **1**=roman, **2**=italic, **3**=bold
    (3322222)
HP   heading level point size
Li   list indent (5)
Ls   list spacing between items (6)
Pi   value of paragraph indent (5)
Pt   paragraph type (2)
Si   display indent (5)
Tb   table counter

C SYSTEM CALLS

variables with no declarations are **int**

access(file,mode) check mode access of file
char *file;   mode = **4**(read), **2**(write), **1**(execute)

alarm(seconds)   receive alarm signal
unsigned seconds;

char *brk(addr) set lowest location to *addr*

chdir(dirname)   change working directory
char *dirname;

chmod(name, mode)   change mode of file
char *name;   (for *mode* see **chmod** p. 5)

close(fildes) close a file

creat(name, mode)   creat a new file
char *name;   (for *mode* see **chmod** p. 5)

dup(fildes)   duplicate an open file descriptor

dup2(fildes, fildes2)   integer *fildes2* set to refer to *fildes*

execl(name, arg0, arg1, ..., argn, 0)   execute a file
char *name, *arg0, *arg1, ..., *argn;

execv(name, argv)   execute a file
char *name, *argv[ ];

execle(name, art0, arg1, ..., argn, 0, envp);   execute a file
char *name, *arg0, *arg1, ..., *argn, *envp[ ];   with an environment

execve(name, argv, envp);   execute a file with an environment
char *name, *argv[ ], *envp[ ];

exit(status) terminate process

fork( )   spawn new process

fstat(fildes, buf)   get status of open file
struct stat *buf

getpid( )   get process id

getuid( )   get real user ID

geteuid( )   get effective user ID

getgid( )   get real group ID

getegid( )   get effective group ID

gtty(fildes, argp) get typewriter status
struct sgttyb *argp;   include file **sgtty.h**

kill(pid, sig)   send signal to process; see **kill** p. 8

link(oldname, newname)   link to a file
char *oldname, *newname;

long lseek(fildes, offset, whence)   move read/write pointer
long offset;   whence **0**(*offset*), **1**(+*offset*), **2**(end+*offset*)

mount(special, name, rwflag) mount file system
char *special, *name;

nice(incr)   lower program priority; **0** < *incr* <= **20** (least)

open(name, mode)   open for reading(**0**) writing(**1**), or both(**2**)

pause( )   wait indefinitely (or for alarm)

pkoff(fildes)   turn off packet driver

pkon(fildes, size) turn on packet driver; **32**≤*size*≤**4096**

pipe(fildes)   create an interprocess channel
int fildes[2];   read[0], write[1]

profil(buff, bufsiz, offset, scale)   execute time profile
char *buff;

ptrace(request, pid, addr, data)   process trace
int *addr: *request* has the following meanings;
   0   process to be traced by parent
   1,2 return value at *addr* in child; for separate I&D
       1=I space, **2**=D space
   3   returns value at *addr* in system's per-process data space
   4,5 *data* is written at *addr*; **4**=I space, **5**=D space
   6   *data* is written at *addr* in system's per-process
       data space
   7   continue child at *addr* with signal *data*;
       data = (**int ***)**1** means continue from where stopped
   8   terminates traced process
   9   continue as **7** but stop with **SIGTRAP** as soon as possible

read(fildes, buffer, nbytes)   read from file
char *buffer;

char *sbrk(incr)   add to data space

setgid(gid) set process group id

setuid(uid) set process user id

(*signal(sig, func))( )   catch or ignore signals; see **kill** p. 8
(*func)( );   **func**=**SIG_DFL** default, **SIG_IGN** ignore
       must include **signal.h**

stat(name, buf)   get file status
char *name;   must include **sys/types.h sys/stat.h**
struct stat *buf;

sync()   update super-block

stty(fildes, argp) set typewriter modes
struct sgttyb *argp;   must include **sgtty.h**

long time(0);   get date and time since 00:00:00 GMT, Jan. 1, 1970

long time(tloc)   store date and time in *tloc*
long *tloc;

ftime(tp)   store data and time in *tp*
struct timeb *tp; must include **sys/types.h sys/timeb.h**

times(buffer)   get process times
struct tbuffer {
     long proc_user_time;
     long proc_sys_time;
     long child_user_time;
     long child_sys_time;
} *buffer;

umount(special)   remove file system
char *special;

umask(complmode)   set file creation mode mask
     (for *complmode* see **chmod** p. 5)

unlink(name)   remove directory entry
char *name;

utime(file, timep) set file times
char *file;   must include **sys/types.h**
time_t timep[2];

wait(status)   wait for process to terminate
int *status;

write(fildes, buffer, nbytes)   write on a file
char *buffer;

C STDIO ROUTINES

#include <stdio.h>   include file for definitions

In the following routines variables must be declared as:
FILE *stream;
char *type;   where "**r**" =read, "**w**"=write, "**a**"=append
char *filename;
char *format;
char *s;
char c;
all other variables are **int** unless otherwise specified
clearerr(stream) resets error indication

fclose(stream)   flush and close **stream**

FILE *fdopen(fildes, type)   returns stream associated with **fildes**

feof(stream)   returns non-zero on EOF

ferror(stream)   returns non-zero on read/write error

fflush(stream)   flush **stream**

int fgetc(stream) function like macro **getc**

char *fgets(s, n, stream)   returns **n**−1 characters in **s**

fileno(stream)   returns integer file descriptor

FILE *fopen(filename, type) open a stream

fprintf(stream, format [, arg ...]) output to **stream**
      see **printf** for form of **format**

fputc(c,stream)   function like macro **putc**

fputs(s,stream)   output a string

fread(ptr, sizeof(*ptr), nitems, stream)   read

FILE *freopen(filename, type, stream)   use **filename** for open **stream**

fscanf(stream, format [, pointer ...])   input and convert
      format is of the form:
        %[*][fw]c
      where * suppresses assignment and *c* is one of
      [cdDefoOsxX] optionally preceeded by l as in **printf**
      or [...] where characters are input until
      the first one not between the brackets or [^ ...] where
      characters are input until the first one between the brackets

fseek(stream, offset, ptrname)   **ptrname**=**0**(beginning),
long offset;   **1**(current place), **2**(end)

long ftell(stream) returns current offset

fwrite(ptr, sizeof(*ptr), nitems, stream)   write

int getc(stream)   returns next character; **EOF** on EOF or error

int getchar()   returns next character from **stdin**

char *gets(s)   returns string from **stdin** in **s**

int getw(stream) returns next word

pclose(**stream**) to close stream opened with **popen**

FILE *popen(**command, type**) create a pipe
char *command, *type;

printf(**format** [, **arg** ...]) output to **stdout**
    format consists of characters and conversion
        specifications of the form:
            %[−][*fw*[.*d*]*c*
    where − specifies left adjustment; *fw*, field width,
    d, precision; and *c* may be
            [l]d   decimal (l or **D** =long)
            [l]o   octal (l or **O** = long)
            [l]x   hexadecimal (l or **X** = long)
            [l]u   unsigned integer (l or **U** = long)
            f   float of form [−]dd.ddd
            e   float of form [−]d.dde±dd
            g   float using minimum space(**d**, **f**, or **e**)
            c   character
            s   string
            %   escape %

rewind(**stream**) rewind

int putc(c, **stream**) output a character

putchar(c) output a character to **stdout**

putw(w,**stream**) output a word

puts(s) output string to **stdout**

scanf(**format** [, **pointer** ...]) read **stdin** and convert
        see **fscanf** for form of **format**

setbuf(**stream, buf**) buffer i/o in **buf**
char buf[BUFSIZ];

sprintf(s,**format** [, **arg**...]) output to string **s**
        see **printf** for form of **format**

sscanf(s,**format** [, **pointer** ...])read from string *s* and convert
        see **fscanf** for form of **format**

ungetc(c, **stream**)push c back on input **stream**

C LIBRARY ROUTINES

#include <**math.h**> include file for math functions
double x, y; declaration for **x** & **y** in math functions

abs(i)absolute value of **i**

double acos(x) arc cosine function; range 0 to π

double asin(x) arc sin function; range − π/2 to π/2

double atan(x) arc tangent function; range − π/2 to π/2

double atan2(x,y)arc tangent of *x/y*; range − π to π

double atof(nptr)converts ascii to float
char *nptr;

atoi(nptr) converts ascii to integer
char *nptr;

long atol(nptr) converts ascii to long integer
char *nptr;

double cos(x) cosine function

double cosh(x) hyperbolic function

char *ctime(clock) converts time to ascii
long *clock;

char *ecvt(value, ndigit, decpt, sign) converts *value* to ascii
double value;
int ndigit, *decpt, *sign;

double exp(x) exponential function

char *getenv(name) search environment for **name**
char *name; returns **NULL** for not found; value for found

double log(x) natural log function

double log10(x) log function base 10

char *malloc(size) memory allocation
unsigned size; release with **free(ptr)**

    char *realloc(ptr, size) change block size or compact

    char *calloc(nelm, elsize) allocate & clear array space
    unsigned nelm, elsize;

char *mktemp(template) make unique file name
char *template; **template** of form *name***XXXXXX**

perror(s) print **s**: last error from system call
char *s;

double pow(x,y) power function; returns x^y

qsort(base, num_elts, width, compar) quicksort
char *base;
int (*compar)();

rand() random number generator; initialized with **srand(seed)**

double sin(x) sine function.

double sinh(x) hyperbolic function

sleep(seconds) suspend execution
unsigned seconds;

double sqrt(x) square root function

system(string) sends **string** to system for execution
char *string;

double tan(x) tangent function

double tanh(x) hyperbolic function

INDEX

Index

414

Index

Index

Index

Index